In Search of Our
Warrior Mothers

In Search of Our Warrior Mothers

*Women Dramatists of the
Black Arts Movement*

✦

La Donna L. Forsgren

NORTHWESTERN UNIVERSITY PRESS
EVANSTON, ILLINOIS

Northwestern University Press
www.nupress.northwestern.edu

10 9 8 7 6 5 4 3 2 1

Library of Congress Cataloging-in-Publication Data

Names: Forsgren, La Donna L., author.
Title: In search of our warrior mothers : women dramatists of the Black Arts
    movement / La Donna L. Forsgren.
Description: Evanston, Illinois : Northwestern University Press, 2018. | Includes
    bibliographical references and index.
Identifiers: LCCN 2017041790 | ISBN 9780810136939 (pbk. : alk. paper) | ISBN
    9780810136946 (cloth : alk. paper) | ISBN 9780810136953 (ebook)
Subjects: LCSH: American drama—African American authors—20th century—
    History and criticism. | American drama—Women authors—20th century—
    History and criticism. | Black Arts movement. | Feminist theater. | Teer,
    Barbara Ann—Criticism and interpretation. | Charles, Martie—Criticism and
    interpretation. | Sanchez, Sonia, 1934—Criticism and interpretation. | Franklin,
    J. E. (Jennie Elizabeth), 1937—Criticism and interpretation.
Classification: LCC PS153.N5 F677 2018 | DDC 812/.54099287/08996073—dc23
    LC record available at https://lccn.loc.gov/2017041790

For Martie Evans-Charles, J.e. Franklin,
Sonia Sanchez, Barbara Ann Teer,
and warrior mothers everywhere

CONTENTS

Acknowledgments   *ix*

Preface   *xi*

Introduction   *3*

Chapter 1
"Set Your Blackness Free": Barbara Ann Teer's Art and Activism   *17*

Chapter 2
"We Black Women": Martie Evans-Charles and the Spirits of
Black Womanhood   *37*

Chapter 3
"Armed Prophet": Sonia Sanchez and the Weapon of Words   *67*

Chapter 4
"Bring Your Wounded Hearts": J.e. Franklin and the Art
of Liberation   *107*

Epilogue
Let the Search Continue   *145*

Appendix A
Chronology of Barbara Ann Teer   *153*

Appendix B
Chronology of Martie Evans-Charles   *157*

Appendix C
Chronology of Sonia Sanchez   *159*

Appendix D
Chronology of J.e. Franklin   *163*

Notes   167

Bibliography   187

Index   195

ACKNOWLEDGMENTS

I would like to begin by thanking Sonia Sanchez, J.e. Franklin, George Lee Miles, Adrienne Charles, Sade Lythcott, Nabii Faison, and Shirley Faison for graciously sharing their life experiences and unpublished plays with me. This book literally could not have been written without you. Chelsea Hall and Charlie Van Duyn, thank you for transcribing these interviews.

My journey through academia has not been easy. Thankfully, I have been blessed with supportive mentors, friends, and family who continually nourish my spirit. I would like to thank Harvey Young for his constant support throughout my graduate study at Northwestern University. My sincerest appreciation for encouraging and mentoring me beyond the life of a dissertation. Anyone fortunate enough to be mentored by Harvey knows that the only thing that exceeds his wonderful scholarship is his incredible kindness. Special thanks to the following individuals for supporting my intellectual journey: Megan Sanborn-Jones, Sandra L. Richards, Susan Manning, Rodger Sorenson, Eric Samuelsen, Karen Jean Martinson, Tracy C. Davis, Bob Nelson, Richard Davis, Addyse Palagyi, Lundeanna Thomas, Theresa May, Paul Bryant-Jackson, and the late Kate Bosher. I have learned a great deal from your example.

I remain indebted to my cohorts from Brigham Young University and Northwestern University: Billy Gunn, Matt Hill, Shelly Graham, Emily McVey, La Been, Keith Byron Kirk, Rashida Shaw McMahon, Katie Zien, Nathan Hedman, Sara Armstrong, Louise Edwards Neiman, Gina Di Salvo, Paul Thelen, Ruth Hays, Lisa Biggs, Sage Morgan-Hubbard, and so many others. Your offer of friendship and camaraderie will forever remain dear to my heart.

This book would not have been possible without Northwestern University Press, generous research support, and the Schomburg Center for Research. I would like to thank editors Gianna Mosser, Mike Levine, and Nathan MacBrien for believing in this project. Thank you Maggie Grossman, JD Wilson, Greta Bennion, Steven Moore, Paul Mendelson, and the Northwestern University Press staff for making my vision a reality. Thank you to Mike Sell and Sandra Adell for reading the manuscript. Thank you anonymous peer reviewers for your encouragement and help in clarifying my argument. Any fault with this book is completely due to my error. Early stages of this project were funded by Northwestern University's Graduate Research Grant and the Department of African American Studies Small Research Grant, Luther

College and the Consortium for Faculty Diversity at Liberal Arts Colleges. The University of Notre Dame's Institute for Scholarship in the Liberal Arts graciously supported the indexing of this book. Special thanks to the archivists at the Schomburg Center for Research for helping me locate the unpublished plays of Martie Evans-Charles.

Finally, I would like to thank my family for their love and support. My mother Brenda Branch who raised eleven children on her own. My wonderful siblings and their partners: Michael Harris, Jennifer Taylor, Crystal Rounsaville, Raushanna Majeed, Monica Fields, Tina and Mark Madsen, Tanya Pratt, Veronica and Brian Miller, Angel Pratt, and Star Briney. My best friend, Kristen Larson, and family by choice: Bonnie and Hal Forsgren, Christina and Eric Forsgren, Elizabeth and Ryan Forsgren, Chantel and Kyle Sharp, Caleb and Holly Forsgren.

Last, but certainly not least, I would like to thank my own little family. Jacoby Thomas, Piper McKay, Braxton Cruser, and Emmett Christopher: this book would not have been completed without your patience, silly jokes, and sticky kisses. You teach and inspire me every single day. *I'll love you forever*. Layne, I would not be where I am today without your love, encouragement, and unwavering belief in my abilities. Next time I'll use your idea.

PREFACE

When this project began more than a decade ago I was not yet a mother. Yet the issues surrounding black motherhood remained dear to my heart. Having been raised by a single mother with ten daughters, I have always been surrounded by incredibly strong, talented, and independent women. As I entered adolescence, however, I quickly realized the vast disparity between my own and society's perception of black womanhood and motherhood. How does a black mother socialize her children to successfully navigate a world that does not recognize their humanity? How does a black mother teach her children self-worth, pride, and resiliency while enduring ideological, economic, and political oppression? At the time, I did not realize that my questions and concerns were, in fact, extensively addressed within the African American literary tradition.

My journey to understand how women writers of the Black Arts Movement (1965–76) represented black womanhood and motherhood did not begin until graduate school. I first encountered the Black Arts Movement while serving as a graduate teaching assistant at Brigham Young University. I was invited to provide a twenty-minute presentation on the Black Arts Movement to a group of white, twenty-something, middle- and upper-class Mormons. While I had never even heard of the Black Arts Movement, I readily agreed to do the lecture for the opportunity to hone my teaching skills. However, after reading LeRoi Jones's (later Amiri Baraka's) provocative manifesto "The Revolutionary Theatre" (1965), I quickly realized that I might have bitten off more than I could chew. Despite my hesitations, the lecture went very well. The students surpassed my expectations with their willingness to discuss racism and racial violence in the United States. One particular student, however, noticed that I only mentioned leading male playwrights of the era. *What were black women writing about during the 1960s and1970s?* Aside from Adrienne Kennedy, I did not have a clue. And so the search began.

I first crossed paths with Sonia Sanchez when I read her poem "blk/rhetoric" (1970). Sanchez not only answers Baraka's famous call in the poem "SOS" (1969), but also gives more meaning to the original message by challenging audiences to make change in their lives. Sanchez writes:

> who's gonna make all
> that beautiful blk/rhetoric
> mean something
> . . .

    this is an S.O.S.
    me. calling . . . .
    calling . . . .
    some/one.
    pleasereplysoon.[1]

This poem helped me to realize how Sanchez's remarkable poetry supported
black nationalist discourse, yet also provided an important critique of detrimental rhetoric and practices of the time. She did not hold back. I wanted to
know more and eventually discovered her equally poignant dramas.

Discovering Sanchez's poetry and dramas led to other black women
playwrights, some of whom appear in this book. The incredible works of
playwrights such as Aduke Aremu (Gwen Jones), Hazel Bryant, Martie
Evans-Charles, Glenda Dickerson, J.e. Franklin, PJ (Patricia Joann) Gibson,
Micki Grant, Gertrude Greenidge, Elaine Jackson, Josephine Jackson, Judi
Ann Mason, Barbara Molette, Salamu (Nettie McCray), and Barbara Ann
Teer were popular during their time, yet many of their names had fallen
into obscurity. Why are their names only briefly, if ever, mentioned in current narratives of Black Arts Movement theater? Why have their works been
neglected by contemporary scholars? Their writings have always been there.
Waiting. Waiting to be reclaimed. It is my hope that this book begins the
process of recovery.

In Search of Our
Warrior Mothers

Introduction

I don't recall the exact moment I set out to explore the works of black women. . . . My discovery of them—most of them out of print, abandoned, discredited, maligned, nearly lost—came about, as many things of value do, almost by accident. As it turned out—and this should not have surprised me—I found I was in need of something that only one of them could provide.
—Alice Walker, 1983

In 1987, the black feminist scholar Barbara Christian issued a call to reclaim the literature of black women writers by creating in-depth studies of their works, writing, "I think we need to read the works of our writers in our various ways and remain open to the intricacies of the intersection of language, class, race, and gender in the literature."[1] Her concern for the continuation of black women's literary tradition remains relevant today, as black women playwrights continue to encounter marginalization and co-optation. The playwright Katori Hall perhaps best expressed this concern after learning about Kent State University's decision to cast a white actor to play the role of Martin Luther King in their production of her 2009 play *The Mountaintop*: "Our stories are worthy of the pedestal we call the stage, and our black bodies must stand unaltered in that spotlight, so that our skin, like King's, can reflect back our own humanity and we can all see ourselves in it."[2] In this instance, removing the black body from the theatrical stage symbolized the historical erasure of the black subject from the world stage. Hall's statement and subsequent efforts to prohibit experimental casting follow a tradition of black women writers who used their agency not only to resist controlling images but also to affirm black humanity. *In Search of Our Warrior Mothers: Women Dramatists of the Black Arts Movement* foregrounds the sociopolitical factors that have led to the marginalization of black women's culture and literary tradition.

Similar to Alice Walker's search to recover the works of Zora Neale Hurston, this book recuperates the theories and dramatic work of four leading women playwrights of the Black Arts Movement (1965–76): Barbara Ann Teer, Martie Evans-Charles, Sonia Sanchez, and J.e. Franklin. Despite operating within a masculinist context that equated the collective well-being of black people with black male agency, these warrior mothers centered their dramas around black women, validated female aspirations for autonomy, and explored women's roles in the struggle for liberation from white hegemony.

The rise of black feminist drama was a development within the Black Arts Movement, not a sharp break from it. The movement consisted of poets, theorists, playwrights, artists, dancers, and musicians who advocated a black aesthetic as a means to promote racial solidarity and incite community activism against racist social and institutional practices in the United States and abroad. "The Revolutionary Theatre" (1965), written by the prominent Black Arts Movement leader, theorist, and playwright Amiri Baraka (LeRoi Jones), is often used to capture the dominant ethos of this era. Baraka writes:

> The Revolutionary Theatre must EXPOSE! . . . It must stagger through our universe correcting, insulting, preaching, spitting craziness . . . but a craziness taught to us in our most rational moments. . . . We will scream and cry, murder, run through the streets in agony, if it means some soul will be moved, moved to actual life understanding of what the world is, and what it ought to be.[3]

Baraka's manifesto conceptualizes "Revolutionary Theatre" as a theater of action, meant to incite actual change in black people's lives. While many Black Arts theorists and artists, including Evans-Charles and Sanchez, were inspired by Baraka's revolutionary writings, their ideological beliefs and artistic practices were by no means consistent with his. Others still, including Franklin and Teer, resisted any dogma that limited their creative sensibilities. Thus, it is misleading to use the writings of male luminaries to encapsulate the entire movement. In some ways the perspectives of Teer, Evans-Charles, Franklin, and Sanchez were consistent with prevailing Black Arts philosophy and Black Power discourses, but in other ways they diverged. Crucial is how their woman-centered dramas express black female subjectivity and how their works relate to the subsequent emergence of black feminism.

Attending to the works of artists such as Teer, Evans-Charles, Sanchez, and Franklin uncovers a significant moment within Black Arts and Black Power discourses wherein the recuperation of black women's culture became an integral element of black empowerment. Such attention disrupts mythologies of a homogeneous Black Arts ideology and a fixed divide between the Black Power and feminist movements, revealing the nuanced tensions between and among these artistic and activist traditions. In-depth study of these playwrights thus not only recuperates a chapter in the history of black women writers who were able to resist both racial and sexual hegemony, but also revises current understandings of the growth of black feminist drama in the United States. While women dramatists of the Black Arts Movement engage with many of the concerns that black feminists would later explore, to label their work "feminist" would not only directly contradict their perception of their work, but also flatten the dynamic relationship between the black liberation and feminist movements. Family members and colleagues describe Teer, Evans-Charles, Sanchez, and Franklin as strong mothers, resourceful women, and talented artists who fostered a more inclusive artistic community in Harlem. Their writings attend to the intricacies of gender and racial inequality, yet they did not consider themselves "feminists" nor did they ever identify their works as "feminist" texts. Evans-Charles's ambivalence toward the second wave feminist movement is perhaps best illustrated in her popular play *Jamimma* (1970). The play includes a didactic scene wherein a group of young black men and women debate the efficacy and relevance of the feminist movement in the lives of black people. Predating the term "intersectionality"[4] by nearly two decades, the black women discuss the problems of gender-specific movements, arguing that their femaleness *and* blackness contribute to their oppression. The women also understand that categorizing gender as mutually exclusive allows white women to ignore their racial privilege and remain complicit in the marginalization of black women. This scene, therefore, not only demonstrates an awareness of racism within the feminist movement but also offers an important critique about the importance of intersectionality. Teer also disavowed the feminist movement, asserting that its divisiveness destroyed creativity. "The women's movement, the feminist [movement], . . . reinforces the same separation, it highlights the same isolation, so that you got women over here, men over there. I think it's not about an individual, it's about a collective, and it's about balance. There's no limits to your creative possibility," remembers Teer.[5] The assertion that the feminist movement served as a divisive tool was espoused by many of her male and female comrades. More than forty years after the demise of the Black Arts Movement, Franklin and Sanchez continue to distance themselves from the feminist movement because of its perceived racism and its isolation from the black community. In addition to their own rejection of the feminist movement, many of the works of Evans-Charles, Franklin, Sanchez, and Teer predate the rise of second wave feminism.

In more recent years, Sanchez has situated her dramas as an early expression of Alice Walker's concept of *womanism*, a social theory deeply rooted in black women's unique traditions and activism. According to Walker, a womanist is a "woman who loves other women, sexually and/or nonsexually. Appreciates and prefers women's culture, women's emotional flexibility (values tears as natural counterbalance of laughter), and women's strength. . . . Committed to survival and wholeness of [an] entire people, male *and* female."[6] Indeed, Sanchez's dramas, as well as many of those written by her female peers, reflect black women's concerns and culture and yet remain fully committed to the liberation of black women, men, and children.

Rather than attempt to attribute a feminist consciousness as expressed today to women playwrights of the Black Arts Movement, this study analyzes how black feminist attitudes emerge from moments of engagement with patriarchal discourses. Black feminist attitudes include an awareness of how

ideological, economic, and political forces oppress black women; the valorization of black women's everyday knowledge, history, and culture; and the
desire to provide a counter-discourse through the creation of multiple visions
of black womanhood. In so doing, Teer, Evans-Charles, Sanchez, and Franklin
used their own experiential knowledge to create a distinctively black female
worldview. Their works consistently reject Black Power rhetoric that equated
black liberation with the acquisition of manhood and instead offer a more
powerful vision of black liberation centered on the survival of black families.
These dramas laid the groundwork for a wave of black feminist drama that is
often attributed to the 1976 New York premiere of Ntozake Shange's highly
popular play *for colored girls who have considered suicide/when the rainbow
is enuf.*

The Black Arts Movement

While immensely popular and critically acclaimed during the 1960s and
1970s, the early dramas of Teer, Evans-Charles, Sanchez, and Franklin have
been relatively ignored by contemporary scholars. This is due in part to the
inaccessibility of their plays and to sexism and racism within the academy.
Indeed, few of their works were published, yet these works were frequently
performed in Black Arts theaters, Off-Broadway, community theaters, and
colleges across the country. Lacking accessible evidence to explore the writings of women playwrights, theater scholars have focused on the plays of
leading male figures, dismissed the agency of female writers, and positioned
the contributions of female playwrights as anomalies. Historians of black
cultural nationalism have also contributed to the erasure of black women
activists by constructing narratives that focus on the contributions of a single
male leader. The historian Komozi Woodard's *A Nation within a Nation:
Amiri Baraka (LeRoi Jones) and Black Power Politics* (1999), for example,
analyzes the politics of black cultural nationalism from the perspective of
Baraka, whom he perceives as the "father" of the movement. While a groundbreaking study of the rise of black nationalism, Woodard's historical narrative
places one male star figure at the center and does not attend to the contributions of female participants.[7]

More recently, historians have made concerted efforts to attend to the
intricacies of gender and Black Power politics. James Smethurst's *The Black
Arts Movement: Literary Nationalism in the 1960s and 1970s* (2005), for
example, contends that gross generalizations of the Black Arts Movement as
homophobic and sexist contribute to the further dismissal of female artists.
Smethurst's study not only considers the importance of regional variation, but
also positions Sanchez and Teer as "the most active and influential national
and regional figures of the movement" and concedes that black women
"often did contest expressions of misogyny and male supremacy within the

movement from the inside."[8] While Smethurst briefly addresses black female agency, he neglects to analyze the concrete ways in which the Black Arts Movement provided a forum for black women to express their thoughts and opinions. *In Search of Our Warrior Mothers*, however, places female artists at the center of analysis in order to investigate the ways in which they created and interpreted Black Arts theory and drama.

While none of the dramatists discussed in this book identify as "black feminists," they certainly used their agency to encourage racial solidarity *and* resist sexism and racism from both within and outside black communities. As the historian Kimberly Springer demonstrates in *Living for the Revolution: Black Feminist Organizations, 1968–1980* (2001), black women used their agency to form their own feminist groups, join predominately white feminist organizations, and "espouse feminist ideals within black nationalist organizations."[9] In so doing, an indirect exchange of antisexist ideas circulated among black feminists and black women working within black nationalist organizations. Similar to the activists in Springer's study, the art and activism of Teer, Evans-Charles, Sanchez, and Franklin also challenge traditional conceptualizations of feminist activism to include critiques of both racism and sexism.[10]

Similar to black women poets of the Black Arts Movement, women dramatists also used their agency to carefully negotiate black nationalist patriarchy. Furthermore, black women artists were aware of and sometimes identified with the basic tenets of the women's liberation movement and negotiated "'within' and 'without' the circle of Black Arts Movement" compatriots.[11] As Cheryl Clarke's *After Mecca: Women Poets and the Black Arts Movement* (2006) demonstrates, at times this negotiation included both challenging prescribed gender roles and "subscrib[ing] to the dictates of womanhood within their circle."[12] In keeping with women poets of the era, the plays written by Teer, Evans-Charles, Sanchez, and Franklin celebrate black women's distinctive worldview, yet remain deeply committed to improving the lives of poor black men, women, and children in their communities.

The socioeconomic conditions, grassroots activism, and artistic community of Harlem greatly impacted the careers of Teer, Evans-Charles, Sanchez, and Franklin. Historically, Harlem has served as an important site of black intellectual thought and culture. During the 1960s and 1970s Harlem remained a vital artistic community, serving as the home to Baraka's Black Arts Repertory Theatre/School (BART/S; 1965), Robert Macbeth's New Lafayette Theatre (1967–72), Teer's National Black Theatre (1968–present), Ed Bullins's Black Theatre Workshop (1968–72), Woodie King Jr.'s New Federal Theatre (1970–present), and the Harlem Writers Guild (1950–present). The establishment of BART/S, often marked as the institutional origin of the Black Arts Movement,[13] provided an opportunity for Sanchez to listen to the woman-centered writings of the jazz singer and civil rights activist Abbey Lincoln. Hearing Lincoln recite "Who Will Revere the Black Woman?" in fact, provided the initial inspiration for Sanchez's woman-centered dramas. At the National Black Theatre, Teer taught Sanchez the nuances of audience engagement, teaching her strategies to perform her poetry for audiences. Teer, incidentally, formulated her concept of a national black theater during informal conversations with the New Lafayette Theatre founder Robert Macbeth at Harlem's Shalimar Club.[14] Evans-Charles's writing likewise grew out of her involvement with the writing community of the Black Theatre Workshop. The esteemed Harlem Writers Guild also fostered the development of Franklin's writing career, introducing her to the woman-centered poetry and novels of Rosa Guy, Alice Childress, and Maya Angelou.

Memory, Orality, and the Written Word

Creating an oral history provided the means to recover the intellectual thought and experiences of women playwrights of the Black Arts Movement. Interviews with Franklin and Sanchez not only provide vital biographical information, but also yield dynamic accounts of how black women negotiated their interests within the artistic community of Harlem. Sanchez's first-person narrative, for example, contradicts previous academic scholarship that critiques the Black Arts Movement as hopelessly misogynistic. Sanchez explains that the Black Arts Movement never had predetermined roles for women and that it embraced women artists. Furthermore, it was not until the 1970s, as so-called revolutionary organizations were formed, that prescribed gender roles were discussed among black activists. Sanchez bases her opinion upon her experiences of being mentored by Bullins and Baraka, both of whom made a conscious effort to include women at poetry readings and public events. Indeed, interviews with other informants confirm that Bullins, in particular, fostered an inclusive artistic community through his mentorship of women playwrights and publication of their works. Franklin, however, remembers experiencing both support and ostracism from both experimental and mainstream commercial theaters. She insists that in general, women playwrights did not fare well in American theater during the 1960s, given that none of their works were produced in commercial theaters. Yet she also notes that the producers Woodie King Jr. and George Houston Bass served as mentors, creating a space for her to develop and produce her works. These differing accounts help situate the Black Arts Movement as a continuously shifting field of negotiation for black women playwrights.

Interviews with Teer's family and colleagues not only demonstrate black women's bold negotiation of male-dominated theater spaces, but also reveal how they directly influenced later dramatic experimentation. Teer's daughter, Barbara "Sade" Lythcott, remembers her mother receiving both the support of male colleagues and ostracism from the larger theater community because of her outspokenness. Quite simply, Teer dared to do what many defined as a "man's job" by founding her own theater. As founder and artistic director of the National Black Theatre, Teer not only produced her own works, but also mentored talented young women dramatists. Teer's colleague Nabii Faison, for example, remembers Ntozake Shange frequently visiting the National Black Theatre. "[Shange] would give deference of credit to NBT because the choreopoem [*for colored girls*] was an outgrowth of the work that we did here," remembers Faison.[15] Shange has also acknowledged her complicated relationship with the Black Arts Movement, stating "I am a daughter of the black arts movement (even though they didn't know they were going to have a girl!)."[16] When combined, Shange's and Faison's statements suggest that while Teer's innovative performance practices greatly influenced Shange's dramatic experimentation, Shange's plays also marked a departure from the previous generation of male writers.

Despite the wealth of knowledge gained from creating oral history narratives, there are also challenges associated with this venture. To begin with, the untimely deaths of Teer, Evans-Charles, and many others preclude the possibility of original interviews. In such cases previously published interviews; discussions with offspring, friends, and colleagues; and secondary literature were used to fill in these silences. In addition, in many instances informants were asked to recall events that occurred more than forty years ago, which sometimes led to vague answers or inaccurate information. Occasionally an informant's current interpretation of her work contradicted her original writings. When discussing the character Sister's submissiveness in the final scene of *Uh, Uh; But How Do It Free Us?* (1974), for example, Sanchez dismissed the implications of her actions, asserting that Sister breaks up with her boyfriend. The stage directions, however, imply that Sister will continue to submit to her emotionally and physically abusive boyfriend. "I might be rewriting my play right now," Sanchez conceded upon further questioning.[17] Moments such as this remain important because they not only illustrate how an artist's ideology changes over time, but also underscore a critical tension between memory, orality, and the written word.

Black Women Writers: Images, Subjectivity, and Mythologies

The experiences of Teer, Evans-Charles, Sanchez, and Franklin as black mothers, educators, artists, and grassroots activists provided an important catalyst for their intellectual thought. Moreover, situating them within black women's intellectual traditions answers the black feminist scholar Patricia Hill Collins's challenge to locate and celebrate the everyday experiences of black women who are not perceived as "intellectuals," such as mothers, artists, and political activists.[18] Indeed, their writings demonstrate how black women's intellectual tradition, often located outside the academy, offers a "distinctive standpoint on self, community, and society."[19] Central to black women's intellectual tradition has been a keen understanding and resistance to the economic, political, and ideological oppression of black women. Dominant groups have responded to this potentially empowering tradition by purposefully and systematically suppressing it by exploiting black women's labor, denying black women citizenship, and perpetuating controlling images to justify the oppression of black women. Collins writes that this very suppression leads to the conditions that foster black women's outsider-within stance, allowing them to create "an independent, viable, yet subjugated knowledge."[20] The distinctive worldview of Teer, Evans-Charles, Sanchez, and Franklin allowed them to continue the black women writer's tradition of "speak[ing] from a multiple and complex social, historical and cultural positionality."[21] Collectively, their works demonstrate incredible artistic skill, encourage racial solidarity, and clarify black women's subjectivity, attributes that garnered for them critical acclaim and attention during the 1960s and 1970s.

Women playwrights of the Black Arts Movement followed a tradition of black women intellectuals who actively resisted controlling images of black womanhood. Cultural images of black women as asexual mammies, emasculating matriarchs, confrontational bitches, long-suffering superwomen, or hypersexual jezebels have been used to not only justify the exploitation of black women's labor and bodies, but also explain white cultural, economic, and political hegemony. Racist ideologies perpetuate these distorted images of black womanhood, wreaking havoc in the lives of black women. Controlling images not only limit black women's social mobility, but also deny their humanity. Black women intellectuals have responded to black women's invisibility by revealing the disparity between controlling images and the actual experiences black women have in their everyday lives. "This tradition of resistance suggests that a distinctive, collective Black women's consciousness exists," argues Collins.[22] While the writings of Teer, Evans-Charles, Sanchez, and Franklin vary in terms of genre, tone, and style, all of their works engage with black women's tradition of resistance.

Teer, Evans-Charles, Sanchez, and Franklin follow a tradition of black women writers who have responded to their invisibility by disrupting the prevailing ideologies of womanhood. Under the slave system, black females were marked as immoral, animalistic, and sexually depraved. Their labor outside of the home provided further evidence that black females were incapable of fulfilling a woman's traditional role within the family. Reduced to their biological being, black women were not afforded protection under the cult of true womanhood, a revered status that only white middle- to upper-class women could obtain. Because they were deemed sexually deviant, society perceived black females as sexually available to any man, black or white. After enslavement, black women remained vulnerable to the threat of rape as they continued to labor in close proximity to white males as domestics. Black women could not rely on the law for protection against sexual assault and were forced to develop strategies of resistance and coping mechanisms in order to function in a society that maligned their very existence. Rather than use black women as the scapegoats for the ills within black communities, black female playwrights' dramas celebrate black women's standpoint, history, and culture. In so doing, their dramas critique dehumanizing mythologies and reveal the ways in which institutionalized racism harms black women, families, and communities.

Women dramatists of the Black Arts Movement clarify black female subjectivity, meaning black women's consciousness, perspective, and experiences. Their works privilege the everyday struggles of various black women, including mothers, grandmothers, teachers, students, and prostitutes. The historian Darlene Clark Hine stresses the importance of creating a visual history of black women's lives. "We have seen Black women's faces and bodies shamed and exploited. What we have not seen nearly enough is the simple truth of our complex and multidimensional lives," writes Hine.[23] Creating multiple visions of black womanhood allowed Teer, Evans-Charles, Sanchez, and Franklin to attend to the specificity of black female subjectivity, as well as provide a broader critique of how oppressive systems disenfranchise all black women, regardless of their social status. All of their plays, for example, feature prostitutes or express concern with the rise of prostitution in Harlem. Rather than present these black women as sexual deviants, their dramas reveal how limited educational opportunities, unemployment, poverty, and lack of community support have led to their prostitution. Despite their trade, audiences discover that these women do not make their decision to sell their bodies to white men out of uncontrollable sexual desire. Abandoned by black men and excluded from the world economy, these black mothers must sell their bodies in order to feed their children. Through passionate speeches, these mothers call audiences to action by using heteronormative constructs to implore black men to help black women raise strong black families. In so doing, their works not only create a counter-discourse, but also illuminate how dominant ideological, economic, and political forces marginalize black women and families.

Prior to the rise of black feminist organizations and theories, women playwrights of the Black Arts Movement offered a powerful critique of detrimental ideologies perpetuated by both the federal government and black male leaders of the Black Power Movement. Their dramas directly address the harmful effects of myths perpetuated by *The Negro Family: The Case for National Action* (1965), also known as the *Moynihan Report*.[24] Headed by Assistant Secretary of Labor Daniel Patrick Moynihan, the report finds that discrimination contributes to the underpayment and underemployment of black men. Their inability to adequately provide for their families forces black mothers to work outside of the home, leading to a matriarchal structure, or "the reversed roles of husband and wife."[25] Black matriarchy emasculates fathers, causing them to either divorce or abandon their families. Without the support of fathers, black children become more likely to "flounder and fail" academically and become criminals, delinquents, or a burden to society through government welfare programs.[26] While the erroneous concept of black matriarchy existed prior to the *Moynihan Report*, the landmark study helped legitimize and transmit this mythology to a national audience. More than a decade prior to Michele Wallace's controversial book *Black Macho and the Myth of the Superwoman* (1978), which condemns the report for perpetuating a myth that would inspire black machismo within the black community, black women playwrights used their outside-within stance to critique such harmful mythologies. Working within the Black Power milieu, women dramatists of the Black Arts Movement resisted black machismo and defined empowerment in terms of the liberation of black men, women, and children.

Women playwrights of the Black Arts Movement generated a counter-discourse to black matriarchy and controlling images through the construction of the mythological warrior mother. Following in the tradition of black female writers who employ myth as "a metaphorical revisioning of experiential knowledge,"[27] Teer, Evans-Charles, Sanchez, and Franklin used their experiential knowledge to create new images of black feminine strength. Their representations of strong black motherhood were meant to counteract erroneous mythology and controlling images of black womanhood. While emotionally strong, the warrior mother avoids attributes of the superwoman stereotype. Wallace describes the superwoman as "a woman of inordinate strength, with the ability of tolerating an unusual amount of misery and heavy, distasteful work. [She] believes herself to be and is, in fact, stronger emotionally than most men."[28] In contrast, Teer, Evans-Charles, Sanchez, and Franklin's representations of warrior mothers express the pain associated with their invisibility. These warrior mothers desire to work with black men to build strong black families and nations. Analogous to black mothers socializing their children to live in an oppressive society, the warrior mother also teaches her community how to withstand the forces of institutional racism. Deeply rooted within Black Arts ethos, these warrior mothers often use Yoruba religious practices to offer godlike protection for their families or communities. This vision of black feminine strength encourages the liberation of the black consciousness and inspires revolutionary action. Indeed, these warrior mothers challenge black audiences to unify and eliminate the destructive behaviors within their own communities after the performance event itself.

Women playwrights of the Black Arts Movement refashioned the Black Arts warrior image to suit their own particular needs. Teer, Evans-Charles, Sanchez, and Franklin's concern with motherhood, which was also taken up by second wave feminists, stems from a desire to subvert racist ideologies and sanctify the black female body. The warrior mother image directly contradicts Smethurst's assertion that the "Black Arts warrior" was "both implicitly and explicitly male" and that "some black women writers in the post-Black

Arts era . . . introduced figures of the woman warrior and the Amazon (with a lesbian subtext) into their work."[29] While Teer, Evans-Charles, Sanchez, and Franklin's dramatic representations of strong black female leadership did, in fact, avoid lesbian subtexts, the warrior mother also importantly critiqued the practice of consigning women activists to the margins of the black liberation movement. Sanchez remembers challenging the sexist practices of black nationalist leaders, yet she lacked the courage to explore black lesbian relationships in her early dramas. She did, however, greatly admire writers who did not avoid lesbian subtexts. She describes Bullins's choice to write *Clara's Ole' Man* (1965), a play about black lesbians, as "brave" because this was "at a time when nobody would touch that."[30] Despite the heteronormative nature of the warrior mother, this image of black womanhood remains important because she not only resists dehumanizing icons of the past, but also demonstrates a continuum of African culture within contemporary black communities.

The dramas of Teer, Evans-Charles, Sanchez, and Franklin were meant to alarm, question, and provoke action. Influenced by the ethos of the Black Arts Movement, as well as by black women's tradition of resistance, most of their dramas feature poor black female protagonists who encounter oppressive forces from both within and outside of their Harlem community. These protagonists provide an important lens that allows the author to expose black women's unique struggles, as well as how these challenges relate to the collective struggles of the entire black community. In many ways, their plays realize Baraka's vision of creating revolutionary theater that would *move* audiences "to actual life understanding of what the world is, and what it ought to be."[31] Their dramas correct, insult, preach, and use dramatic irony to help audiences understand how both racism and sexism exclude black women and families from the world stage. Collectively, their works issue a call to black audiences to liberate their minds, bodies, and spirits from the political, economic, and ideological prisons of the past and present. This holistic understanding of black liberation was intended to ensure the survival of strong black families, the core foundation of any true revolution.

Historical Recovery

Chapter 1 of this book investigates Barbara Ann Teer's contributions to the Black Arts Movement, analyzing how her early experiences as an international dancer, Broadway actress, entrepreneur, and activist influenced her innovative art and her administration of the National Black Theatre. Teer wrote, performed, directed, and choreographed three "ritualistic revivals" during the Black Arts Movement: *A Ritual to Regain Our Strength and Reclaim Our Power* (1970), *A Revival: Change! Love Together! Organize!* (1972), and *Soljourney into Truth: A Ritualistic Revival* (1974). Coined by Teer, ritualistic revivals used elements of Pentecostal and Holy Roller church practices, Yoruba religion, and African aesthetics to eliminate traditional divisions between performer and audience. She envisioned ritualistic revivals as a holistic performance event that would educate blacks about destructive behaviors in their communities, create new mythologies of black womanhood, and celebrate the African continuum. Central to Teer's efforts was a desire to heal the psychological wounds of ideological, economic, and political oppression. The use of music, song, movement, chant, and testimonials gave "liberators" and "participants" (i.e., performers and audiences, respectively) an opportunity to not only create meaning in their lives, but also commune with one another. The chapter concludes by discussing the legacy of the National Black Theatre and other black women warriors who founded theaters and performance companies during the Black Arts Movement.

Chapter 2 examines the didactic and woman-centered dramas of Martie Evans-Charles, exploring how the performance careers and everyday knowledge of Evans-Charles's mother and aunts shaped her early conceptualization of drama. Evans-Charles's experiences living among a circle of talented black women not only influenced her appreciation of black women's culture, but also shaped her career as a dancer, educator, audience developer, actor, and playwright. Ed Bullins's mentorship, her service as a playwright-in-residence at the New Lafayette Theatre, and participation in the Black Theatre Workshop greatly impacted her development as a formidable Black Arts Movement playwright. Five of Evans-Charles's plays were produced during the Black Arts Movement: *Where We At?* (1969), *Black Cycle* (1970), *Job Security* (1970), *Jamimma* (1970), and *Asante* (1974). These works incorporate African cultural and spiritual practices, including conjuration, ritual, testimony, storytelling, and incantation, in order to teach, edify, and alarm audiences. Collectively, her works invite audiences to unify and to expel negative forces from their lives.

Chapter 3 explores the womanist dramas of the prolific poet Sonia Sanchez, detailing the ways in which womanist theology influenced her early conceptualization of drama. She later incorporated these insights, as well as knowledge gained from her experiences as a student, educator, and political activist, into her highly militant dramas. Described by the scholar of African American literature Joanne Veal Gabbin as an "armed prophet," Sanchez equipped herself with the weapon of words.[32] Her five dramas written during the Black Arts Movement are *The Bronx Is Next* (1968), *Sister Son/ji* (1969), *Dirty Hearts* (1971), *Malcolm/Man Don't Live Here No Mo'* (1972), and *Uh, Uh; But How Do It Free Us?* (1974). These dramas boldly expose the destructive attitudes and behavior within and outside of black communities in order to inspire positive change. In so doing, Sanchez's dramas recover black women's silenced history, voice the ongoing concerns of black women, and challenge black men and women to work together to eliminate all forms of oppression. Perhaps most important, Sanchez's dramas position female leadership and the survival of black women and families as vital to the achievement of black liberation.

Chapter 4 examines J.e. Franklin's development as an artist and theorist, noting the ways in which her early upbringing, political activism with Mobilization for Youth, membership in the Harlem Writers Guild, and experiences as a domestic worker and educator shaped her theories of performance and her concept of liberation. As a black woman intellectual, Franklin envisioned performance as a liberatory act that not only validates experiential knowledge, but also fosters embodied learning. Eleven of Franklin's plays were produced during the Black Arts Movement: *The In-Crowd: A Rock Opera in One Act* (1965), *Two Flowers* (1966), *Miss Honey's Young'uns* (1966 as *Mau Mau Room*), *The Prodigal Daughter* (before 1972), *Black Girl* (1969), *The Enemy* (1973), *Four Women* (1973), *MacPilate* (1974), *The Prodigal Sister* (1974) with Micki Grant, *The Creation* (1975), and *Another Morning Rising* (1976). While clearly engaged with the concern for black liberation, Franklin's refusal to adhere to the dominant set of artistic standards and practices of the era marked her as an outsider to the inner circle of Black Arts compatriots. Despite her uncomfortable relationship with Black Arts Movement rhetoric, Franklin worked with many of the leading black producers, directors, and composers of the era, including Woodie King Jr., George Houston Bass, Shauneille Perry, and Micki Grant, all of whom greatly impacted her career. Careful negotiation allowed Franklin to see her musicals, "straight plays," children's plays, and experimental works produced for television, film, and prominent Black Arts theaters.

"Let the Search Continue" marks the conclusion of *In Search of Our Warrior Mothers*. This epilogue notes the artistic legacies of Teer, Evans-Charles, Sanchez, and Franklin, as well as recovers the names of other women who inspired, developed, and critiqued Black Arts discourse. While these lists are helpful for further study, the gesture is not enough. Further sustained study of black women playwrights, directors, producers, and managers is needed in order to fully understand the myriad of ways that black women contributed to the artistic flowering known as the Black Arts Movement. This book, therefore, serves as a tribute to black warrior mothers—named and still unknown—whose tremendous talent, vision, and sacrifice made it possible (to paraphrase Katori Hall) to see black women's bodies stand unaltered on the pedestal called the stage.

Chapter 1

✦

"Set Your Blackness Free"
Barbara Ann Teer's Art and Activism

> Her eyes, opening like crystals, looked back to Africa, forward
> to the Caribbean, upward to America, told us to "take God
> out of the sky and put God into our hearts." . . . This woman,
> heavy with the smell of herstory and history, put her foot on
> this American spine and bid us look up at her gospel hands
> hanging bamboo poems of life.
>
> —Sonia Sanchez, 2008

Barbara Ann Teer's ritualistic revivals and theoretical writings reveal the
unique ways in which black women intellectuals of the Black Arts Movement
used their agency to actively conceptualize their own framework for black
empowerment. Her important theories of performance challenge the current
historical fallacy that there were no female theorists of the Black Arts Movement. This chapter critically examines Teer's holistic performance theories,
critical essays, and unpublished ritualistic revivals to demonstrate a continuation of black women's intellectual traditions from within Black Power
discourse. This study contends that Teer's intellectual and artistic endeavors
redefined revolutionary theater of the Black Arts Movement by incorporating a holistic approach to performance that privileged the spiritual, artistic,
and psychological liberation of both participants and performers. Furthermore, Teer's grassroots efforts created a new woman-centered African-based
mythology and promoted community activism by providing a platform to
discuss the devastating effects of racism and the need to form productive
relationships among black men and women of Harlem.

Teer's politically and socially conscious art embraced African aesthetics
and rejected traditional theatrical notions of time and space by eliminating
the divisions between actor and audience and encouraging all to use the performance event itself as an opportunity to bring about social change. Her
ritualistic revivals were much more than entertaining "plays," and were
meant to have lasting effects far beyond the scope of the event itself. Teer

used the terms "liberator" and "participant" in order to illustrate the active roles that both the performer and audience must undertake in order to bring about a cultural revolution. She encouraged liberators to approach performance holistically by utilizing chants, sermons, testimonials, music, song, dance, and structured improvisation to guide participants along a spiritual journey of self-identification and empowerment. A community was formed during the ritualistic revivals as participants were exposed to the problems facing Harlem, taught black cultural pride through the infusion of African mythology into contemporary life, and encouraged to take part in bettering their own community. Teer's didactic, emotionally engaging, and entertaining ritualistic revivals successfully fused a dramatic premise with music, movement, poetry, and religious practices. During the Black Arts Movement, Teer wrote, choreographed, and developed three important ritualistic revivals: *A Ritual to Regain Our Strength and Reclaim Our Power* (1970), *A Revival: Change! Love Together! Organize!* (1972) cowritten with Charlie Russell, and *Soljourney into Truth: A Ritualistic Revival* (1974).[1]

While Teer's performance theories and ritualistic revivals were critically acclaimed during the Black Arts Movement, her contributions to Black Arts theory and performance have been almost entirely overlooked by contemporary theater historians and feminist scholars. While Smethurst's important study *The Black Arts Movement: Literary Nationalism in the 1960s and 1970s* (2005) acknowledges Teer's National Black Theatre (NBT; 1968–present) as a "pioneer of black ritual theater," he remains doubtful of the "long-term impact of Teer and the NBT on the Black Arts Movement."[2] To further exacerbate this historical erasure, Teer's writings remain unpublished. Lacking accessible evidence to explore her ritualistic revivals, many theater historians continue to ignore her literary and artistic achievements.

To date, the most significant study of Teer's work remains theater historian Lundeana Thomas's *Barbara Ann Teer and the National Black Theatre: Transformational Forces in Harlem* (1997), written twenty years ago. While Thomas has written a remarkable biography about Teer's efforts to found the NBT, her study does not provide an in-depth analysis of how Teer implemented her performance theories within actual performances of her ritualistic revivals. Thomas's article "Barbara Ann Teer: From Holistic Training to Liberating Minds" (2002), however, provides more information about performance practices at the NBT. Thomas writes:

> The ritualistic revivals conducted by Teer were visions of spectacle aimed at enlightening and inspiring the audience. Each performance was a celebration of life, of identity, and artistic expression. . . . Special greetings, music, singing, dancing, chanting, high energy, audience interaction, and spontaneity were elements that engaged the NBT's audience in unusual ways. Some were not as successful as others in their implementation, but each distinguished the NBT as a group that

entertained its audience in ways not always familiar in the American professional theatre.[3]

This chapter also engages with the performative aspects of ritualistic revivals, paying particular attention to the participatory and communal nature of Teer's ritualistic revivals. This study departs from Thomas's work by utilizing the black feminist theories of Patricia Hill Collins, Teer's performance theories and unpublished play scripts, production recordings, and original interviews with Black Arts Movement artists in order to understand how Teer used her agency as an artist and Black Power activist to implement innovative performance practices. This chapter recovers Teer's efforts to galvanize her local community and honors her profound legacy to African American theater history, African American studies, and black feminist scholarship.

Barbara Ann Teer: Black Woman Intellectual

Teer's performance theories, critical essays, and ritualistic dramas demonstrate the continuation of black women's intellectual traditions from within Black Power discourse. Teer used her standpoint as a mother, artist, and activist to empower black men and women. Her ritualistic dramas created celebratory images of black womanhood and honored African American and African cultural traditions in order to empower and inspire unity among black men and women. Similar to the prevalent Black Arts and Black Power rhetoric of the era, Teer's art and activism demonstrated a commitment to developing a "distinctly African American or African culture."[4] Yet Teer did not situate her representations of blackness in opposition to white culture. Rather, she looked inward, focusing her efforts on strengthening the black community of Harlem. She theorized performance practices that would enable her to utilize the rhythms of a black preacher to reeducate participants about their African ancestry and encourage them to work together to eliminate the harmful images and vices within the community.

Teer's intellectual and artistic sensibilities reflect an appreciation of black women's culture and foreshadow the efforts of later womanist writers such as Alice Walker. After enduring a series of discriminatory experiences as an actress on Broadway during the late 1960s, Teer turned away from commercial theater and focused her efforts on the survival of the black community. Defying the popular belief at the time that a viable black theater could not exist in Harlem, in 1968 Teer founded her own experimental theater company, the NBT, to empower her community through the implementation of innovative ritualistic revivals that incorporated the emotions and spirituality of black female cultural practices. Teer, of course, was not alone in her efforts to experiment with black ritual form in Harlem. Robert Macbeth's New Lafayette Theatre (1967–72) produced the works of leading playwright

Figure 1. Dr. Barbara Ann Teer standing outside of National Black Theatre Inc., early 1980s. Courtesy of Dr. Barbara Ann Teer's National Black Theatre.

Ed Bullins and also experimented with ritual form. However, Harlem audiences preferred the spirit of community and the emotional depth of Teer's ritualistic revivals. As Paul Carter Harrison argues in *The Drama of Nommo* (1972), the New Lafayette Theatre's experimentation with ritual form ultimately "fail[ed]" to connect with audiences because of their "overzealous and self-indulgent preoccupation with form" and "nationalism."[5] The NBT, on the other hand, remained a vital theater because it "arous[ed] the spirit, thus heightening the community's consciousness."[6] Indeed, Teer's ritualistic revivals combined elements of ritual drama, Pentecostal and Holy Roller church practices, and the emotional excitement of revivalism in order to teach, cleanse, and unite the Harlem community.

Drawing from black women's cultural traditions, Teer aroused the spirit or what she deemed a distinct "god force" within blacks that she believed was necessary to secure "black survival."[7] She led an emotional release for participants through her captivating performances as a conductor, newly conceptualized deity named Taji and powerful Yoruba goddess Oshun.

Teer showcased her leadership and talents by singing, chanting, playing instruments, and preaching didactic messages of cultural pride and self-determination. By presenting herself as an African goddess onstage and self-fashioning herself as a warrior mother offstage, Teer not only created new African-based mythologies centered on the power of black womanhood, but also reaffirmed her own role as a formidable leader in Harlem.

Teer began to formulate her own artistic theories and develop a holistic approach to acting during and immediately following her career on Broadway in the mid-1960s. While working with the choreographer Alwin Nikolais in New York City, Teer suffered a knee injury that would end her dance career. According to the theater historian Lundeana Thomas, Teer became "[d]epressed by her injury" and "consulted a spiritualist who told her that her power was in her head rather than her feet."[8] Although Teer would go on to learn traditional modes of acting theory from world-renowned teachers such as Sanford Meisner, Lloyd Richards, Paul Mann, and Philip Burton, she used a holistic approach for her own theories of performance. Teer discussed this important phase in her life and the psychological damage of performing in commercial theater in a 1971 interview with NBT playwright-in-residence Charlie L. Russell:

> I became conscious of who I was. A black woman. Politically aware of what a black woman in America means. Over my manager's objections I had cut my hair in a natural. Cutting my hair helped me realize that I was in the wrong place, white theatre. Because of my natural I had my first fight with my manager.[9]

By cutting and styling her hair into a "natural" or afro, Teer symbolically liberated herself from Western standards of beauty and claimed the space she needed to circumvent society's expectations and norms. From this point on she refused to perform stereotypical characters onstage, fired her manager, and began voicing her concerns about the psychological impact of racist performance practices on black actors and actresses in American theater.

In the late 1960s Teer published several crucial essays that focused on the mental health of black actresses who are forced to compete with each other for limited and stereotypical roles. Black actresses are offered only two roles—"domestic" or "sex symbol," argued Teer in her essay "The Black Woman: She Does Exist" (1967) written for the *New York Times*.[10] Contextualizing this plight within the broader framework of black women's history in the Americas, Teer asserted that these limited roles "resulted from racist concepts created in the days of slavery which made the Negro woman either a work animal or a producing animal, consequently stripping her of any traits of intelligence and any attributes of femininity."[11] Deeply concerned with the psychological effects of portraying such distortions of black womanhood, Teer asserted that these stereotypes "greatly, if not completely, stifled the Negro actress' development as an entity in the industry" and caused her to simultaneously "fight the battle of being forced to conform to a Caucasian standard of beauty" and fight "racism which excludes the reality of her existence as a human being."[12] Teer suggested that performing the roles of a domestic or a hypersexualized jezebel not only dehumanizes, but also destroys the creative minds and souls of black actresses. In her 1968 essay "Needed: A New Image," published in *The Black Power Revolt,* Teer put forth a call for black artists to "project an image of love, respect, and solidarity" to counteract stereotypical images of black women.[13] She broadened her concern by requesting that black artists "establish a positive relationship between black men and black women in the theatre and all other mass media."[14] Building upon this essay, that same year Teer published a manifesto, "The Great White Way Is Not Our Way—Not Yet" (1968) in *Negro Digest,* which would be another key turning point in her career. Rather than focus her energy on condemning the media, she issued a call for black artists to build a strong black cultural institution in Harlem that would nurture, teach, and allow young black artists to embrace their identity and "be free to experiment and to create."[15] Teer's manifesto unequivocally severed her ties with what she regarded as the "white establishment" of Broadway, and from this point on she would utilize the talents, resources, and strengths of the Harlem community to realize her vision of founding a black cultural institution.[16]

Teer's theoretical writings suggest that the interdisciplinary nature of theater provides an ideal cultural institution that, if nourished, can become a galvanizing force to empower the black community. She discusses the relationship between black American theater and African culture in her article "We Can Be What We Were Born to Be" (1968) written for the *New York Times.* "To quote Harold Cruse, 'We must cease thinking of black theater purely in European terms the way white artists view the theater. Black theater is, historically, an American development by way of Africa. It is not an American development by way of Europe,'" Teer writes.[17] She envisioned a theater built upon African aesthetics, African ways of knowing, and African ways of being. She believed that a cultural revolution was necessary in order for blacks to become subjects and define their own world instead of being defined by others. Building upon Cruse's call in *Rebellion or Revolution?* (1968) to "transform the [Negro] movement from a mere rebellion" into an active "cultural revolution" that served a "social purpose,"[18] Teer argues:

> The theater should be the forerunner in this cultural revolution because the theater is a form which can encompass nearly all *our* creative endeavors. It can disavow all the stereotypes and replace them with more meaningful images that represent *us* as *we* really are in life. *We* must establish for *ourselves* what is beautiful, ugly, clean, pure, dirty, correct, incorrect, good, bad, sexy, violent, nonviolent, criminal—what is really meaningful to *us*.[19]

Teer advocated for blacks to establish a theater that would provide black artists with a safe space to create and construct visions of their past, present, and future conditions. By the very nature of this mission, Teer's theater would function as a cultural institution, revolutionizing black art and promoting self-determination within black communities.

Teer experienced backlash from black artists in New York City because of her rejection of commercial theater, criticism of the state of black theater, and promotion of a separate black theater. She was unprepared for the harsh criticism. Barbara "Sade" Lythcott, her daughter and the current president of the NBT, recalls:

> At one point my mom was becoming very hot [i.e., passionate]. What she was saying was so revolutionary—this happens oftentimes—that black people maybe [we]re not ready to embrace something so radical. But white people [we]re very intrigued by it and she wrote several articles for the *New York Times*. When you write something and you put it out in the public, you have to be open for criticism.[20]

"White people, black people, actors alike" disapproved of her mother's vision and "the criticism really destroyed her."[21] Lythcott remembers that her mother "didn't feel safe in public anymore," was deeply hurt by what she felt was a "betrayal," and "became fiercely private, which [is] why she's never written a book."[22] Although Teer continued to write plays, poetry, and theories of performance, she ceased publishing for fear of further ostracism. She did, however, continue to publish press releases, nurture young artists at the NBT, and collaborate with spiritualists and African artists who shared similar beliefs.

Teer faced challenges as an artist, activist, and entrepreneur because she refused to conform to someone else's standards of black femininity. In a 1971 *Essence* magazine interview, Teer remarked that she saw her critics as "militants who called themselves nationalists. . . . Frustrated men who wanted to define for me my role as a black woman. Insecure men who felt that the woman's place is in the home having babies, walking six steps behind, and speaking only when spoken to."[23] Teer recognized that in order to found a black cultural institution in Harlem, she had to negotiate a space among so-called militants who upheld such double standards. She self-fashioned her own public image as a "warrior mother" to allow her to fulfill her responsibilities as creator, performer, and artistic director of the NBT.

Teer had to develop a warrior mother persona and display what she identified as "ruthless compassion" to succeed in the male-dominated theaters of New York City.[24] In a 2010 interview, former liberator Nabii Faison argues that because of her race and gender, Teer's intelligence and ability to finance and manage a cultural institution were constantly under scrutiny. Channeling her feminine warrior strength, however, helped Teer establish her leadership within her community. In a 1994 interview with the theater historian Rebecca Daniels, Teer discusses ruthless compassion and the process of embracing her feminine warrior strength. Teer defines ruthless compassion as "a combination of the warrior/masculine side and the mother/feminine side so that . . . your love for that somebody or that something . . . may look very hard or very cold or unfeeling."[25] There were times when she admittedly tried to "avoid" displaying her warrior strength so as not to intimidate insecure men who were in control of the resources she needed.[26] By delicately balancing her feminine strength, artistic sensibilities, and entrepreneurial spirit, Teer was able to cultivate a warrior mother public persona and successfully navigate her interests within the male-dominated New York theaters.

Teer's warrior mother persona complemented her matriarchal approach to innovative theater management. She modeled her management of the NBT after the "black family structure"[27] and likened the theater to "a family base."[28] Interestingly, the NBT did not include a patriarch. Teer utilized total cooperation as the core of her administration; yet as the matriarch, she guided every aspect of the NBT. Teer's unique administrative practices included the removal of specialization within theater management. Liberators, for example, not only performed, but also painted sets and contributed their talents wherever needed. In her 1971 interview with NBT playwright-in-resident Charles L. Russell, Teer explained that rather than delineate specific roles for men and women, "most" responsibilities were "interchangeable."[29] Her only exception to gender-neutral tasks pertained to security of facilities—only men performed this task. Security, in fact, became an important feature at the NBT after so-called militants threatened Teer's life for her outspokenness.[30]

Male and female compatriots gravitated toward Teer because of her incredible intelligence, undeniable talent, and powerful vision of a black cultural revolution. Male members of the NBT "caught hell from many outsiders" because they "belong[ed] to an organization run by a woman" who was supposedly "trying to do a man's job," Teer recalled in her interview with Russell.[31] Regardless of the criticism, Faison remembers his great admiration for her inner strength, passion, business savvy, and leadership skills:

> I've always said—and it's always been said—that if Barbara was a man she'd probably be dead because she had the energy of a warrior [or] samurai to be more accurate. [Teer was] just an incredible, non-stop, no-prisoners, don't-take-no-for-an-answer, unconditional loving soul and as a result it intimidated the hell out of most men. It intimidated women in a positive way because Barbara was living the dreams that most women had: to be themselves. Not what they're supposed to be. She was charming. Engaging. . . . There [we]re men in the sixties that'd get in her face like they talk to a man. She'd just diffuse it. She'd just look at them and they shifted. I never saw her back down in my life.[32]

Whether actively cultivated or as a consequence of working alongside Teer, women members of the NBT also shared her self-confidence.[33] She praised her female colleagues and described them as "all very much like me, very assertive and clear and powerful."[34] The now-legendary black producer Woodie King Jr. recognized Teer's intelligence and tenacity upon first meeting her in the 1960s. In an interview with Ted Wilson following Teer's death in 2008, King describes a young Teer as "a stunning beauty—thin, tall, free and fierce."[35]

By the mid-1970s, Teer's fierce determination to succeed resulted in numerous awards, including the inaugural AUDELCO Recognition Award for Excellence in Black Theatre. New York Congressman Charles Rangel recognized her efforts in 1975, declaring the NBT "one of the most valuable, worthwhile and exciting programs in our community . . . [the NBT] ha[s] been a positive force in Harlem, asking people indirectly to confront their own lives and celebrating constantly the achievements and experience of Black writers, artists and scholars."[36] Teer's legacy continues strong as the NBT remains one of the few surviving Black Arts theater institutions in the United States.

During the theater's first year of operation in 1968, Teer developed the "Five Cycles of Evolution," an innovative theory of acting designed to liberate the consciousness of black performers and participants. She formulated her theories through observations at bars and churches, as well as discussions with local preachers, deacons, church sisters, and singers. The theater critic Jessica B. Harris commended Teer's holistic theories of performance, stating that they provided a "major innovation" for black theater by allowing "the black actor to . . . return to himself, to his culture, to his heritage and to his people."[37] Faison likewise confirmed the benefits of Teer's holistic approach to acting, having experienced the process firsthand during his early career as a liberator. Teer taught self-awareness and "created a space of love where stories could be shared to heal our psychic distortion, to heal our mental breakdown" caused by self-hatred, says Faison.[38] NBT liberators underwent Teer's process of "decrudin," or what Harris describes as "a purification," to become self-aware and therefore a positive force in the Harlem community.[39] In his brief analysis of Teer's efforts, African American theater historian Mance Williams explains that the "intention" of Teer's "decrudin" was to "return Blacks to their spiritual base so they can rediscover their individual identities and their collective identity."[40] Liberators (and eventually participants) had to willingly embark on a spiritual journey through the "Five Cycles of Evolution." Teer describes the five levels of black consciousness during her interview with Russell:

> *The Nigger*, . . . he has strong materialistic and individualistic values; *The Negro*, he is also individualistic and materialistic, accepts white cultural standards . . . ; *The Militant*, an aware *Nigger* . . . not for real change, and is only angry and frustrated because the system won't let him in; *The Nationalist*, being non-materialistic, he is intellectually

for the collective. This is the first step into true blackness, where you
develop a consciousness and a love for your people; *The Revolutionary* . . . deal[s] with the spirituality of blackness. You know who you
are, what you have to do, and you simply go about doing it.[41]

Unification and a love of blackness served as the crucial first step in developing a black consciousness. Teer theorized that the spirituality of blackness
did not function as a reaction against white hegemony, but rather helped
revolutionaries to remain self-aware, confident, and take action to meet the
needs of the collective community. She discussed the need to teach liberators
to (1) analyze each evolutionary type from a "social," "religious," and "political point of view," (2) take part in "a total educational process" by living and
dressing in the mode of their cycle, (3) record their findings, and (4) embody
their findings during ritualistic revivals.[42] By 1975 the theater critic Tony Best
praised Teer's experimentation, noting the NBT's well-deserved reputation as
a "creative factory" among the theater community.[43]

Teer hosted seminars and community workshops and set forth new artistic standards to educate critics and participants about her creative work.
Her artistic mission was to "enlighten participants" by sharing "knowledge
and truth" about the black condition.[44] She believed that people of African
descent were a spiritual people who possessed a distinctive energy force,
and she would dedicate the next decade of her life to theorizing ways to
uncover and utilize this energy during her performance events. In so doing,
Teer created what she deemed "a Standard of Criticism of Black Art" by
which critics and theatergoers could evaluate NBT events. "Theatrical pre-
sentations" had to fulfill five criteria: "(1) Raise the level of consciousness . . .
(2) Be Political . . . (3) Educate . . . (4) Clarify issues [and] (5) Entertain."[45]
Teer actualized her artistic mission by hosting workshops and creating performances that raised awareness on pertinent issues impacting the local
community. She invited locally and internationally known guest speakers
to educate her community about spirituality, health and wellness, politics,
and African culture. Her most notable guests included the Black Arts writers
Sonia Sanchez and Nikki Giovanni; Student Nonviolent Coordinating Committee leaders Stokely Carmichael, H. Rap Brown, and James Foreman; and
the award-winning actress and activist Ruby Dee. The NBT also organized
relevant topical seminars ranging from "Man-Woman Relationships" and
"Liberation Theory and Practice" to "Community Organization" in order
to empower Harlem citizens. In a 1971 article on black theaters in the New
York City metropolitan area, the critic Peter Bailey noted that the NBT successfully "replac[ed] the sermon with seminars."[46] Bailey's comment signaled
an important shift within the Harlem community: blacks were now turning
to the NBT for spiritual nourishment. Teer's ritualistic revivals, in particular, fused religious practices with secular sociopolitical messages to educate,
unify, and spiritually nourish participants.

Heavily influenced by pan-Africanist philosophy, Teer conceived of ritualistic revivals as revolutionary events that could educate, unify, and edify blacks through the valorization of African cultural aesthetics. While there are various historical and critical understandings of pan-Africanism, P. Olisanwuche Esedebe offers a useful definition of its core values: a collective concern for identifying Africa as the homeland of Africans and those of African descent, pride in African history and culture, "belief in a distinct African personality," and "solidarity among people of African descent."[47] Teer's ritualistic revivals were revolutionary events because they actualized pan-Africanist sentiments by cultivating black love, pride in African aesthetics, and solidarity. She expressed her pan-Africanist vision in an early NBT press release, "Letter by Barbara Ann Teer":

> The National Black Theatre is calling for a return to the basic foundation of African traditional Culture and folklore for we believe that this is the ultimate solution to the elimination of 400 years of Black oppression. Our first Revival deals with elimination of drugs, evil, and vice because our drug and crime rate have drastically increased in the last five years. And we feel that this is the most serious internal issue confronting our communities today. So the Revival becomes more tha[n] dynamic entertainment. It becomes an educational vehicle that is designed to remove those negative influences from the Harlem community and move it back toward love. And Black Theatre should be concerned with the survival of its' people, i.e. its' Culture. For a race without a solid, strong spiritual foundation and a positive cultural thrust will never survive.[48]

Blacks had the power to heal their communities through the promotion of culture, or the ability to define and express truth about oneself. Teer believed that her ritualistic revivals functioned as "a revolutionary act" by the simple fact that they promoted "Black Love" and uncovered the latent "god force" within participants.[49] All peoples of African descent had a powerful energy from within that, if properly channeled, could become a healing force.

Theory in Practice: Ritualistic Revivals at the NBT (1968–76)

Teer's ritualistic revivals borrowed heavily from the structure of ritual drama, church service practices, and the emotional exuberance of revivalism in order to elicit audience participation. In "The Way to Viable Theatre?: Afro-American Ritual Drama" (1973), the playwright and scholar Carlton W. Molette explains that the structure of ritual drama utilizes a "dramatic premise" and the "patterned arrangement of actions" rather than a traditional plot.[50] Similar to preacher sermons, the success of ritual dramas rests upon "not *what* you say and do but *how* you say and do it."[51] In concrete terms, the dramatic happening should build in intensity to bring forth an emotional response from participants. As with ritual drama, Teer used rhythm, or the repetition of speech, music, and movement, to build and eventually reduce the emotional intensity of participants. Teer likened participants to a congregation and explained that her revivals offered participants "a holy experience" whereby blacks could "mold, meet, and merge into one" and "feel, laugh, cry, and experience life together."[52] Equally important for Teer was that participants should experience a spiritual cleansing during the performative event. In a review of *A Ritual to Regain Our Strength and Reclaim Our Power* (1971), Teer explains that "like the Christian concept of Easter, our ritual serves to help with the revitalization, a rebirth, a cleansing, a lifting, a loving."[53] Her emphasis on the importance of emotional cleansing during her ritualistic revivals reflects a major tenant of Holiness, Baptist, and Pentecostal church worship practices. As a place of worship, Teer's ritualistic revivals used the entire performance space and included incantations, meditations, sermons, and testimonials from both liberators and participants. Teer effectively altered traditional divisions between spectators and performers by removing both emotional and spatial barriers. Spectators arrived with a desire to emotionally participate, Faison recalls. Seemingly improvised interactions with liberators or the high energy of fellow participants often persuaded speculative participants to contribute to the performance event.

Teer's ritualistic revivals utilized structured improvisation to cultivate total cooperation between liberator and participant. She developed these revivals through experimental workshops with liberators that included poetry readings and musical sessions. Liberators then used the acting theories and methods of structured improvisation taught by Teer during actual revivals to greet and interact with participants. Perhaps the best example of the use of structured improvisation occurs in *Soljourney into Truth* (1974), Teer's third ritualistic revival. The unpublished manuscript states that liberators (who use their actual names) should begin the ritual by asking participants a series of questions. The question "What do you expect to happen tonight on this Soljourney?" allows liberators to assess participant's expectations and willingness to take part in the ritual.[54] After receiving responses from participants, the stage directions state that liberators rejoin, "Well, you're gonna get an opportunity to feel real good inside," and then implore participants to "choose one example from their experience" of feeling "good inside."[55] Teer's script provides three possible experiences for liberators to state in order to prod participants to vocalize their thoughts: "Eat the last mouthful of a good meal," "Buy a brand new outfit," and "Get a beautiful gift you weren't expecting from a person you really love."[56] Liberators then inform participants that they will be invited to sing songs, hold hands, and close their eyes.[57] If participants agree to actively participate in the ritual, liberators state, "Great! You're ready to fly," and begin the ritual.[58] If participants refuse, liberators must repeat the series of questions. This moment of structured improvisation at the beginning of *Soljourney* was an important device that fostered total cooperation and set the tone for a holy experience. In a 1985 interview with the playwright and theater historian Karen Malpede, Teer likened total cooperation to a holy experience:

> In those days people used to get possessed . . . The drums would take them out. They would talk in tongues, and they would tell stories, and they would share with me all kinds of things when they came back. They experienced a freedom I had never seen before. . . . I began creating exercises and processes and techniques to handle the energy and I continued to go to my mentors, who were church people.[59]

The high level of energy would become the most notable feature of Teer's productions and elicit favorable reviews from critics.[60]

Promoting a pan-Africanist vision based on an appreciation of black women's culture remained at the center of Teer's early revivals. *The Ritual*, a filmed recording of her first ritualistic revival, *A Ritual to Regain Our Strength and Reclaim Our Power* (1970), illustrates her concern for participants to recognize their strength and reclaim their African heritage. Faison remembers that Kwame Azular's poem "What If," which was developed during workshops, provided the inspiration for the ritualistic revival. Azular's poem suggests the need to return to an African cultural base by repeatedly asking, "What if we did not come *from* Africa, but *to* Africa."[61] In contrast to her later works, *The Ritual* uses the plight of a black girl named Young Girl to answer these profound questions. Young Girl, dressed in unkempt baggy clothes, represents those who struggle to survive in an economically depressed urban neighborhood. The liberators, clothed in vibrant red, black, and green ankle-length robes, represent a pan-Africanist vision. The liberators attempt to reeducate Young Girl and the participants about their place within the African continuum throughout the course of the event. Ayedelo informs Young Girl of the destructiveness of drugs, while Tunde tries to instill black pride in her by reminding her that blacks are "kings and queens" who must help build the "nation."[62] Young Girl remains unconvinced, however, until the female liberators take on the rhythms of black preachers. A strong sisterhood is formed as the women testify to black women's resilience in surviving their history of rape and exploitation in the United States, preach Malcolm X's message of love between black men and women, and exhort Young Girl to love herself. These sermons allow Teer to simultaneously recover black women's unique history in America while celebrating a shared African heritage among black men and women.

The ultimate success of *A Ritual* and the later televised production rested upon Teer's performance as the conductor. Following the revival's initial success at the NBT, Ellis Hazlip produced *The Ritual* on New York City's Public Broadcasting System *Soul* program in February 1970. While Faison contends that the film version did not precisely capture the emotional interactions between liberators and participants, he says the film accurately represented Teer's gift for guiding ritualistic revivals. According to Faison, Teer functioned as "the conductor of the ritual" and effectively "weaved the story" for participants.[63] With music underscoring her words, Teer begins *The Ritual* by creating a communal space through the celebration of blackness. After encouraging participants to hold hands, Teer reminds participants of their shared cultural heritage and challenges them to "see if we can find our way home."[64] With incense burning and the conga drum gently beating, Teer, along with a fellow liberator, proceeds to open the ritual by softly chanting, "Set your blackness free."[65] Thus initiating the revival, participants in the film recording unabashedly cry during testimonials, sway to the beat of the conga drum, mingle with liberators on the three-quarter stage, and enthusiastically shout "Yeah!" during moments of call and response. Teer closes *The Ritual* by directing participants to hold hands, stand up, and form a "love chain."[66] Seemingly aware of the various energy levels around her, Teer begins to dance and play the tambourine while issuing humorous yet important challenges to participants to increase their involvement. She calls in a lighthearted tone, "I bet you can't shake hands! . . . Let me see you grab someone and hug 'em!," and begins chanting, "Hey! Hey! I feel alright!"[67] Participants respond to Teer's call by chanting "Hey! Hey! I feel alright," touching one another, forming a love chain, and jumping up and down to the beat of the conga drum throughout the entire performance space. The challenges issued by Teer help participants to not only form a cooperative community, but also to actively affirm their humanity as black Americans.

The national broadcast of *The Ritual* brought recognition to Teer's artistic vision, a vision that she refused to compromise for monetary gain. In her article "Ritual and the National Black Theatre" (1987), Teer reflected upon the revival's initial success, noting that the filmed production garnered the NBT "a semi-visibility in the black world."[68] Although she received multiple job offers as a consequence of the broadcast, she refused them all because she believed the proposals were "all too commercial" and "would water-down" her artistic vision.[69] Instead of pursuing fame or fortune, Teer opted to maintain control over her artistry and toured the production at colleges and universities to enthusiastic youths. She did, however, form a partnership with the NBT's writer-in-residence Charlie L. Russell for her second ritualistic revival, *A Revival: Change! Love Together! Organize!* (1972). In the press release, she notes that while Russell provided the "story line and characters," she "incorporated" this information "spiritually and artistically" into her own "unique ritualistic form" which took three years of development to complete.[70] The dramatic premise of *A Revival* features the struggles of the protagonist Toussaint, leader of a young revolutionary group known as the Kabakas. Toussaint works passionately to teach black love, eliminate drugs, and save the citizens of Harlem from a sure cultural and spiritual

Figure 2. Dr. Barbara Ann Teer performing in a National Black Theatre ritualistic revival, 1970. Courtesy of Dr. Barbara Ann Teer's National Black Theatre.

death. Similar to his namesake Toussaint Louverture, the captivating leader who successfully led enslaved San Domingans against Napoleon Bonaparte's forces during the Haitian Revolution (1791–1804), Teer and Russell's Toussaint also attempts to conquer a seemingly more powerful foe: Walt Chapman, the most powerful drug dealer in Harlem.

Of Teer's three ritualistic revivals, *A Revival: Change! Love Together! Organize!* remains the most overtly didactic. The ritualistic revival begins with the Kabakas informing participants that although blacks comprise "only 11%" of the American population, they "drink more than 33% . . . of all the orange sodas," "consume over 50% of the Scotch," "bought over 25% of the hats! And spent over 9 million dollars on neck-ties!"[71] By critiquing the disproportionate consumption of alcohol, poor dietary habits, and frivolous spending within the black community, the Kabakas first attempt to "decrud" participants by drawing awareness to the problems facing Harlem citizens. The Kabakas then proceed to galvanize participants into action by repeatedly chanting, "Build black institutions if you wanna be free. Support black institutions, that's your responsibility."[72] The Kabakas urge participants to effect positive social change outside of the performance event itself by developing black businesses and buying products made within their community. Immediately following intermission, "a montage of taped sounds" of the black nationalist leaders Malcolm X, H. Rap Brown, and Stokely Carmichael are played.[73] These audio recordings of contemporary black leaders delivering inspirational messages reinforce Teer's message of community activism. This black nationalist rhetoric is put into action as liberators and participants prepare for a community revival known as "The Meeting." Participants are "ushered under a heavy chain and into the Temple of Liberation," a peaceful space of communal worship, says the theater critic Jessica B. Harris.[74] From this point onward the dramatic premise ceases altogether as liberators and participants hold each other, chant, meditate, worship Yoruba gods and goddesses, and call upon Oshun, the beautiful Yoruba mother goddess of rivers and fertility, for guidance. As with all of her ritualistic revivals, *A Revival: Change! Love Together! Organize!* closes with a call to arms to improve the Harlem community. Unlike the previous ritual, liberator Mamadou, rather than Teer, issues the call, stating: "We are now releasing this cone of harmonious energy out into our community, and as it flows, we will each begin to feel a change. The change will help us love together, and then we will move to organize."[75] *A Revival: Change! Love Together! Organize!* thus provided the assurance that black men and women had the capacity to liberate themselves by changing their mind-sets and organizing collectively to become an independent and economically viable community.

In *A Revival: Change! Love Together! Organize!* the character Oshun functions as a didactic tool to educate participants about the importance of Yoruba culture and demonstrate the limitless power of black female deities. The dramatic premise reveals that Oshun has become the forgotten mother goddess of Harlem. Undervalued and cast aside, Oshun must watch while her children destroy themselves with drugs, alcohol, prostitution, and crime. Although wise and powerful, Oshun cannot offer advice, safety, or protection to the black community of Harlem unless they invoke her through prayer and ask for her guidance. Oshun (Teer) pleads with her children, "Oh spirit faced people, you are lost from your source / We have come over to help you grow and grow and get you—all our children, back on the right course."[76] Toussaint, who hears Oshun's plea, exhorts the street people and participants to "return to our gods" since "our Gods [are] the original source of power," and invites them to attend "The Meeting" to summon Oshun.[77] Once gathered, liberators and participants perform a Haitian voodoo rites ceremony to summon Oshun and ask her for protection. She answers their call by providing a solution to their problems: unification and love. During this ceremony the performance space becomes a sacred place where the "god force" can be unleashed. Teer's work reflects what Carlton and Barbara Molette argue is the "goal" within black revolutionary theater: to "recapture a lost sense of [ancestral] values" by "adapt[ing] traditional Black ritual concepts to contemporary African-American culture."[78] By connecting Yoruba mythology with the struggles of everyday urban life, Teer not only fulfilled her purpose of returning to African culture and folklore, but also created new mythologies centered upon feminine strength and wisdom.

A Revival: Change! Love Together! Organize also provided the opportunity for Teer to cultivate her own role as a fearless warrior mother by performing as Oshun. The mythology of Oshun's management of the world and Teer's management of the NBT mirror each other. In *Òsun across the Waters: A Yoruba Goddess in Africa and the Americas* (2001), the art historian Cornelius O. Adepegba describes Oshun's difficulties as a female deity among male deities:

> Osun was one of the Yoruba primordial deities. Yet she was at first not considered to be a fellow deity by her peers. . . . She was at first not involved in the management of the world because she alone was a woman. But the sixteen deities were having problems until they went to God for direction and were told to invite Osun to all that they wanted to do, for normalcy to be restored. According to God, she should be involved because she was as powerful as men. It was when they were inviting her to join them as God directed that she was addressed by the male deities as . . . *Ìyá Ìjùmú, òyéyé ní imò*, meaning, "The mother . . . of Ijumu that is full of understanding."[79]

Similar to the Yoruba deities, Teer's male peers lacked faith in her abilities because of her gender. They told her that as a woman, she could not successfully purchase and manage a theater in Harlem. Both Oshun and Teer utilized their intelligence and motherhood to secure their authority among powerful men. Just as Oshun became the wise mother of Ìjùmú, Teer cultivated the image of a warrior mother as a source of empowerment to successfully negotiate a space for herself within a male-dominated sphere of New York theater. Oshun's tale reflects the importance of black female leadership and the dangers of undervaluing black womanhood. Without Oshun's management, other male deities experienced "problems" and the world did not experience "normalcy" until she was fully accepted by her peers. By performing as Oshun, Teer symbolically positioned her own leadership as not only normal, but also necessary to the survival of black culture.

Teer's third ritualistic revival, *Soljourney into Truth* (1974), symbolically takes black participants to Africa to connect back to their African religious practices and spiritually cleanse themselves of negative forces. As the title suggests, Teer was concerned with the "souls" of participants and their "true" essence as black Americans. Unlike her previous ritualistic revivals, *Soljourney into Truth* abandons traditional narrative structure and relies upon total cooperation between participants and liberators. Participants become protagonists of the ritual event as they are invited by liberators to imagine that they are in a waiting area of the Black Star Line about to board the Sun Ship. Teer's incorporation of the Black Star Line pays tribute to the pan-Africanist vision of Marcus Garvey, founder of the Universal Negro Improvement Association (1914–30). In 1919 Garvey organized the Black Star Line to transport merchandise as well as black Americans back to Africa. Esedebe explains Garvey's influence: "Without setting foot on African soil he created for the first time a real feeling of international solidarity among Africans and persons of African stock."[80] By incorporating the Black Star Line into the ritual event, Teer not only honored Garvey's entrepreneurial spirit, but also realized his back-to-Africa vision by symbolically leading participants back to their African roots. In order to board the Sun Ship, liberators take participants through a series of exercises to help them discover "the true you" by eliminating the toxins of fear, oppression, hate, and any negative forces from their lives.[81] Having been "decruded," participants board the Sun Ship where they are encouraged to provide more "fuel" for the ship by talking to each other, holding hands, chanting, singing, sharing testimonials, interacting with Yoruba gods and goddesses, forming a dancing love train, and "rock[ing] to and fro."[82] Not content to merely eliminate toxins, near the conclusion of the ritual Teer also encouraged participants to take on the difficult task of empowering themselves.

Soljourney into Truth provided a safe space for participants to actively create new images of black identity that reflected their innermost truths. Performing as a goddess named Taji, Teer "descended from a throne" and guided participants throughout their spiritual journey of self-discovery.[83] Teer begins this process, according to the stage directions, by taking on the "preacher rhythm"[84] and performing an inspirational sermon, stating:

> Harlem . . . just like that tree planted by the water, we shall not be moved. Cause Harlem is a mighty, mighty place, it's filled full of a mighty glorious race and this mighty[,] mighty place called Harlem is now and forever more, I said Harlem is the cultural capitol of the world! And from that cultural capitol of the world comes a divine army of trained Liberators.[85]

Similar to black activists of the 1930s, who altered the lyrics of the slave spiritual "We Shall Not Be Moved" to the anthem "We Shall Overcome," Teer uses the slave spiritual to suit her own rhetorical needs. She constructs a romantic vision of Harlem filled with liberators leading a cultural revolution. Teer's emphasis on the importance of Harlem, delivered in preacher rhythm, was meant to inspire black pride, provide a powerful call to arms, and position the Harlem community as an integral force behind a "divine" cultural revolution.

Teer's cultural revolution began during the ritual itself as she challenged participants to cooperate and take an active role in their own psychological liberation. During *Soljourney into Truth* Teer invites participants to complete five exercises to test their willingness to bring about positive change. The script suggests that she began this process by asking participants to hold hands, forming a communal space. She invites participants to share

Figure 3. Dr. Barbara Ann Teer, 1990s. Photo by Bernard Fairclough. Courtesy of Dr. Barbara Ann Teer's National Black Theatre.

their inner emotions by looking each other in the eyes and telling how they "honestly feel."[86] Building in difficulty, Teer's third challenge requires participants to close their eyes and "manufacture new thoughts" by creating "new images," or "a picture that reflects who we really are."[87] Having recognized the power of images during her Broadway career, Teer wanted to empower participants by helping them understand their own worth and humanity and teaching them the skills to define themselves. Teer's final two tests incorporated call and response and self-affirming chants. The script states that Taji (Teer) teaches participants the following chant: "You're the only one who can make yourself happy, / You're the only one who can fill your life with joy, / You're the only one who can make yourself happy, / Cause nothing can happen to you unless it passes thru your mind."[88] After teaching the chant, Taji (Teer) divides participants into groups "A" and "B" and while ad-libbing, encourages participants to chant to each other and applaud their own efforts. Teer's communal chant served three purposes: (1) to teach participants that they are ultimately responsible for determining their own happiness, (2) to remind blacks that they have a responsibility to support and uplift each other, and (3) to demonstrate how chants of self-affirmation can transform one's consciousness and therefore one's life. *Soljourney into Truth* not only entertained participants through self-affirmation chants, but also empowered them by helping them understand how self-determination and racial solidarity can be used as weapons to revolutionize Harlem.

Teer's career defies traditional notions of black power and feminist activism. Although Teer did not join a feminist group or organization, nor did she endorse equality among men and women, she did foster a cooperative learning environment and advocate mutual respect between black men and women. In a 1996 interview with the theater historian Rebecca Daniels, Teer argued that although gender was "biological," this did not mean that black women were "weak" or should "be victimized, or taken over."[89] Sexism was "wrong-headed," and she refused to submit to "somebody else's idea of somebody else's world."[90] At the same time, Teer likened feminist movements to commercial theater and argued that both led to "separation" and "isolation" by focusing on the "individual" instead of the "collective."[91] Teer's remarks suggest that while she understood the power of black solidarity, her conceptualization of gender and feminism were somewhat limiting. Her art and activism, however, demonstrates an appreciation for black women's culture and a genuine concern for the spiritual well-being of her entire community.

Teer, of course, was not alone in her efforts to found a theater that would give voice to the concerns of black women from within the Black Power milieu. Teer worked among other black women who also founded successful theaters and cultural centers in New York City; among them are Vinnette Carroll's Urban Arts Corps, Hazel Bryant's Richard Allen Center, Rosetta LeNoire's AMAS Repertory Theatre, Marjorie Moon's Billy Holiday Theatre, Cynthia Belgrave's Acting Studio, and Yvonne Madison/Sister Lubaba Lateef's Brownsville Laboratory Theatre. However, there is little sustained research on their contributions to black theater. Although these women were pioneers in their own right, Teer's career remains unique in that she not only formulated holistic theories of performance, but also actualized her call for a black cultural revolution through innovative ritualistic revivals. As Sonia Sanchez says in her eulogy, Teer will always be remembered as a woman "heavy with the smell of herstory and history" who "put her foot on this American spine and bid us look up at her gospel hands hanging bamboo poems of life."[92]

Chapter 2

✦

"We Black Women"

Martie Evans-Charles and the
Spirits of Black Womanhood

People who don't know who they are or what they are about can easily be controlled by those who do. Too many sisters don't know themselves. . . . We start out at five or less wishing for blond hair and blue eyes, and we end up trying to be a carbon copy of the covers of *Harpers* & *Vogue* . . . being what someone else says they should be . . . never realizing or even resenting the fact that the *Seventeens* & *Brides* & *Harpers* magazines were never talking to or about us.

—Martie Evans-Charles, 1972

As a black woman intellectual, Martie Evans-Charles centered her dramas on black women's history and culture. Collectively, her works validate the everyday concerns of black women, demystify black women's oppression, and resist controlling images of black womanhood. Rather than use a black male as a representative of black experiences in America, Evans-Charles's dramas employ black females as emblems of black history and culture. Influenced by Afrocentric discourse, Evans-Charles's dramas function as corrective texts that educate audiences about their African past and cultural strength. Yet, also inspired by her experiences as a mother and public school teacher, her plays explore how Eurocentric education negatively impacts the young black female psyche. Throughout the Black Arts Movement she remained closely linked to the New Lafayette Theatre (1967–72) of Harlem, which has been deemed "one of the most important [theater] groups in the Black Arts Movement" by the theorist Larry Neal. The New Lafayette Theatre housed Ed Bullins's Black Theatre Workshop (1968–72), an artistic endeavor that workshopped many of Evans-Charles's early works.[1] Her dramas were so well received by audiences and critics alike that by 1972 the theater critic Lisbeth Gant would describe her as "an important playwright"[2] and the

Figure 4. Martie Evans-Charles at the New Lafayette Theatre's Black Theatre Workshop (1968–72). Courtesy of Dr. Adrienne Charles.

director Shauneille Perry would herald her as "one of the more powerful new playwrights on the scene."[3] During the Black Arts Movement Evans-Charles wrote six plays: *Where We At?* (written 1969), *Black Cycle* (written 1969), *Job Security* (published 1970), *Jamimma* (performed 1970), *Asante* (written c. 1974), and *Friends* (written c. 1973–75). Yet her name and artistic legacy have been lost within current narratives of the Black Arts Movement theater.

This chapter critically examines Evans-Charles's intellectual and artistic development, noting the ways in which her deep appreciation for black women's culture contributed to the success of the New Lafayette Theatre. Evans-Charles's dramas use dramatic irony and black women's culture to expose the horrors of slavery, the so-called freedoms of emancipation, and the psychological trauma of racism. As various historical, mythological, and everyday women encounter oppressive forces, Evans-Charles reveals the healing power of African spiritual practices. In so doing, Evans-Charles conjures the spirits of black womanhood as a transformative vehicle for black empowerment.

Evans-Charles honed her writing skills and discovered her passion for ritual performance while working at the New Lafayette Theatre. Evans-Charles's daughter Adrienne Charles notes that her mother gained entrance into the close-knit community through her family, who were also New Lafayette Theatre company members. Evans-Charles, in fact, spent much of her childhood and early adulthood observing rehearsals, attending productions, and performing in theater with her mother, the actress Estelle Rolle, and maternal aunts, the actresses Esther Rolle[4] and Roseanna Carter.[5] After a brief career as a dancer working alongside Rolle at Asadata Dafora's African dance troupe Shogola Oloba, she became a formal member of the New Lafayette Theatre.[6] As a company member, Evans-Charles contributed her talents as an actor, audience developer, and playwright. Most notably, she performed as Toni, a social worker, in Robert Macbeth's 1971 production of Bullins's *The Fabulous Miss Marie*, and as Eitram in the company's 1970–71 ritual *The Devil Catchers*.[7] As an audience developer, her responsibilities included increasing public awareness about New Lafayette Theatre productions. Charles remembers that her mother cultivated audiences by passing out flyers and speaking to Harlem church members, community organizations, and radio stations about upcoming plays and ritual performances. Evans-Charles then participated in the Black Theatre Workshop and eventually became a playwright-in-residence alongside Bullins, J. E. "Sonny Jim" Gaines, and Richard Wesley. Although considered a credit to the New Lafayette Theatre, the artistic director and founder Robert Macbeth never selected Evans-Charles's works for their main stage. Rather, her popular plays were developed and produced at the Black Theatre Workshop and later performed at surrounding Harlem theaters.

While Evans-Charles's writings encompass themes which later black feminist artists would address, her works have only been explored by the scholars Rosemary Curb, Beatrix Taumann, Isabel Wasgindt, and Elizabeth Brown-Guillory (née Brown). Curb's "'Goin Through Changes': Mother-Daughter Confrontations in Three Recent Plays by Young Black Women" (1979) provides an admirable comparative analysis of the struggles of black female adolescence in Evans-Charles's *Black Cycle*, J.e. Franklin's *Black Girl*, and Elaine Jackson's *Toe Jam*. However, her article does not examine Evans-Charles's provocative invocation at the beginning of *Black Cycle*, nor situate her play within the broader framework of black revolutionary theater. Taumann's book *Strange Orphans: Contemporary African American Women Playwrights* (1999) provides a history of contemporary African American women playwrights and recognizes the importance of both Evans-Charles and J.e. Franklin's dramas. While Taumann acknowledges that their works "differ greatly from those of their male counterparts by focusing on subjects which are of a special interest for black women," resist stereotypes of black womanhood, and "anticipate central themes of feminist theater which will emerge almost a decade later," she does not provide further analysis.[8]

Brown's dissertation provides textual analyses of dramas written by black women dramatists from 1950 to 1980. She situates *Black Cycle* as a form of "'protest' drama," arguing that Evans-Charles's works "advocate that blacks should disassociate themselves from whites and strive toward black unity."[9] Brown further argues that Evans-Charles's plays, along with other contemporary female writers, "for the most part" present "positive" images of black women as survivors.[10] Wasgindt's dissertation *Martie Charles and Black Revolutionary Theatre* (1994) provides the only in-depth textual analyses of four of Evans-Charles's six dramas written during the Black Arts Movement.

This chapter departs from previous studies by examining Evans-Charles's critical writings, previously published interviews, and unpublished program notes and play scripts, as well as original interviews with her daughter Adrienne Charles and Black Arts Movement artists. This study seeks to understand how Evans-Charles used her agency to negotiate a space for herself and her woman-centered dramas within Black Arts institutions. In so doing, this chapter celebrates Evans-Charles's contributions to Black Arts Movement theater, Afrocentric thought, and black feminist scholarship.

Martie Evans-Charles: Black Woman Intellectual

Evans-Charles's intellectual and artistic sensibilities reflect a deep appreciation of black women's culture. She began experimenting with theater at an early age and wrote her first play, *Every Inch a Lady*, as a junior high school student. Although the manuscript has been lost, the title suggests that even as an adolescent, her writings focused on womanhood. After earning an A.B. in speech at Fisk University and an M.A. in speech pathology at Hunter College, she followed in her mother's footsteps and became a teacher at Harlem public schools. Several years later she married, became a mother to her only child Adrienne Charles, taught speech and drama at Medgar Evers College in Brooklyn, and continued to pursue a professional career in playwriting. Charles recalls that black women were the original audience for her mother's works. "We sat around and would listen to her scenes as she developed her plays. It would be my grandmother, my Aunt Rosa, my Aunt Esther. They would critique her work and discuss it and ask her reasons for why she chose particular things which would make her really think about her characters," says Charles. Patricia Hill Collins's *Black Feminist Thought: Knowledge, Consciousness, and the Politics of Empowerment* (1990) stresses the importance of conversation in black women's lives. "In the comfort of daily conversations, through serious conversation and humor, African-American women as sisters and friends affirm one another's humanity, specialness, and right to exist," writes Collins.[11] Conversations among this circle of black women not only provided an intellectual and artistic community for Evans-Charles, but also a cultural foundation that shaped her writings.

Figure 5. Martie Evans-Charles, 1993. Photo by Dr. Adrienne Charles. Courtesy of Dr. Adrienne Charles.

Evans-Charles's dramas also emphasize the importance of conversation and forming genuine relationships among black women. In *Jamimma*, for example, she depicts the destructiveness of competition among black women. At the beginning of the play, the protagonist Jameena, formerly known as Jamimma, appears to have her heart's desire: the love of her partner Omar and friendship with Vivian. Ironically, audiences realize long before Jameena does that Vivian masks a hidden agenda: she wants a sexual relationship with Omar. Although Vivian achieves her goal, she ultimately loses her self-worth and friendship with Jameena as she becomes a shell of her former self and the victim of Omar's verbal and physical abuse. Charles remembers that the purpose of *Jamimma* was "to show that women should be genuine with each other and sincere in their friendship and not give up their friendships for perceived better relationships with men." Evans-Charles's writings, therefore, demonstrate the importance of sisterhood in black women's lives.

While private conversations among black women played a key role in her intellectual and artistic development, Evans-Charles publicly praised leading male figures of the New Lafayette Theatre and positioned her genesis as a playwright within a masculine culture. Her program notes for the New Federal Theatre's 1972 production of *Jamimma* best exemplify her origin story. Evans-Charles writes that externally defined images of blackness formulated by the media dominated her sense of self early in life. Her father Walter Evans, brother Charles Evans, and cousin Ronald Evans, however, began the process of opening her mind so that she could begin the process of forming a "concept of self."[12] While her critical racial consciousness bloomed in the wake of the 1964 Harlem riots, she still felt dissatisfied with her ignorance and sought the mentorship of Bullins. Her note concludes by specifically crediting Bullins, Robert Macbeth, and Woodie King Jr. for their "influence" on her development as a playwright.[13] By positioning herself as her father's daughter and aligning her work with leading male artistic figures in New York, Evans-Charles locates herself and her artistry within a patrilineal heritage. Creating an origin story rooted in masculine culture allowed her to carefully negotiate a space for her woman-centered work within the male-dominated theaters of New York. Her program note also suggests that she utilized a culture of black masculinity to speak directly to black women. "All praises to our warriors to our / Brother men. / I say all praises to our warriors / to our Brother men. / In whose eyes we sistuhs can / dig the condition we in," writes Evans-Charles.[14] While it honors the warrior spirit of black men, this African-inspired praise poem also challenges black men to help black women understand the nature and significance of the black female condition.

Evans-Charles's dramas exemplify the ethos and artistic standards put forth by the New Lafayette Theatre's Black Theatre Workshop. Located within the heart of Harlem on 108 West 112th Street, the Black Theatre Workshop served as an important artistic outlet for young black playwrights and actors. New Lafayette Theatre playwright-in-residence Richard Wesley writes that young artists were first taught that "Black Art was a collective effort, and that it grew out of the consciousnesses [sic] of the Black community in which it exists."[15] Evans-Charles and her fellow Black Theatre Workshop participants were encouraged to work collaboratively with one another, contribute to every aspect of production from set construction to publicity, and incorporate the "sights, sounds, smells, and rhythms of Harlem" into their artistry.[16] Inspired by the writings of Maulana [Ron] Karenga and Bullins, the Black Theatre Workshop also set forth a "Black artistic standard," producing art that "reflects the condition, wants, needs and desires of our people."[17] Evans-Charles's dramas realize this artistic standard by critically examining the condition of black women, men, and children who live, love, and work in Harlem. Thus Harlem becomes more than a mere location for all of her plays. Urban life in Harlem acts as a guiding force that shapes every aspect of her dramas from central conflicts to character occupations, objectives, and speech patterns. Indeed, one of the unique features about Evans-Charles's writing style is her ability to artfully combine African spiritual practices and folklore with urban daily life via three-dimensional characters drawn from the black underclass.

Evans-Charles's dramas typify what the theater historian Mike Sell has described as the "New Lafayette School of playwriting." Developed under the tutelage of Bullins, the New Lafayette school of playwriting "focuses on the everyday lives of the African American urban underclass, uses a range of vernaculars, favors sudden shifts between dramatic modes, and favors irony over dramatic resolution."[18] Bullins cultivated this form of playwriting at the Black Theatre Workshop, where he provided playwrights the opportunity to hear their scenes read aloud and participate in playwriting exercises. Former New Lafayette Theatre company member, director, and workshop participant George Lee Miles remembers "working with dialogue," "sub-character," and "all of the things that go into the playwriting aspect" during workshop sessions.[19] Evans-Charles honed her skills at the Black Theatre Workshop, eventually mastering this style of playwriting in four important ways. First, her dramas explore the concerns of the black underclass of Harlem through finely crafted characters. Second, her dialogue seamlessly weaves patterns of speech characteristic of the Harlem neighborhood. Third, at times her dramas unapologetically abandon Western dramatic realism in favor of an African-based aesthetics that includes ritual, conjuration, testimony, and incantation. Last, and perhaps most importantly, her plays utilize dramatic irony to validate the everyday concerns of black women and encourage audiences to expel negative forces from within the black community. Charles remembers her mother's plays receiving standing ovations because her works were "very accessible" to audiences due to her construction of relatable, three-dimensional characters.[20] Miles also remembers that Evans-Charles's dramas "resonate[d] with members of an audience" because of her honest depiction of the "human condition" and "the issues of that time." Both Charles and Miles suggest that Evans-Charles used the journeys of imperfect characters to educate audiences about immediate concerns within the Harlem community.

Evans-Charles's engagement with experimental ritual performances at the New Lafayette Theatre influenced her use of African spiritual practices within her own writing. Miles remembers that Evans-Charles "got that [incantation and ritual] out of the ritual stuff that we were doing [at the New Lafayette Theatre]." The New Lafayette Theatre first began experimenting with African-based rituals in 1969, the same year Evans-Charles wrote *Where We At?* at the Black Theatre Workshop. Within three years, the New Lafayette Theatre produced five rituals: *A Ritual to Bind Together and Strengthen Black People So That They Can Survive the Long Struggle That Is to Come* (1969), *To Raise the Dead and Foretell the Future* (1970), *A Black Time for Black Folk* (1970), *The Devil Catchers* (1970–71), and *Psychic Pretenders* (1971). While Evans-Charles attended rehearsals for all these rituals, she only performed in the company-conceptualized ritual *The Devil Catchers*. Described by the theater critic Lisbeth Gant as a "red, eerie world of sights and sounds," *The Devil Catchers* utilized the African concepts of Nommo and hoodoo to create "the world to come, in which everyone except the devils had been reduced to either a devil catcher or a devil guide."[21] The New Lafayette Theatre's experimentation with ritual received unfavorable reviews, with critics arguing that the rituals lacked both substance and connection with Harlem audiences. The critic Peter Bailey, for example, wrote that New Lafayette Theatre rituals lacked recognizable content and simply buried "the meaning . . . under a plentiful supply of lights, sounds, gimmicks, and obscurity."[22] Contemporary scholars consider the New Lafayette Theatre's inability to relate to Harlem audiences as a contributing factor to the theater's demise. The historian of African American theater Errol G. Hill, for example, notes that while "no group symbolized the new black theatre more dramatically than the New Lafayette Theatre," they "failed to make themselves an integral part of the community or present plays in a genre familiar to the audience."[23]

In contrast to the New Lafayette Theatre, Evans-Charles's use of ritual met with success because she incorporated ritual elements into a genre already familiar to audiences. Indeed, while Evans-Charles's dramas use conjuration, testimony, storytelling, and incantation, her woman-centered plays maintain traditional Western play structure. Her play *Asante* (1974), for example, incorporated ritual into the traditional musical form. This character-driven musical features rhythmically pleasing songs and yet also includes an African healing ritual performed by the protagonist, Denise, to expel controlling images from her black female psyche. Denise's ritual allowed Evans-Charles to not only reclaim black womanhood but also encourage unification through the remembrance of a shared ancestry. Her use of traditional character-driven plots and contemporary music provided a comfortable point of entry for Harlem audiences who may have been unfamiliar with Denise's use of Swahili and African ritual practices.

In addition to the New Lafayette Theatre, Evans-Charles also used the Nation of Islam's teachings to negotiate a space to discuss black women's subjectivity, history, and culture. Similar to Sonia Sanchez, Evans-Charles joined the Nation of Islam for the educational opportunities it afforded her daughter. Charles remembers that Nation of Islam schools were "very supportive of women" and her mother "just felt that it was a more nurturing situation analogous to historically black colleges and universities." Although Evans-Charles never held a leadership position in the Nation of Islam, she actively participated in the organization from 1969 until shortly after the death of Elijah Muhammad in 1975. She was, however, asked to use her talents to create a drama for a special luncheon held in honor of Wallace D. Muhammad's 1974 visit to New York. While the drama is no longer extant, Evans-Charles discussed her inspiration and outline for this work in progress in her article "The Confrontation" (1975). "My aim was to write a script based on the thoughts of the Black woman of America from the time she

Figure 6. Martie Evans-Charles at daughter Dr. Adrienne Charles's 1998 graduation. Photo by Amos Charles. Courtesy of Dr. Adrienne Charles.

stepped upon these shores on to today; and after hearing the Supreme Minister's enlightening teaching on the woman and on the impact of Eve, Delilah and Jezebel images upon the woman's self-concept and the resulting behavior these images generate, my work took on even greater meaning," writes Evans-Charles.[24] With these opening remarks, Evans-Charles demonstrates her desire to use the celebration of Wallace D. Muhammad to honor black women's thought, history, and culture. Framing her discussion within a religious context allowed her to also critique how systems of oppression have regulated and exploited black women's sexuality from the time of creation. In so doing, Evans-Charles carefully negotiates a space within the Nation of Islam to discuss and celebrate black women's resilience without alienating male audiences.

Similar to later black feminist activists, Evans-Charles believed that controlling images of black womanhood concerned the entire black community. "The Confrontation" demonstrates that her critical consciousness included an understanding of how sexual politics have been used to construct racial difference, justify the exploitation of black women's bodies, and oppress black women. Evans-Charles writes:

> So often the Black woman is labeled as the one female on earth who is available to any and every man on the planet. Whenever we look for ourselves in the literature, it is the concept of the "free woman" that is put before us, and so it was my hope to locate the work of those who understood what was happening and did not yield mentally to the oppressive conditions in which they found themselves, but who cried out thru [sic] their writings against injustice, and whose beings fought the images that were forced upon them. I wanted to structure a work that would highlight such thought chronologically, thus revealing to the audience the development of the mind in its ability to articulate to a greater and greater degree what was happening to us as a people, with emphasis on the woman.[25]

Evans-Charles understood that Western gender ideologies marked the black female body as animalistic and sexually deviant. During enslavement one could not "rape" a black woman, since her supposedly uncontrollable sexual appetite made her sexually available to all men. She explicitly sought to craft a play that would educate both men and women of the Nation of Islam about the black experience in the United States, but from the black female subject's perspective. Yet, not content to only explore black women's history of rape and exploitation, she also wanted to reclaim black women's sexuality by creating new images of black femininity and masculinity. Her plays feature female protagonists who all, in varying degrees, resist controlling images of black womanhood and seek self-definition. The plays' black female antagonists, on the other hand, embody an attitude of contempt toward the black community. They lack a critical understanding of how black female sexuality has been used to stigmatize black bodies and culture. Although not all of Evans-Charles's female characters fully realize their potential, by the conclusion of her plays many develop strong friendships with other women, find joy in their sexuality, or experience the beginnings of a critical racial consciousness.

As a black woman intellectual and playwright, Evans-Charles sought to transform the critical consciousness of her audiences by educating them about the failures of the public school system. She addressed this concern while participating in the 1976 Frank Silvera Writers' Workshop[26] symposium "The Dilemma of the Black Playwright":

> If we want to reach our people, we have to educate them. The job of education is long and hard. . . . To reach an audience, we must understand something about how people listen and how they see in order to know when and where to put those potent statements that

we feel will help to advance people's understanding in terms of what we want to show them.[27]

Evans-Charles believed that her dramas could educate audiences and transform their critical consciousness. Influenced by her experiences as a mother, public school teacher, and professor, she wanted audiences to understand *how* and *why* the public education system fails black children. Her plays depict public schools as oppressive institutions that teach black children from an early age to believe in their own inferiority through the purposeful distortion of their history and culture.

Evans-Charles most overtly addresses her concern for the education of black girls in *Job Security* (1970) and *Black Cycle* (1969). *Job Security* takes place at a Harlem public school run by an absent white principal. Conflict arises when a young black girl named Ella questions the ethics of her black teachers who blindly enforce the detrimental practices of white school administrators in order to preserve their jobs. After enduring years of psychological abuse or "poisoning" of her mind by her teachers, Ella finally reaches her emotional limit and enacts her own justice by literally poisoning her teachers. Conflict also arises in *Black Cycle* when a teenage girl named Jeannie not only defies her school administration, but also her mother Vera by leading a student boycott to protest her private school's racist ceremonial practices. Through Ella and Jeannie's experiences, Evans-Charles reveals that more than a decade after the desegregation of schools, the public school system remains steeped in racist ideologies and practices that undermine the psychological well-being of black children.

Evans-Charles's dramas work to counteract racist ideologies and practices by presenting new, internally defined images of black femininity and masculinity. Evans-Charles understood the devastating effects of controlling images upon the lives of black women and men. *Jamimma* (1970) most overtly critiques the controlling image of Aunt Jemima, the legendary pancake-toting happy slave image first performed by Nancy Green at the 1893 Chicago World's Fair.[28] Evans-Charles takes on Aunt Jemima because she not only represents historical amnesia within popular culture (i.e., slavery as idyllic), but also the commodification of black women's bodies. Evans-Charles's Jameena, formerly known as Jamimma, changes her name and migrates from North Carolina to Harlem for a better life. Through Jameena's journey, Evans-Charles essentially frees Aunt Jemima from the pancake box and allows a new image of a beautifully flawed, three-dimensional black woman to emerge. Her lover Omar also avoids stereotypical representation. In contrast to the black macho image, Evans-Charles depicts him as a contemplative and emotionally conflicted young man who is only just discovering his talent as a musician. Critics admired Evans-Charles's depiction of black femininity and masculinity and her ability to inspire racial solidarity. Rather than present black men as simply "jive," Evans-Charles was applauded by the theater critic Kushauri Kupa for "paint[ing] her men with touches of humanity so that they do not remain totally trapped within the restrictions of being stereotypes."[29] Evans-Charles created these new images in order to subvert racist icons of the past and, hopefully, empower audiences to define themselves through the reaffirmation of black humanity, history, and culture.

Herstory Speaks: Locating Iconic, Mythological, and Everyday Women

Where We At? (1969), which premiered at the Negro Ensemble Company's 1972 "Works in Progress" series, functions as a parable for teaching black sisterhood and solidarity. Evans-Charles, in fact, refashions the New Testament's parable of the Good Samaritan[30] in order to discuss the immediate secular needs of the black community. Similar to the story of a priest and Levite who shirk their Christian duty and walk past a half-dead man, Evans-Charles's Fannie has just returned from church service yet steps over a drunken Hazel in order to stand closer to the bus stop sign. In contrast to the parable of neighborly love, Evans-Charles incorporates black sisterhood as a galvanizing force for black love and solidarity. After witnessing Fannie's behavior, Peaches acts as the Good Sister by lifting Hazel up from the ground and admonishing Fannie. "Humans people, don act like that. . . . You bin on yoh knees communin with the blue eyed devils. Drinkin they potions. Thas why you have no room in yo heart foh our BLACK Sistuh," says Peaches.[31] In contrast to the parable of the Good Samaritan, *Where We At?* denounces white Christian culture as dehumanizing and instead promotes African spirituality. Peaches then utilizes an African incantation that conjures a Masked Figure and a group of Drab Figures composed of a "Whore," "Pimp," "addict," and "wino" to assist in her ritual of expelling Fannie from the black community.[32] Rather than depict the morally repugnant as impediments to social change, Evans-Charles positions their participation as an *essential* element in the process of expunging negative forces from within the black community.

Fannie's expulsion from the black community not only leaves her open to sexual assault, but also forms a tangible link between the African past and the present-day circumstances of black women. The play ends with White Faced Cop erroneously accusing her of theft, fondling her breasts, and promising to let her return to her domestic job after sexually satisfying him. From the mouth of a modern-day police officer, Evans-Charles suggests that black women's silenced history of rape continues to repeat itself. Fannie's sexual assault by a representative of the state, therefore, becomes an important symbol of racial oppression. Ultimately, Evans-Charles's parable asks black audiences to consider their own standpoint, or where they are at in the fight for black liberation. Will blacks choose individualism and assimilation (i.e., victimization by white society) or black sisterhood and unity (i.e., protection and empowerment)?

Writing against the (then) current scholarship that minimalized the contributions of black female vocalists in the early production of blues, Evans-Charles's one-act play also recovers the legacy of blues women who used their agency to express black women's standpoint.[33] Collins writes that "[t]he lyrics sung by many of the Black women blues singers challenge externally defined controlling images used to justify Black women's objectification as the Other."[34] Evans-Charles follows this tradition by dramatizing images of black womanhood within Nina Simone's 1966 hit song "Four Women."[35] Told from the perspective of four black women, Simone's haunting song evokes black women's silenced history of rape and resistance in the United States. "My skin is brown / And my manner is tough / I'll kill the first mother I see / Cos my life / has been too rough / I'm awfully bitter these days / because my parents were slaves / What do they call me / My / Name / Is / PEACHES," declares Simone in her final verse.[36] Simone's lyrics suggest that the dehumanizing practices of slavery, including rape, continue to inform Peaches's present-day circumstances. Evans-Charles's dramatization recovers the warrior-like spirit of blues women through the character Peaches, who maintains the "tough" manner of her original incarnation. In so doing, Evans-Charles anticipates similar recuperation efforts of black women writers such as Toni Cade Bambara, Gayle Jones, Sherley Anne Williams, and Alice Walker. In *Where We At?* Evans-Charles uses the confrontation between Peaches and Fannie to demystify how racism, sexism, and poverty oppress black women and therefore harm the entire black community. Peaches rejects Fannie's excuse that Hazel is simply "a fallen woman who brought this on huself" and instead attempts to teach Fannie about the importance of sisterhood.[37] Similar to the women's blues tradition, *Where We At?* engages with and finds meaning in the everyday problems facing poor and working-class black women like Hazel.

Where We At? engages with central themes found within black women's blues tradition, including travel, sisterly advice, and abandonment.[38] Black feminist and activist Angela Davis writes that travel themes in the blues tradition "rearticulated the collective desire to escape bondage that pervaded the musical culture of slavery."[39] Early blues women often evoked the theme of travel in terms of women "forever walking, running, leaving, catching trains, or sometimes aimlessly rambling" in order to move toward or away from lovers.[40] In *Where We At?* Fannie and Hazel attempt to travel home. Just as blues women offered advice to other women, Peaches admonishes Fannie to help her fellow sister and to remember: "We women. We Black women. An we have a sistuh who caint do foh huhself."[41] Fannie and Hazel's situations represent a larger concern for unity among black women, and their travel serves as a metaphor for returning home to the black community. Alcoholism has left Hazel stricken on the ground and unable to return home to the bosom of the black community. A desire to assimilate has likewise left Fannie isolated from the black community. Indifferent to the needs of blacks, and harboring a deep disdain for her own community, Fannie attempts to advise Peaches, stating: "I know you young an wanna do foh yoh people an all that, but you gotta face reality, niggas is one mess uh people that you caint do nothing foh, so stop wastin yoh time. Jus git whatchu cain for yaself. Thas the bes you can do in this life."[42] Outraged by Fannie's contemptuous speech, Peaches curses Fannie so that she will "[n]ever . . . live among black people again" and will wander "aimlessly," experiencing "life without Black love."[43] Fannie's "lover," or the black community, abandons her and leaves her to fight negative forces on her own.

Peaches, who embodies the warrior spirit of Nina Simone, provides a new image of feminine strength. Evans-Charles's dramatization reinforces critical interpretations that Simone's Peaches reflects the blues woman's own militant stance.[44] Simone first became aware of her political consciousness after the 1963 assassination of the NAACP field secretary Medgar Evers and the bombing of the 16th Street Baptist Church in Birmingham, Alabama. "I suddenly realized what it was to be black in America in 1963, but it wasn't an intellectual connection of the type Lorraine [Hansberry] had been repeating to me over and over—it came as a rush of fury, hatred and determination. In church language, the Truth entered into me and I 'came through,'" writes Simone.[45] After learning about the deaths of five black girls killed in the bombing, Simone fashioned a "zip gun" with the intent to enact violence. Only after calming down did she make the important decision to use her voice as a weapon against such atrocities. She then composed her legendary protest song "Mississippi Goddam."[46] "[F]or the next seven years I was driven by civil rights and the hope of black revolution. . . . My music was dedicated to a purpose more important than classical music's pursuit of excellence; it was dedicated to the fight for freedom and the historical destiny of my people. I felt pride when I thought about what we were all doing together," Simone writes.[47] Influenced by the ideologies of the Student Nonviolent Coordinating Committee former chairman Stokely Carmichael,[48] as well as Black Panther Party cofounder Huey Newton, Simone expressed her revolutionary message of black power and pride by becoming "the first popular African American entertainer to wear her hair 'natural'"[49] and began performing at civil rights rallies and marches. Similar to Simone, Evans-Charles's Peaches not only expresses anger over racial injustices, but also asserts the need for black pride and racial solidarity. In one of the most meaningful moments of the play, Peaches assumes the legacy of Malcolm X, stating: "Like Brother Malcom [sic] say. What happen ta one uh us happen ta all uhus."[50] Unfortunately, Fannie remains unmoved by Peaches's concern for the collective health and safety of blacks. Just as Simone's song conjures the spirits of black women from centuries past, Peaches conjures a Masked Figure spirit to help her protect black women and the greater black community against further psychological abuse.

Figure 7. Martie Evans-Charles and daughter Dr. Adrienne Charles attend the National Medical Association annual conference, Hawai'i, 2002. Courtesy of Dr. Adrienne Charles.

Evans-Charles's second play, *Black Cycle* (1969), also grapples with the psychological effects of racism, everyday concerns of black women, and legacy of enslavement. George Lee Miles directed the 1969 premiere of *Black Cycle* at the New Lafayette Theatre's Black Theatre Workshop.[51] The *New York Amsterdam News* reported that the production was "very popular" and "played to capacity audiences."[52] As implied by the play's title, *Black Cycle* focuses on the cyclical nature of trauma experienced by black women. The majority of *Black Cycle* takes place in Paradise, a Harlem beauty salon owned by a black single mother named Vera. Similar to Fannie in *Where We At?* Vera has also internalized racism and expresses contempt toward poor black women in her community. Vera enrolls her daughter Jeannie in a prestigious private high school in the hope that her daughter will form a relationship with a white student. Conflict arises as Jeannie's racial consciousness blooms and she organizes a boycott against an award ceremony designed to humiliate her black schoolmates. Through the use of a provocative invocation, as well as multiple representations of black womanhood, *Black Cycle* breaks the cycle of silence regarding black women's history of rape and abuse from both within and outside of the black community and reclaims black women's pursuit of sexual pleasure. In so doing, the play disrupts the mythology of black matriarchy and a supposedly pathological black family.

Black Cycle begins with an invocation that conjures the spirits of black womanhood in order to educate black women about their history of enslavement in the United States. Similar to rituals at the New Lafayette Theatre, the poetic invocation completely abandons Western dramatic play structure. Stage directions note that "one female voice in total blackness"[53] accompanied by drums should state: "Spirits of black womanhood, surround me /

Spirits of black womanhood, surround me / Spirits of black womanhood, be with me. / Fill every pore of my being with knowledge of who I am."[54] Time becomes cyclical as the female speaker uses repetition to form a spiritual connection with her female ancestors, enabling her to understand how her present circumstances have been shaped by the experiences of her foremothers. Audiences serve as witnesses to a spiritual act as the female speaker testifies to how black women suffered "many rape-filled nights," having their bodies "used . . . as receptacles, sucklers, fodder / Fodder in the building of our nation."[55] Indeed, antebellum ideologies justified the rape of female slaves by marking their bodies as animalistic and hypersexual. Although the female speaker rightly testifies to the vulnerability of female slaves to sexual assault, she ignores the possibility that black men could also perpetrate these crimes. "The female slave lived in constant awareness of her sexual vulnerability and in perpetual fear that any male, black or white, might single her out to assault or victimize," writes the black feminist scholar bell hooks.[56] By only singling out white men as sexual predators, the speaker creates a shared history of victimization among blacks and avoids intracultural conflict.

The female speaker's testimony disrupts the (then) traditional narrative of slavery, which focuses on loss of manhood and either diminishes or ignores the impact of slavery on the lives of black women. hooks critiques this historical fallacy in *Ain't I a Woman: Black Women and Feminism* (1981). "Sexist historians and sociologists have provided the American public with a perspective on slavery in which the most cruel and de-humanizing impact of slavery on the lives of black people was that black men were stripped of their masculinity, which they then argue resulted in the dissolution and overall disruption of any black familial structure," hooks writes.[57] While the female speaker acknowledges that black men experienced mutilation and death, she does not use the emasculation of black men as a symbol of the dehumanizing effects of enslavement. Rather, black women's suffering serves as an emblem of oppression. The female speaker uses her disembodied voice to echo slavery's impact on the black female consciousness.

Black Cycle's invocation reveals the psychological trauma of enslavement and how antebellum ideologies continue to impact the consciousness of black women. Angela Davis's groundbreaking essay "Reflections on the Black Woman's Role in the Community of Slaves" (1971), published just two years after *Black Cycle*, chronicles the psychological warfare inflicted upon enslaved women and their resistance to sexual assault. Davis argues that the sexual assault of slave women reflects the slave master's desire to reduce her "to the level of her *biological* being" by situating "her as a female *animal*."[58] Davis describes the institutionalized rape of female slaves as a method of "terrorism" used to repress black women's agency as well as "demoralize" the entire slave community.[59] *Black Cycle*'s invocation reveals how this psychological trauma continues to haunt black women. "Peel my brain / Remove the layers of white thought, white talk / Gouge out the inner eye, implanted in my mind oh so long / ago by / The devil beasts . . . / Root out that devil inner eye, programmed to destroy / blackness. / . . . Spirits of Black Womanhood, cast out this curse," pleads the female speaker.[60] According to the female speaker, the reprogramming of the black female consciousness began when slavers "tore us from our homeland."[61] During the Middle Passage slavers attempted to break the spirits of blacks in order to transform the African personality into that of a slave. Slavers not only removed "any overt sign of African heritage," including African names, status, and kinship, but also terrorized African men and women in the form of rape, beatings, and mutilations so that they would "adopt the slave identity imposed upon them," writes hooks.[62] Black women did not fare better on the shores of America.

At the time of *Black Cycle*'s publication, slavery had been abolished for a hundred years, and yet the female speaker argues that this psychological trauma continues to inform the present. As the invocation suggests, black women's ability to mother became another aspect of trauma under enslavement. Despite incentives to reproduce the next generation of slaves, some women used what little agency they had to commit infanticide, rather than perpetuate this heinous system of oppression.[63] Harriet Jacobs, best known for her autobiography *Incidents in the Life of a Slave Girl* (1861), perhaps best expresses the emotional trauma of motherhood under the institution of slavery. "I loved to watch his infant slumbers; but always there was a dark cloud over my enjoyment. I could never forget he was a slave. Sometimes I wished he might die in infancy. . . . Death is better than slavery," wrote Jacobs.[64] The female speaker not only expresses this pain, but also reveals how centuries of programming to believe in one's own inferiority have continued to disempower blacks. After delivering this provocative thesis, *Black Cycle* provides a contemporary case study to explore the ways in which racist antebellum ideologies continue to oppress black women.

Vera represents the countless black women who have internalized externally defined visions of black womanhood. She suffers from historical amnesia and views other black women with contempt. Disconnected from the plight of other black women, yet experiencing the same effects of disenfranchisement, Vera seeks relief from poverty through assimilation into white culture. According to Vera's logic, Jeannie will be saved from "trouble" such as drug addiction, incarceration, and teen pregnancy by avoiding relationships with black men.[65] Vera, in fact, would rather Jeannie "turn up dead"[66] than repeat her life as a poor, uneducated teen parent. Vera's pursuit of white men has stifled any meaningful relationship she could have with black men, including Jeannie's father Florida. According to Florida, Vera used him as a resource to get "off the streets" and then left him once she had "gotten all [she] could."[67] Instead of recognizing that Florida, black female patrons, and the greater black community have supported her business, she perceives them as a hindrance to her social mobility. Vera states that she will not "be lettin' 'em hold me back" and refuses to allow black students to do the same to her daughter.[68] As a result of her ignorance, Vera cannot comprehend her daughter's bourgeoning activism, nor form true friendship with her patron Sadie.

Evans-Charles provides a much-needed glimpse into the inner lives of poor black women through Sadie's experiences as a domestic servant, wife, and mother. Within the confines of the Paradise beauty shop, Sadie talks openly about her former life as a domestic and her decision to quit her demeaning job so she can care for her six children. At the time Evans-Charles wrote *Black Cycle*, black women's employment in the domestic servant sphere had radically declined. Anthropologist Leith Mullings writes that "[i]n 1940, 60 percent of all African-American women workers were domestic servants; by 1967, the number declines to 24.5 percent."[69] Sadie represents both the hundreds of thousands of black women who migrated north during the world wars to urban centers in order to find employment and the more recent massive exodus from domestic labor. With little education and few job opportunities, Sadie became a domestic servant in a white household. While she received sparse compensation for her actual labor, her employment provided some personal autonomy. In a private conversation with Vera, Sadie reveals her inner thoughts that were formulated while working as a domestic servant. Sadie concludes that whites act "like a bunch uh pigs."[70] By likening whites unto pigs, Sadie linguistically disrupts the association of black women with animalistic behavior, thus reaffirming her own humanity. While Sadie's disclosure suggests contempt for her employers, she likely managed to maintain her job by remaining silent and bearing the indignities. The historian Darlene Clark Hine writes that during the late nineteenth and early twentieth centuries, black domestics developed a "self-imposed invisibility" in order to have the "psychic space" to resist oppression while working in close proximity to whites.[71] Black women developed a "culture of dissemblance," meaning the "appearance of disclosure, or openness about themselves and their feelings, while actually remaining enigmatic," writes Hine.[72] The culture of dissemblance also allows Sadie to maintain her dignity while suffering in an abusive relationship and rearing six children within an oppressive society.

Sadie's experiences as a wife and mother disrupt mythologies of black matriarchy. When audiences first meet Sadie, she has already endured years of domestic servitude and has now become a stay-at-home mother. Unable to find traditional employment, her husband Jerome finds extralegal work as a numbers runner. Unfortunately, Jerome cannot financially provide for her or their children, which causes friction in their relationship. When Sadie pleads for money, Jerome calls her a "bitch," beats her in front of their daughter Carolyn, and tosses five dollars on the street.[73] The stage directions indicate that Sadie is "exhausted" when she returns to Vera's shop, yet she does not berate Jerome or express any desire to leave him.[74] When Vera indicates that she would never endure such public humiliation, Sadie articulates her experiential knowledge. "Thas cause you ain't never had to do it. And you ain't got no six kids," responds Sadie.[75] While Evans-Charles does not provide a

solution to Sadie's predicament, her provocative portrayal of domestic violence does break the cycle of silence regarding the abuse of black women
from within their communities. Rather than present Sadie as an emasculating matriarch or manipulative welfare queen, Evans-Charles depicts her as a
simple woman who tries her best to work with Jerome to keep their family
intact. Regardless of whether or not audiences agree with Sadie's decision to
beg Jerome for financial help, she believes she is fulfilling her obligation as a
mother. In this instance, Sadie's inability to leave an abusive husband reflects
a very real problem within black communities.

Jeannie and Carolyn's pursuit of self-definition and sexual pleasure break
the cycle of emotional, physical, and sexual abuse experienced by previous
generations of black women. Through their everyday conversations about
love, sex, motherhood, and politics, Jeannie and Carolyn validate each other's
humanity and form a strong sisterhood. "For a young Black woman growing
up involves not only experiencing the usual traumas of adolescence but the
germinating consciousness of the double curse she bears in a racist and sexist
society," writes Curb.[76] Jeannie and Carolyn are aware of the particular challenges they face as young black women. Rather than continue to be defined
by their mothers or other external forces, they take steps to define themselves.
For example, both Carolyn and Jeannie embrace their "natural" beauty by
sporting afros, both forge relationships with racially conscious black men,
and Jeannie celebrates her African heritage by learning Yoruba. Jeannie,
however, moves beyond an awareness of racial oppression to actively fight
for social change. Jeannie defiantly declares "I'm black"[77] in response to her
mother Vera's argument that she "don't have the same problem"[78] as the
other black students. Jeannie, in fact, understands identity politics and uses
blackness as a unifying weapon to galvanize her peers and undermine racist
practices at her school. Although Carolyn does not actively join Jeannie's
boycott, she provides friendship and emotional support. Within the confines
of Carolyn's kitchen, the two friends laugh and cry together as they discuss
Carolyn's impending motherhood and the challenges of being poor, black,
and female. As Jeannie ponders aloud what having sex would feel like, Carolyn answers, "It's goooooooooooooooood."[79] In so doing, Evans-Charles
grants young black women agency to pursue sexual pleasure. With Carolyn's
encouragement, Jeannie develops a sexual relationship with Calvin, a young
hustler who encourages her to fully develop her racial consciousness. *Black
Cycle* concludes on the optimistic note that perhaps Jeannie and Calvin's
healthy relationship will break cycles of abuse and division among black men
and women.

Evans-Charles's next drama, *Job Security* (1970), also explores the demoralizing effects of racism on the black female psyche. *Job Security* remains
unique, however, in that the play features an all-female cast and focuses on
a poor black girl's pursuit of an education within a hostile environment.
Throughout the one-act play the protagonist, Ella, not only critiques the

ineptitude of her teachers and the hypocrisies of the public school system, but also resists the psychological and physical abuse of the parent-volunteer Mrs. Douglas. Ironically, instead of helping Ella reach her academic potential, the assistant principal Mrs. Johnson, the teachers Mrs. Russell and Mrs. Chase, and the absent principal Mr. Levy ignore, demean, or respond indifferently to Ella's plight. Eventually Ella realizes that her teachers purposefully maintain the status quo in order to ensure their own paychecks. The scholars of African American theater James V. Hatch and Ted Shine validate Evans-Charles's critique of New York's public school system. Hatch and Shine write:

> For many years the only job offering security and respectability for black college graduates (aside from medicine, law, and the ministry) was teaching. Since only a limited number of teachers were hired each year, it was not unusual to find blacks with college degrees employed as postal workers, waiters, red caps, and Pullman porters. Often individuals hired to teach had no interest in the profession but took the job because of the status and the regular salary check. The result was dissatisfied people playing roles at the expense of innocent students.[80]

Evans-Charles worked as a Harlem public school teacher while writing *Job Security*. Her firsthand experience allowed her to understand why public schools systematically fail black children. As *Job Security* attests, much of the blame falls on the shoulders of apathetic teachers and absentee administrators who only become teachers in order to gain job security. Once Ella is finally pushed to her mental breaking point, she uses feminine wit, trickery, and her street smarts to resolve her troubles. Taken at face value, Ella's solution appears sadistic at best. When placed within the framework of animal trickster tales, however, Ella's antics acquire a revolutionary significance for black audiences.

Evans-Charles's adaptation of animal trickster tales for contemporary audiences demonstrates a profound appreciation of both African folklore and black women's culture. Within African folklore, animal tricksters are "weak, relatively powerless creatures who attain their ends through the application of native wit and guile rather than power or authority," writes the historian Lawrence Levine.[81] During enslavement, animal trickster tales not only taught "important lessons about authority" but also provided enslaved blacks with "psychic relief" from oppression through "symbolic assaults upon the powerful."[82] Indeed, using animals as symbols provided storytellers the opportunity to freely express their inner thoughts about slavers, the hypocrisies of enslavement, and the "meaninglessness of the status quo."[83] Tales of Brer Rabbit's exploits, for example, celebrate his ability to manipulate the natural order by not only defeating his larger enemies and surviving, but also gaining wealth and power to improve his condition. While slavers perceived these tales as mere child's play, these stories proved subversive because they granted enslaved blacks symbolic victory over a larger society that denied their very humanity.

At the time Evans-Charles wrote *Job Security*, scholars and critics minimalized the significance of female tricksters in mythology and folklore.[84] Lawrence Levine's seminal book *Black Culture and Black Consciousness: African-American Folk Thought from Slavery to Freedom* (1977), for example, notes that "in general women played a small role in slave tales."[85] Female animals served "as attractive possessions to be fought over" by competing animals or were used to "symbolically" represent "freedom," writes Levine.[86] Evans-Charles, however, celebrates and recovers the history of females in trickster roles through Ella. As young, poor, black, and female, Ella ranks among the lowest of the low in a society dominated by white patriarchal, middle-class ideologies. Her vulnerability due to her age, class, race, and sex makes it necessary for her to use trickery, deceit, street smarts, and feminine wit to manipulate her enemies so that she may improve her condition. Just as in animal trickster tales, Ella's more powerful enemies exemplify hypocrisy. Her teachers express moral outrage at her thievery, violent temperament, and profuse cursing, yet spend most of their time oppressing Ella through psychological and physical abuse. As with any animal trickster tale, Ella's plight represents a greater concern within the black community, namely a generational divide about the use of violence within the black revolution.

Ella's trickster tale not only offers vicarious pleasure to those who witness her socially unacceptable behavior, but also educates and galvanizes audiences to resist oppressive authority. Operating in a liminal space between chaos and fixed social norms, Ella finds enjoyment in stealing candy from the parents' room at school because this allows her to transgress established customs. Using stealth to acquire food—or candy in Ella's case—plays a vital role in trickster tales. Considering that slaves were afforded minimal rations, the acquisition of food and the means by which the food is obtained take on an important meaning within trickster tales. Levine writes that in Brer Rabbit tales, for example, food symbolizes "enhanced status and power" because he obtains it "through the manipulation and deprivation of others."[87] Ella's ability to steal her enemy's candy and not get caught likewise symbolizes her burgeoning sense of power. During the interrogation over the missing candy, Ella skillfully performs verbal acrobatics in order to mock, confuse, and undermine her teacher's authority and nonsensical school policies. Ella insolently asserts her opinion that Mrs. Johnson should fulfill her responsibilities as assistant principal, rather than terrorize students for not having hall passes. In so doing, Ella reveals the hypocrisy of her teachers and asks: why does the theft of candy produce moral outrage while inept teachers continue to profit off of the victimization of children? Much to Ella's delight, Mrs. Russell provides an inadequate justification for the assistant principal's actions. "That's not the point!" Mrs. Russell retorts.[88] Ella responds by chanting, "That's not the point."[89] Completely baffled, yet incensed by Ella's actions, Mrs. Douglas deems Ella "crazy" and suggests that she "ought to be in a mental institution."[90] Aware of the dysfunctional world that she inhabits, Ella replies, "I am in one (*looking around*) just don't you worry bout it."[91] Wise beyond her years, Ella invites audiences to also recognize the absurdity of the public school system.

In addition to her intelligence, Ella utilizes deceit and trickery to transgress social boundaries. The day after her interrogation, Ella arrives at school in disguise. Sporting a "white party type dress" with her hair "dressed with white ribbons," Ella appears as pure and innocent as possible.[92] Her appearance, in fact, harkens back to Norman Rockwell's painting *The Problem We All Live With* (1964), which captures six-year-old Ruby Bridges on her way to a newly desegregated New Orleans public school. The painting presents the iconic image of a young black girl with white ribbons in her hair and a white party dress. Standing center, she clutches her school supplies while surrounded by faceless officers with the words "NIGGER" and a smashed tomato above her head. Like Bridges, Ella is surrounded by a world of violence. In order to survive, Ella conceals her true feelings and endures violence and insults in order to gain her teacher's trust. Ella offers an insincere apology to Mrs. Douglas and then proceeds to entice her to take two pieces of poison-laced candies. Once her teachers begin to heave and writhe in pain, Ella celebrates her coup by taunting her opponents. "[G]lory, glory halleluiah, my teacher hit me with the ruler, the ruler turned red and the teacher dropped dead, no more school for me," sings Ella.[93] Her adaptation of "The Battle Hymn of the Republic" (1861), a derivative of the Union marching song "John Brown's Body" (1860), connects the emancipation of enslaved blacks with her own present-day liberation. Just as the abolitionist John Brown advocated armed insurrection as a tool to abolish slavery, Ella exerts extralegal efforts to free herself from an oppressive school system.

Ella's resilience and ultimate triumph over verbal and physical abuse provides vicarious pleasure to audiences. Evans-Charles's daughter performed the role of Ella during early readings of *Job Security*, including a locally televised reading on Channel 5's "Black News." The Black Magicians then premiered *Job Security* at the Third World Theatre in 1970. The critic Paulette Perrier's review of the production provides a glimpse into the various audience responses to Ella's actions. "Although the over-30 Brothers and Sisters winced at the deaths, i.e. kids don't really do THAT!—poison their teachers. Answer: but they do beat them up every now and again, curse them out . . . . The younger Black folk in the audience got the message. It is the same message which was recently expressed in the Cultural Revolution in China: those who are not with us are truly against us," wrote Perrier.[94] According to Perrier, a generational divide led to two distinctive interpretations of the production: older audiences questioned the plausibility of Ella's violent actions, while younger audiences related to Ella's plight and inspirational message of armed resistance. Although Perrier's remarks create an oversimplified generational binary, they are important because they demonstrate that not all audience members understood the symbolic meaning of the play. Some audiences, however, did appreciate Evans-Charles's efforts to demonstrate the physical and emotional abuse inflicted upon poor inner city children. Throughout the play, Mrs. Douglas attempts to brainwash Ella into believing in her own inferiority. Mrs. Douglas begins this process by referring to Ella as a "little monster"[95] and threatening to throw her out of a window, before "*mov[ing] in for the kill*."[96] "Don't nobody want you. . . . The school don't want you. The teachers don't want you, even yuh own mama don't want you," states Mrs. Douglas.[97] In just a few sentences, Mrs. Douglas attempts to "kill" Ella's spirit by making her feel unwanted. Ella, however, responds by calling Mrs. Douglas a "white bitch."[98] Identifying Mrs. Douglas as an enforcer of the white administrator's racist ideologies and practices allows Ella to maintain her fighting spirit while in a hostile environment. Ella's plight also demonstrates that the desegregation of public schools has had a minute impact on the quality of education afforded black children in Harlem. As a mother and public school teacher, Evans-Charles understood firsthand the debilitating effects of underfunding predominately black schools, as well as the psychological trauma that incompetent teachers could inflict upon children. The deaths of Ella's teachers provide an important lesson against profiting off of black children's subjugation.

Evans-Charles's full-length drama *Jamimma* (1970) explores the impact that controlling images and the public school systems have on the black female psyche. *Jamimma* focuses on the everyday struggles of a young idealistic woman named Jameena Caine. Through carefully crafted exposition, Evans-Charles reveals the psychological trauma Jameena endured at school because of her birth name. According to her sister Viola, the other high school students "almost crucified" Jameena because of the legacy that her birth name evoked.[99] Ironically, while Jameena may have figuratively escaped the pancake box by moving to Harlem, she remains in the kitchen as a virtual slave to her boyfriend Omar. Jameena remains vulnerable to manipulation because she lacks the ability to define herself. Instead, she subscribes to an idealized vision of black womanhood created by external forces. In so doing, Jameena continues to live a life of subjugation.

Jamimma evokes the iconic image of Aunt Jemima as a lens to critique modern-day idealized representations of black womanhood. Perhaps no other controlling image has more effectively mitigated the horrors black women suffered during enslavement than that of Aunt Jemima. "[The trademark's] success revolved around the fantasy of returning the black woman to a sanitized version of slavery. The Aunt Jemima character involved a regression of race relations, and her character helped usher in a prominent resurgence of the 'happy slave' mythology of the antebellum South," writes the African American studies scholar Kimberly Wallace-Sanders.[100] Aunt Jemima's delicious pancakes and jovial attitude perpetuated the belief that black women

were not only natural cooks, but also enjoyed their status as eternal servants. Perhaps most importantly, her dim-wittedness, gargantuan size, black
skin, and grotesque smile masked any belief that her close proximity to
whites could result in sexual relations with white men. History, of course,
suggests otherwise. Pressured by growing criticism of the derogatory image,
the Quaker Oats Company radically transformed the Aunt Jemima trademark during the Black Power era by lightening her complexion, slimming
her ample body, and eliminating the handkerchief on her head and toothy
grin. These cosmetic changes, however, did little to eliminate the mammy-
type figure from popular memory. For writers such as Evans-Charles, Aunt
Jemima continued to symbolize the legacy of enslavement and black oppression. Evans-Charles eradicates the stereotype of Aunt Jemima by allowing a
beautiful, three-dimensional vision of black womanhood to emerge from her
dust. Jameena recognizes the destructiveness of controlling images and resists
the negative imagery of Aunt Jemima by changing her name. Yet she ultimately suffers because she remains mostly ignorant of her own identity, lacks
self-worth, and easily accepts "positive" stereotypes of black womanhood.

Jameena represents black women who settle for prescribed gender roles
instead of taking on the more difficult task of self-discovery. Throughout the
play Jameena displays her talents as a singer, dancer, musician, and seamstress.
Her emotional insecurities, however, leave her vulnerable to the machinations
of her unfaithful boyfriend Omar, who shapes her into his idealized woman.
During the course of the play, Jameena spends most of her time cooking
and tending to Omar's needs. As his loyal, unpaid domestic servant, Jameena
even allows Omar to move Vivian, her former friend and his new lover, into
her apartment with them.[101] Jameena justifies her passivity by explaining to
Vivian that her primary objective in life is to simply be Omar's "woman."
Aware of her insecurities, Omar controls Jameena through emotional abuse.
For example, although aware of the emotional trauma associated with her
birth name, Omar condescendingly refers to her as Jamimma. He also recalls
the visual imagery of the Aunt Jemima trademark to further humiliate her.
According to Omar, Jameena "was grinning all over [her]self" when they
finally reconciled their differences after an eight-month separation.[102] Just as
the grinning Aunt Jemima lived to serve her white master, Jameena's identity
and world revolve around pleasing Omar. Through this irony Evans-Charles
demonstrates the dangers of stereotypes. "Replacing negative images with
positive ones can be equally problematic if the function of stereotypes as
controlling images remains unrecognized," writes Collins.[103] Jameena does
not recognize that she continues to limit herself by allowing Omar's romantic
vision of black womanhood to shape her own consciousness.

Jameena's predicament provides an important lesson for black female audiences: in order to have productive romantic relationships, one must first gain
a knowledge of self. When a black female audience member asked her why
she allowed Jameena to "take all of what she did from him," Evans-Charles

explained that Jameena simply "could not see."[104] As their conversation continued, Evans-Charles further clarified that Jameena represents "an attitude, a conglomeration of women, a pattern of behavior."[105] Jameena dreams of having a home and family, and willingly accepts Omar's abuse in the hopes of obtaining this goal. In order to maintain the illusion of familial bliss, however, she must also ignore Omar's unfaithfulness, which causes additional emotional suffering. "But had she possessed a greater knowledge about herself, and a better understanding of the concept of woman and of being true to yourself and your human dignity before you can be true to anyone else, she would have done a better job of solving her problems," writes Evans-Charles.[106] Jameena thus serves as an important example of black women who recognize their problems but only take the initial step toward self-definition.

Jamimma was both Evans-Charles's most celebrated and most controversial play. The Black Theatre Workshop's 1970 premiere of *Jamimma* played to sold-out audiences and the majority of theater critics praised Evans-Charles for crafting a well-developed plot, an emotionally compelling heroine, and authentic supporting characters. The *New York Amsterdam News* critic Vivian Robinson, in particular, commended Evans-Charles for her use of black vernacular and the ability to write about "readily identifiable experiences."[107] The *New York Times* critic Howard Thompson also lauded Evans-Charles's writing skills and Shauneille Perry's direction of the New Federal Theatre's 1972 production of *Jamimma*.[108] "Miss Evans-Charles has devised an authentic theatrical microcosm about real, troubled people of today that rings true. . . . Individually and collectively, under Shauneille Perry's direction, a trim cast vivifies and deepens the characters," wrote Thompson.[109] In addition to deeming *Jamimma* an entertaining and "promising" play, the *New York Times* critic Walter Kerr commended Evans-Charles for providing "dignity and attractive resilience to her heroine."[110] Despite *Jamimma's* overwhelmingly positive critical reception, the reviewer Jean Carey Bond considered Jameena's acceptance of Omar's mediocre offerings and emotional abuse as a major flaw within the play. "The playwright wants us to be impressed with Jamimma's ability to GIVE, to love without needing to be loved in return . . . Jamimma, and perhaps Martie Evans-Charles, confuses giving with passive acceptance of abuse, with the refusal to make demands, with a fatalistic acceptance of the status quo," wrote Bond.[111] While she accurately identified emotional abuse as the core problem within Jameena and Omar's relationship, Bond failed to understand that Evans-Charles does not celebrate Jameena's poor choices. Rather, Evans-Charles uses dramatic irony to demonstrate how controlling images—whether positive or negative—disempower black women.

Regardless of whether or not critics agree with Jameena's position, she remains an important character because she represents everyday black women who lack the knowledge to define themselves. Evans-Charles responded to Bond's scathing review as follows:

No m'am. She gets no pleasure from being hurt or mistreated by her partner. Well then what ails the girl? What is she about? Who is Jamimma? I daresay that Jamimma herself doesn't know . . . and people who don't know who they are or what they are about can easily be controlled by those who do. . . . and to answer one critic's complaint that Jamimma's consciousness is never raised . . . I would say that the ability to step away from trying to look like or to be like what we think those models on the covers of magazines are is the raising of one's consciousness. . . . And anyone who is hip to where the minds of many Black sisters are today will realize that Jamimma has taken a giant step in an attempt to take hold of herself.[112]

By resisting the controlling image of Aunt Jemima and white standards of beauty, however, Jameena takes an important first step toward forming her own identity. Unlike Vivian, who sports the popular mod look with heavy eye makeup and an "enormous afro," Jameena foregoes makeup and dresses simply in "wraps and full ankle length skirts," with her hair in braids or a head wrap.[113] Jameena also demonstrates a burgeoning knowledge of her African heritage. For example, during times of emotional distress, Jameena seeks the guidance and support of an unnamed African mother goddess through prayer. Even though Jameena never fully recognizes her strength as a black woman and allows Omar to control her, she does take measured steps toward self-definition. Jameena and Omar's clearly toxic relationship represents the need for black men and women to work together to establish authentic relationships with one another.

After the success of *Jamimma*, Evans-Charles turned her attention toward adapting Rosa Guy's young adult novel *The Friends* (1973) for the stage. Guy's novel, set in 1953/1954, tells the story of two West Indian teenage girls who have recently moved to Harlem. While beautiful seventeen-year-old Ruby easily adjusts to her new life, fourteen-year-old Phyllisia struggles to find acceptance in her hostile school environment. Throughout the novel the two girls encounter the unique challenges of being young, black, and female, as well as the typical concerns of adolescence. As Ruby and Phyllisia adjust to a new city, they struggle to understand life after their mother's death, their father's abuse, romantic relationships, colorism within the black community, and their friends' poverty. The dialogue of Evans-Charles's *Friends* borrows heavily from the novel and represents a faithful adaptation. Unfortunately, Evans-Charles never secured permission to do so and as a result, *Friends* never received a full production. Charles, however, recalls several early readings of her mother's play, including one at Woodie King's New Federal Theatre. In 1992 Barbara Ann Teer's National Black Theatre produced a staged reading of *Friends* as part of its "Women's Reading Series," which celebrates black women in society. While *Friends* has yet to be fully realized onstage, the play remains important because it demonstrates Evans-Charles's appreciation of black women's culture and her commitment to reveal the oppressive forces within black women's lives. She continued to explore this topic in *Asante* (1974), her final play written during the Black Arts Movement.

Asante not only represents an important shift in black musical theater, but also Evans-Charles's growth as a playwright. Her compelling three-act musical uses song to express black women's standpoint and ritual to expel oppressive forces from the black female psyche. The protagonist Denise, a talented singer and dancer, provides the means to seamlessly blend these performance genres into a cohesive whole. Operating under similar circumstances as Jameena, Denise struggles to resist oppressive forces in her life and form a healthy union with her boyfriend Aseebo. In contrast to Jameena, however, Denise fully understands her worth as a black woman and performs a ritual to expel the "prisons" of her mind.[114] In so doing, Denise breaks ties with past trauma, forges her own identity, and obtains wedded bliss with Aseebo. Although sources indicate that *Asante* was never professionally produced, the musical remains important because it reflects black women's standpoint and is indicative of an important shift in black musical theater. Evans-Charles wrote *Asante* during what the scholar Allen Woll regards as the "revival of the black musical on Broadway."[115] New black-created musicals such as *Purlie* (1970) and *Eubie!* (1978) garnered critical acclaim while resisting the "sunny optimism of the white-created black musical" of the past.[116] These new musicals examined the criminal underclass and addressed previously taboo topics such as enslavement, racism, and teen pregnancy. In keeping with the problem musicals of the era, *Asante* boldly explores racism and its impact upon the black female psyche.

Incorporating song into a Black Arts ethos allowed Evans-Charles to more fully express black women's subjectivity. Original songs such as "In the Garden of My Mind" afford audiences a glimpse into the mind of a black woman. Denise begins by singing:

> I'm gonna plant a garden in my mind
> I'm gonna plant a garden in my mind
> Gonna plant a garden in my mind
> With the roots buried in my soul

Denise continues to sing that she's "gonna plant seeds" called "know myself," "charity," "love one another," and "do for one another."[117] Denise's "garden" and "seeds" represent her mind and thoughts, respectively. Her song also presents black women as active agents. Denise, after all, controls her "mental garden," and only she has the power to plant positive ideas. "In the Garden of My Mind" also demonstrates Denise's desire to give back to her community and work productively with others. However, Denise naively discounts the influence of external forces in her life until Aseebo explains to her that "whoever is in power" manipulates and defines her.[118] Denise's wardrobe, in fact, supports Aseebo's assessment. Paradoxically, while Denise disavows outside influences on her consciousness, she dresses as a quintessential all-American teen complete with a cheerleader skirt and form-fitting sweater. While Denise can plant charity and love in her mind, she will not gain self-knowledge until she identifies and casts aside the outside forces, or "prisons," that subconsciously entrap her mind.

Similar to Peaches in *Where We At?* Denise performs a ritual of expulsion in order to liberate herself from the oppressive forces that entrap her psyche. While Denise enters into a trance, Aseebo "calls out the prisons that entrap us, causing us to hold on to that which inhibits growth and to shun that which encourages it."[119] These five prisons are poverty, jealousy, hate, self-contempt, and fear.[120] Of all the prisons, self-contempt proves the most insidious because it infiltrates the minds of black women at an early age and leads to a fractured sense of self. Denise reveals that she developed self-contempt when Little White Girl at school teased her about her "funny" hair.[121] This experience prompts her to wear a mop on her head, much to her mother's dismay, and the two have the following conversation:

> DENISE: Mommy, when I grow up will I have blonde hair like the other girls at school?
> MOTHER: No, honey don't be silly. You will have what mommy has.
> DENISE: A wig?[122]

Evans-Charles uses dramatic irony to demonstrate the process of socializing black girls to hate their own beauty. Denise's mother's statement that she "will have what mommy has" does not provide psychic relief because even as a child Denise recognizes that a mop and a wig similarly mask their natural hair. Denise's idealization of white standards of beauty (i.e., straight blond hair) becomes a tool of oppression. While remaining in a trance, Denise reveals how her early feelings of inadequacy blossomed into self-contempt. "I'm not at all like you. Who am I, huh? Just who am I? Who am I like? Where are my images? What am I, some split personality pieced together by this fractured world," Denise says to her mother.[123] With these words Denise describes a mental tension that is a unique experience for black women. She must reconcile her internal concept of self with the outside world's distorted representations of black womanhood in order to function in the world. Patricia Hill Collins describes this process as a "series of negotiations" that black women must undergo in order to "reconcile the contradictions separating our own internally defined images of self as African-American women with our Objectification as the 'Other.'"[124] Lacking positive images of black womanhood, Denise reconciles this mental tension by submitting to the will of outside forces. "We are formed by the outer forces and the outer forces of this world have deemed us to be nothing and so we are nothing. We are only shadows in their consciousness, and so we live in a shadowy existence," Denise tells Aseebo.[125] The act of ritual, however, enables Denise to free her mind from the prison of self-contempt. No longer a "shadow" in her oppressor's consciousness, Denise can finally resist controlling images of black woman-hood, appreciate her own beauty, and form her own identity. With this ritual performance, Evans-Charles not only promotes a holistic approach to black liberation, but also privileges black women's standpoint and demonstrates a keen understanding of the importance of beauty politics.

After performing a ritual to liberate the black female mind from oppressive forces, the premise of *Asante* shifts to reaffirming the humanity of blacks through the celebration of black history and culture. The title of the musical itself speaks to Evans-Charles's ongoing concern with cultural retention. "Asante" is a variant of the word "Ashanti," which refers to a people in southern Ghana, as well as a dialect spoken by the Ashanti people. As Aseebo sings the title song "Asante" to bar performer Thelma, he teaches both her and the audience about African history and culture:

> Asante speaks of queenly women with genteel loving ways
> Asante speaks of warrior kings and Africa's Golden Age
> Asante, my brother, Asante, my sister
> Is a stepping stone a bridge to our forgotten past
> A Swahili word for thank you, our ancient melody.
> Asante sana, thank you very much
> Asante sana, Asante sana, nende salama
> Thank you very much, thank you very much
> Go in peace[126]

Through the didactic and lyrical title song "Asante," Evans-Charles encourages audiences to embrace their mother tongue and take pride in the tremendous wealth and power that the West African kingdoms of Ghana, Mali, and Song-hay enjoyed during Africa's Golden Age. "Asante" also creates a pan-African consciousness by situating black Americans as the descendants of "queenly women" and "warrior kings." However, Evans-Charles's idealized vision of the African Golden Age, complete with royal titles, unwittingly reinscribes oppressive gender hierarchies, for a "genteel" queen will always be subject to the will of her "warrior" king. Remembering this shared—though highly romanticized—African past unites blacks within this play, regardless of their socioeconomic backgrounds and racial consciousness. Evans-Charles would continue to explore Afrocentrism in her dramas written after the Black Arts Movement.

Although Evans-Charles's early dramas were written more than forty years ago, her insightful plays remain relevant today because they articulate black women's subjectivity and recover black women's history in the United States. Through the everyday conversations of complex female protagonists, Evans-Charles validates black women's humanity and reveals the oppressive

Figure 8. Martie Evans-Charles, early 1990s. Photo by Dr. Adrienne Charles. Courtesy of Dr. Adrienne Charles.

forces within their lives. As these women, to various degrees, resist control-ling images of black womanhood, they gain knowledge about themselves and their African heritage. Perhaps most important, Evans-Charles's dramas grant black women agency to express their innermost thoughts for black audiences to relate to. When asked what people should know and remem-ber about her mother's life's work, Charles does not hesitate: "She loved the theater. She loved drama. She loved to laugh. She loved people and she really enjoyed writing. . . . She wanted to leave a legacy."[127] As a warrior mother in her own right, Evans-Charles's contributions to black revolutionary drama will endure.

Chapter 3

✦

"Armed Prophet"

Sonia Sanchez and the Weapon of Words

If you scratch the surface of any woman of color, you know she's a womanist already. She's had to struggle with men. She had to struggle with her own identity. She's had to struggle in a house, just to be herself. She has to struggle with rape, incest. She's had to struggle to go to school. People have attempted to destroy the power of the word *feminism*. That's why I like "womanist" so much. I like what Alice Walker did with that word. You see if I'm a "womanist," I love myself; then I love other women and I love men also. I love my people too. I can't be on this earth without all of these loves.

—Sonia Sanchez, 2005

Sonia Sanchez's drama privileges the everyday concerns of poor black women and in so doing simultaneously supports, negates, and critiques Black Power rhetoric. Exploring Sanchez's art and activism reveals a significant moment wherein emerging womanist thought became an essential component of Black Arts discourse. While Sanchez's early dramas preceded the term "womanist," her writings nonetheless address many of the concerns associated with womanist thought.[1] Indeed, Sanchez's dramas recover black women's silenced history, articulate the ongoing concerns of black women, and encourage unity among black men and women. Her dramas were influenced by her own experiences as a mother, educator, activist, and poet, as well as by the artistic and political sensibilities of Abbey Lincoln, Malcolm X, Bertolt Brecht, Amiri Baraka, and Barbara Ann Teer. This chapter critically examines Sanchez's development as an artist and black woman intellectual, noting the ways in which her Southern upbringing, political activism, participation in the Black Arts Repertory Theatre/School, and interaction with fellow Black Arts participants shaped her playwriting career.

As an "armed prophet"[2] Sanchez equipped herself with the weapon of words and unapologetically told black audiences what they *needed* to hear.

Sanchez published five popular dramas during the Black Arts Movement: *The Bronx Is Next* (1968), *Sister Son/ji* (1969), *Dirty Hearts* (1971), *Malcolm/ Man Don't Live Here No Mo'* (1972), and *Uh, Uh; But How Do It Free Us?* (1974). While the style and form of her plays vary, Sanchez consistently used theater as a platform to critique actual debates happening within Harlem and the greater black community. Rather than equate the acquisition of manhood with an emblem of black liberation, her plays depict the survival of black women and children as an integral component of black liberation. Collectively, her plays were meant to embolden audiences and encourage strong leadership among black men and women. Yet her plays also reflect her own intellectual growth toward a humanistic vision of the world. Her third play, *Dirty Hearts*, for example, echoes her growing global awareness of how white racism negatively impacts *all* people of color.

Sanchez's experimental dramas not only interpret the black condition from a black woman's worldview, but also create a new image of feminine strength through the warrior mother figure. In her critical essay "Ruminations/Reflections" (1984), Sanchez likens the work of a poet to that of a prophet: "Like the priest and prophet, with whom he/she was often *synonymous*, the poet in some societies has had infinite powers to interpret life . . . to create, preserve, or destroy social values."[3] Sanchez's poetic sensibilities inform her dramatic representation of black life in the United States. Her dramas function as corrective texts that create new images of feminine strength, preserve black women's culture, and work to destroy any destructive behaviors or attitudes that harm black communities. In so doing, Sanchez creates a counter-discourse to prevailing Black Arts images. Indeed, rather than depict the strong black male warrior or submissive African queen, Sanchez's new image demonstrates a deep appreciation of black women's strength, beauty, and humanity. Sanchez's warrior mother experiences pain, loss, and oppressive forces from within and outside of her own community. Yet these trials ultimately motivate her to become a strong leader capable of uniting and galvanizing black men and women. Sanchez's prophetic representation of the black warrior mother, therefore, seeks to destroy old social values.

In addition to the warrior mother image, the most notable features of Sanchez's dramas include her use of ritual, irony, and language to express womanist thought. Sanchez utilized ritual performance and nonlinear episodes to create a non-static representation of time. Doing so allowed audiences to consider how black women's past experiences in the United States continue to inform their present-day circumstances. Dramatic irony allowed Sanchez to not only deconstruct racist archetypes of black womanhood, but also reveal the disparity between romanticized visions of black womanhood and the actual everyday lives of poor black women. Sanchez presents black women from a variety of backgrounds who use poetry, black vernacular, chant, and everyday conversations to demonstrate how prevailing understandings of black empowerment harm black women and families.

Regardless of their age, political beliefs, or lifestyle, all of the black women in Sanchez's plays are unable to satisfy their needs as women and mothers when they defer to prescribed gender roles. These women remain in this terrible emotional state until they use their agency to define themselves. Their newfound confidence allows them to resist controlling forces in their lives and become leaders in the black liberation movement. In so doing, Sanchez not only privileges black women's concerns, but also positions black female leadership and healthy relationships with black men as critical components of black liberation.

While Sanchez's dramas provide an important example of early womanist thought, few feminist scholars and theater historians have explored her important writings. Sanchez, in fact, is better known today as a prolific Black Arts poet than a playwright, even though her poetry and dramas met critical acclaim at roughly the same time.[4] Scholars such as Joyce Ann Joyce, Cheryl Clarke, Elizabeth Frost, and Michelle Nzadi Keita have written remarkable studies that celebrate Sanchez's poetry and distinctive black female aesthetic, yet there has been little sustained analysis of her dramas. Rosemary K. Curb's "Pre-Feminism in the Revolutionary Drama of Sonia Sanchez" (1985) provides one of the earliest critical analyses of Sanchez's dramas in relation to black feminist thought. Curb's article situates Sanchez as a "leading female literary voice of the Black Revolution" and provides close readings of three of her plays in order to understand how her works are similar to and depart from black revolutionary drama.[5] Curb finds that while Sanchez's plays critique sexism within black communities and provide a "preliminary raising of consciousness," they do not affirm "a conscious feminist position."[6] Elizabeth Brown-Guillory's "Sonia Sanchez (1934–)" (1993), a three-page encyclopedia article, adds to Curb's analysis by providing insights into the thematic similarities between Sanchez's poetry and drama.

While previous scholarship attests to Sanchez's ability to critique sexism within the movement, only theater historians Mike Sell and Jacqueline Wood suggest that Sanchez used her agency to consciously promote a feminist attitude or womanist stance. Sell's *Avant-Garde Performance and the Limits of Criticism: Approaching the Living Theatre, Happening/Fluxus, and the Black Arts Movement* (2005) considers Sanchez's artistic legacy and provides an exceptional, yet brief, close analysis of three of her plays. Sell situates Sanchez's dramas as "among the most acutely self-critical, resolutely revolutionary plays of the Black Arts era, articulating a rigorously feminist attitude that one rarely encounters among the artistic and critical works of the movement."[7] Similar to Sell, Wood also locates Sanchez's dramas within both the Black Arts and feminist traditions and provides close readings of three of her plays. Wood's "'Shaking Loose': Sonia Sanchez's Militant Drama" (2007) contends that Sanchez was one of the "most vocal womanist/humanist critics" of the era and contributed to the development of militant drama through her "radicalization of its language," "privileging of women's questions in the movement," and "audacious challenges to form."[8] This study builds on the scholarship of Sell and Wood by situating Sanchez as a black woman intellectual who consciously used her standpoint and artistic agency to create a distinctly womanist aesthetic from within the black revolutionary dramatic form.

This chapter departs from previous studies by analyzing all of Sanchez's plays written during the Black Arts Movement, previously published interviews, and a more recent original interview with Sanchez in order to understand *how* and *to what extent* she negotiated an early womanist stance from within the Black Arts ethos. This study puts Sanchez in dialogue with the multiple discourses in which she engaged, including womanist theology, black feminist thought, Black Arts and Epic theater aesthetics, and American politics. This chapter recovers Sanchez's profound contributions to the development of black revolutionary drama and later black feminist drama.

Sonia Sanchez: Black Woman Intellectual

The womanist theology espoused by her grandmother and the churchwomen of her youth greatly influenced Sanchez's early conception of drama. "Womanist theology is a prophetic voice concerned about the well-being of the entire African American community, male and female, adults and children. . . . Womanist theology attempts to help black women see, affirm, and have confidence in the importance of their experience and faith," writes the theologian Delores Williams.[9] Sanchez recalls that she first learned about drama by listening to black churchwomen affirm each other's humanity and strategize ways to survive oppressive forces in their lives. After the death of her mother, Sanchez and her sister Anita Patricia moved to Birmingham, Alabama, and were raised by their three aunts and paternal grandmother, "Mama."[10] As a deaconess of the A.M.E. Zion Church, Mama often gathered a group of sisters together on Saturdays to cook food for Sunday services. "In that milieu of cooking food and snapping beans there would be conversations about dear Sister Ruth. 'Her husband's beating her again.' And there would be this sigh of, 'hummm.' My Mama would say, 'Sister Louise, I want you to take the little boy because you have a little boy and they can play together. Sister Betty, I want you to take the baby 'cause you still nursin' your baby so she can nurse at your breast,'" recalls Sanchez.[11] In addition to meeting Sister Ruth's immediate needs, the churchwomen helped her strategize ways to resist further abuse. "What they told her is that the next time your husband is sleeping, put some hot grits on the stove or some hot water on the stove. Wake him up and say, 'The next time you hit me and the next time you go to sleep, you gonna wake up with these hot grits on you or this hot water on you,'" recalls Sanchez. These everyday conversations not only established a strong sisterhood but also transmitted black women's wisdom, faith, and as

Figure 9. Sonia Sanchez, late 1970s / early 1980s. Photo by Gordon Robotham. Courtesy of Sonia Sanchez.

Sanchez describes, "a psychology of black women staying alive."[12] Although Sanchez was just a child, Mama allowed her to witness these conversations about black women's resistance in order to prepare her for womanhood. Sanchez's dramas reflect the womanist wisdom imparted by Mama and the churchwomen.

Sanchez's desire to learn about and create black literature was cultivated by the Birmingham public schools and by the distinguished poet Louise Bogan, respectively. Long before joining activist organizations, Sanchez recalls that public school assemblies immersed her in black literature. Birmingham public schools taught her to appreciate the works of poets such as Langston Hughes, Paul Laurence Dunbar, and Countee Cullen. Following Mama's death in 1943, Sanchez moved to Harlem to live with her father Wilson L. Driver and continued to learn about black culture and politics. Her keen mind and interest in social justice enabled her to earn a bachelor of arts degree in political science from Hunter College in 1955. Her passion for reading poetry led to her desire to craft her own original works. She then pursued graduate study in poetry at New York University where she was mentored by Bogan, poet laureate to the Library of Congress. Sanchez continues to credit Bogan for encouraging her to read her poetry out loud so that she could train her ear to "know whether it works or not."[13] Sanchez remembers continuing this practice throughout her career, sometimes even realizing that her poem actually needed dialogue. "There were some poems I've done along the way that I would put in the margins: 'to be sung,' 'clap,' 'stamp your feet.' . . . I wanted the person speaking out loud and I realized that this is very dramatic," recalls Sanchez.[14] These discoveries often led her to craft a poetic play, such as *Sister Son/ji*. Now armed with a knowledge of both poetry and politics, Sanchez turned her attention to bettering her Harlem community.

Sanchez's participation in community activist organizations provided the formal structure she needed to express her knowledge and experiences as a black woman in the United States. During the early 1960s Sanchez taught at Downtown Community School, an experimental and racially integrated school; worked with the social activist group Harlem Youth Opportunities Unlimited; and became an active member of the Congress of Racial Equality's (CORE's) New York branch. Her experience with CORE gave her a greater understanding of black activist traditions. She also learned practical skills in negotiation, such as how to effectively communicate with trade unions and housing developers. Working with CORE also led to a greater awareness of other activist organizations. She read the writings of Martin Luther King and Malcolm X and became acquainted with leftists and participants in other civil rights organizations. Sanchez fondly remembers listening to Malcolm speak on street corners and becoming inspired by his words, even though she did not fully support his vision. "'Mr. X, I didn't quite agree with everything you said.' . . . He looked at me with those eyes, so gentle and loving, and said, 'But you will one day, my sister,'" recalls Sanchez.[15] While Sanchez acknowledges that Malcolm and later Amiri Baraka influenced her interest in black nationalism, she resists any notions that her encounters with them marked an ideological shift from "integrationist" to "separatist." Rather, Sanchez identifies her early activism in terms of "struggling as a young black woman in America" and ongoing efforts of "talkin' about change."[16]

Joining Baraka's Black Arts Repertory Theatre/School (BART/S) in 1965 provided an opportunity to further engage her Harlem community. BART/S not only provided a space for her to hone her poetry skills, but also gave her the opportunity to be a part of a community of musicians, poets, playwrights, artists, and activists. Sanchez initially accepted Baraka's invitation to join BART/S because she believed in the transformative power of art. Sanchez recalls:

> Baraka sent out letters to all the artists that he knew from poets, playwrights, [and] musicians saying, after Malcolm died, "Come and be a part of this great Black Arts Movement where we're going to, in a sense, change the world." . . . We all gathered there [and] listened to the idea of how we could be these transformative people in this building [on] 130th Street. [We began] to talk about art, using art as change for community. It was like going to the community, being in the community, and beginning to talk about art that would transform a community.

Figure 10. Sonia Sanchez, 1980s. Photo by Rich Addlicks. Courtesy of Sonia Sanchez.

As a member of BART/S, Sanchez helped organize poetry readings, community discussions, talks with prominent artists and activists, and workshops for children, in order to bring awareness to social issues impacting her community.

BARTS/S provided the space to engage with other black woman intellectuals, such as Abbey Lincoln. Sanchez remembers that Lincoln's talk, "Who Will Revere the Black Woman?" published the following year in *Negro Digest*, particularly resonated with her sensibilities.[17] Lincoln's brief yet powerful speech boldly revealed how rape, misogyny, domestic violence, the use of black women as scapegoats, and the proliferation of distorted images of black womanhood oppressed black women and crippled their psyche. Lincoln concluded her speech by asking a series of questions: "Who will revere the Black woman? Who will keep our neighborhoods safe for Black innocent womanhood? . . . Black womanhood cries for dignity and restitution and salvation. Black womanhood wants and needs protection, and keeping, and holding. . . . Who will glorify and proclaim her beautiful image? To whom will she cry rape?"[18] Influenced by Malcolm X's teachings, Lincoln essentially

Figure 11. Sonia Sanchez, 1990s. Photo by Marion Ettlinger. Courtesy of Sonia Sanchez.

issued a call for black men to assume the role of benevolent patriarchs as
an act of resistance against black women's oppression. Sanchez's plays, in
fact, further validate Lincoln's critique of misogyny and stereotypes of black
womanhood. *The Bronx Is Next*, for example, features a poor single mother
named Black Bitch who performs sexual acts with White Cop in order to
provide for her sons. Ironically, when the so-called black revolutionary leaders interact with Black Bitch, they also abuse her emotionally, physically, and
sexually. The black men have internalized stereotypes about black womanhood and easily justify their assault on Black Bitch by labeling her a "bitch"
and "black matriarch." While the audience never learns Black Bitch's actual
name, she does express her everyday knowledge, revealing her humanity and
the actual forces that oppress her. In so doing, Sanchez challenges mythologies about black womanhood and critiques any ideology that uses black
women as scapegoats for poverty in black communities.

Sanchez utilized the higher education system as a resource to transmit
black women's intellectual tradition to the next generation. After the closing
of BART/S in 1965, Sanchez moved from New York to San Francisco and

worked alongside Professor Nathan Hare, Amiri Baraka, Ed Bullins, Sarah Webster Fabio, and Marvin X at San Francisco State College to found the nation's first black studies program. She then used her experiences at San Francisco State College to teach "The Black Woman," one of the first college courses in the United States to focus solely on black womanhood. During this groundbreaking course Sanchez taught University of Pittsburgh students how to critically engage with the controversial statements espoused in the *Moynihan Report* (1965). She remembers:

> The heated discussion made me search for another term that would describe the discussion that we found ourselves in. I said at the time that our survival in America was not really patriarchal or really matriarchal. What many of us truly had was a diarchy, that is, in some of these Black families you had a mother and grandmother, a mother and an aunt, a mother and an uncle. And the family survived.[19]

Teaching the next generation of potential activists gave Sanchez the opportunity to resist descriptions of the black family as a model of pathology and to reaffirm black motherhood as integral to the survival of black communities. Sanchez continued to repeat this message to students when she received invitations to speak at colleges and universities. The *New York Amsterdam News* reported that she candidly discussed problems within the black community without in any way blaming black women while speaking to black students at Fairleigh Dickinson University in New Jersey. Sanchez taught that "'drugs undermine the Black man, keep him powerless'" and advised students to make certain that their children "were taught only by loving, black teachers, so that they would not learn to hate themselves."[20] The *New York Amsterdam News* praised her words of wisdom, noting that she was often hailed as "the female LeRoi Jones."[21] Yet a powerful leader in her own right, Sanchez's "voluminous Afro, aggressive poetics, and activist work" soon marked her as "an emblem of powerful black womanhood."[22] Regardless of her similarities to Baraka, by the end of the 1960s Sanchez had firmly established herself as a provocative Black Arts speaker, writer, and activist.

Sanchez remembers the Black Arts Movement as a nonsexist, constantly shifting dialogue that occurred among black artists and theorists. "At the inception of the Black Arts there was no sexism. It didn't come until afterwards in the seventies and it wasn't the Black Arts per se. It was those organizations that began to come out with ideologies as to the role of the black woman. The Black Arts never said at the beginning there is a role for black women," recalls Sanchez.[23] She insists that even when other Black Arts members joined black organizations that endorsed prescribed gender roles—namely the Nation of Islam and Ron Karenga's US Organization—she refused to limit her activism. "I'd say 'No. That's not my role. I'm not gonna be secretary. Get a man to be secretary.' I'm very serious about that. You can understand sometimes why I had trouble. Which is an understatement," remembers Sanchez.[24] Indeed, her refusal to adhere to someone else's vision of black womanhood would lead to a turbulent experience with the Nation of Islam.

Despite her womanist sensibilities, Sanchez joined the Nation of Islam in 1972, after moving from Harlem to teach at Amherst College in Massachusetts. Similar to Martie Evans-Charles, she became a member of the Nation of Islam in order for her children to receive a quality education. "I had gone into the Nation because I was raising my children by myself, and the public school situation was really pathetic. The Nation was one of the places to receive a good education at the time; it was a place to go for some kind of protection," recalls Sanchez.[25] Furthermore, the Nation of Islam's "concepts of nationhood, morality, small businesses, schools" appealed to her.[26] Only later did she realize that she had to meet certain expectations in order to maintain the Nation of Islam's promise of protection. While she wore the traditional head coverings and full-length dresses of female members, Sanchez admits that she did not alter her "basic lifestyle" or modify her militant writings or political activism.[27] "My contribution to the Nation has been that I refused to let them tell me where my place was. . . . One dude said to me once that the solution for Sonia Sanchez was for her to have some babies. . . . I wrote a long satirical poem called 'Solution to Sonia Sanchez,' which was my response," Sanchez recollects.[28] Her response to the man's sexist ideology reflects her feminine wit and keen ability to use her words as a weapon against misogyny.

Eventually Sanchez was unable to reconcile her womanist ideology with the prescribed gender roles outlined by the Nation of Islam. She remembers that despite the Nation of Islam's ideology that "women were supposed to be in the background," she continued to speak at college campuses, travel abroad, and publish plays, two books of poetry, and a book of fiction.[29] Her children's play *Malcolm/Man Don't Live Here No Mo'* (1972), written while a member, not only celebrates Malcolm's life but also provides a subtle critique of the Nation of Islam. The characters within the play encourage blacks to *continue* to cultivate strong leadership within their communities, rather than rely on a slain leader. By 1974, however, Sanchez more openly critiqued the Nation of Islam in her play *Uh, Uh; But How Do It Free Us?* by boldly exposing how the practice of polygamy disempowers black women. She finally left the Nation of Islam and moved to Philadelphia to teach at the University of Pennsylvania when she could no longer endure the Nation's limited vision of black womanhood.

In addition to the Nation of Islam, Sanchez also used her agency to challenge misogyny within the writings of the Black Panther Party (1966–82) leader Eldridge Cleaver. When asked by *Negro World* editors to review Cleaver's memoir *Soul on Ice* (1968), Sanchez provided a scathing critique of his misogynist sentiments. "I thought [Cleaver] was problematic from the beginning. Any man who would write a book that talked about practicing rape on black women in order to rape white women was problematic. I started the review, 'Eldridge Cleaver is not a revolutionary; he's a hustler. I come from New York, and I've seen quite enough hustlers in my time,' " remembers Sanchez.[30] Although *Negro World* reassigned *Soul on Ice* to a male writer and refused to publish her review, Sanchez continued to question the ethics of Cleaver's leadership in *Uh, Uh; But How Do It Free Us?* In this play Sanchez dramatizes Cleaver's perverse ideology through the hateful speeches of a street hustler-turned-revolutionary named Brother Man. Similar to Cleaver, Brother Man has found fame and fortune as a revolutionary leader. While high on drugs, Brother Man brags about his popularity and outlines his plan to finance the so-called revolution by selling drugs to his community. Through Brother Man, Sanchez warns audiences that some black predators are, in fact, profiting off of the revolution, to the utter detriment of black communities. Sanchez's writings continually question the ethics and motivations of male leaders engaged in the struggle for black liberation.

Sanchez credits Ed Bullins for launching her playwriting career and creating an inclusive space for her to develop her womanist dramas. While Sanchez concedes that "women playwrights were working at a disadvantage because most of the playwrights were male," she continues to praise the efforts of Bullins, who used his positions as guest editor for *The Drama Review*, playwright-in-residence of the New Lafayette Theatre (1967–72), and founder of the Black Theatre Workshop (1968–72) to nurture women writers. "I was blessed to have come through with Bullins and Baraka. I was blessed to have been part of a movement where people looked up at some point and said, 'Are there any women who are writing?' Ed [Bullins] and the New Lafayette Theatre did that. No one gives them enough credit for that," recalls Sanchez.[31] Bullins, in fact, sparked Sanchez's initial interest in writing plays and provided the means for her to publish her first drama. He approached Sanchez to contribute a play to *The Drama Review*'s special issue on "Black Theatre." Unbeknownst to Bullins, Sanchez did not have prior experience writing plays. " '[Bullins asked,] Do you write plays, Sonia?' I said, 'Yes.' If someone ever asks you, who is somebody, 'Do you write plays? Do you write poetry? Do you write short stories?' always say 'Yes.' Then proceed home and start reading every short story you can, read every play you can read, and then sit down and write a play. That's what I did," remembers Sanchez.[32] With Bullins's assistance, she wrote and published her first play, *The Bronx Is Next*. The following year Bullins worked with Sanchez again to publish her second play, *Sister Son/ji*, in *New Plays from the Black Theatre: An Anthology* (1969).

While Bullins provided the mentorship Sanchez needed, he did not necessarily provide support for the everyday challenges she encountered trying to find the time to write, work, and raise children. "I'd promised Ed Bullins the play. I had just given birth to the twins—they were about three months old—when he called. I said that I'd just given birth, that I was teaching, that

I was tired and depressed. He said, 'Don't tell me your problems; I just want the play.' I got so mad at him that night I sat down and finished the play [*Sister Son/ji*] at five in the morning," recalls Sanchez.[33] As a semiautobiographical drama, *Sister Son/ji* not only reflects many of the "problems" that Sanchez encountered while trying to survive in America, but also celebrates the resilience of black womanhood. Despite their occasional disagreements, Bullins published her fifth play, *Uh, Uh; But How Do It Free Us?* in his collection *The New Lafayette Theatre Presents: Plays with Aesthetic Comments by Six Black Playwrights* (1974). Sanchez continues to praise Bullins for encouraging her to pursue playwriting and allowing her to use his Black Theatre Workshop to hear her work read aloud. She continues to hold the New Lafayette Theatre in high esteem for providing a space for her to interact with other artists and perform nonspeaking walk-on roles during ritual performances.

While Sanchez often published her plays before they had received full productions, she always wrote with the purpose of galvanizing black audiences. Borrowing from an Epic theater aesthetics, Sanchez incorporated Bertolt Brecht's principle of *Verfremdungseffekt*, or "defamiliarization effect," in order to encourage audiences to avoid passivity and critically examine the debates presented onstage. "I use him [Brecht] as almost a bible sometimes because I like his larger way of looking at the world and I like his politics. I like the human face that he gives to his plays," recalls Sanchez.[34] Her drama *Sister Son/ji*, in particular, demonstrates an appreciation of Brecht's political and artistic sensibilities. *Sister Son/ji* employs techniques such as memory monologues, direct address, a minimalistic set, severe lighting cues, and onstage costume changes in order to elicit responses from the audience. "[What] I have tried to do is to do the writing, to get it out so people can see themselves on stages and change. So they can see other people out on stages and know that they don't want to be like them. So they can see ideas onstage and begin conversations . . . and walk with a different kind of walk when they left that theater," says Sanchez.[35] She also describes *Uh, Uh; But How Do It Free Us?* as "a Brechtian kind of play" because it functions as a corrective text that "spoke to the issues" of the day.[36] *Uh, Uh* presents the plight of three young black women who struggle to find happiness with so-called revolutionaries. Sanchez tells their stories in three separate episodes or "Groups," which are interlaced with a chorus of dancers. In so doing, Sanchez juxtaposes the somber episodes, which contain explicit emotional and physical abuse of black women, with the comedic escapades of the dancers. "I wanted people to see themselves and then to correct themselves, and to see how they were really killing themselves and others," explains Sanchez.[37] While she remembers that the dancers elicited laughter from the audience, she recalls that she received criticism for the play.

In addition to Brecht, Sanchez also incorporated elements of Teer's conceptualization of ritual performance to galvanize audiences. Breaking down traditional divisions between the actor and audience became a notable feature of Sanchez's drama, which she learned by regularly attending Teer's ritualistic revivals and by performing at National Black Theatre workshops. "I was a regular at NBT, seeing what they were doing, how they engaged an audience with their work. There was sometimes no division between the audience and the actors. So what I tried to do as a poet and a playwright and an actor, I tried to make for no division between any of us at all," recalls Sanchez.[38] Perhaps the final scene in *Sister Son/ji* best demonstrates her desire to eliminate barriers and foster unity among blacks. At the close of the play, having taken audiences through her journey of self-discovery, an aged Son/ji directly addresses the audience, stating, "A time for us. blk/ness. blk/people. Anybody can grab the day and make it stop. can u my friends? or may be it's better if I ask: will you?"[39] Her questions boldly challenge audiences to actualize the rhetoric of black love and eliminate the destructive behaviors of the past in order to create a liberated future for black men, women, and children.

The controversial subject matter of both her plays and poetry often received a mixed response from audiences: emboldening some, while offending others. Sanchez admits that she "took a lot of abuse" when she began performing her poetry.[40] The first time she read her poetry in New York, for example, she remembers that some audience members "just sat there" and stared at her until she asserted her right to perform, stating, "I'm a Black woman poet."[41] Even though her more vocal adversaries responded by booing her, she continued to perform her poetry. "I wrote poems that were obviously womanist before we even started talking about it. Men would get up and go on about their business because they said I was reading only for women. So one day I said out loud 'My poetry is just as important as your poetry.' It was at a huge conference. And I was not invited back to a major conference for three years," recalls Sanchez.[42] Regardless of the consequences, Sanchez continued to boldly express womanist thought in both her poetry and plays.

Sanchez's concern for the audience allowed her writings to transcend Western literary divides. For Sanchez, her writings were "always about the audience" and "not just a pen on paper," and she often recorded her poetry and performed live at Black Arts events.[43] As with Teer, performing her own works gave her much more visibility in the black artistic community. "I do believe that many of us who perform our poetry [believe] that it is theater. It is theater. It's not by chance that a lot of poets write plays because their poetry is drama as it were," explains Sanchez.[44] Her efforts were observed by her peers, with Broadside Press founder Dudley Randall celebrating the fact that her "notation . . . preserves much of the sound of an actual oral reading."[45] The literary scholar Elizabeth A. Frost similarly notes that the "visual disruptions"[46] within her poetry provide a footprint for oral reading, serving as a precursor to performance poetry. Sanchez's "then-novel use of slashes, capitals, spaces, and repeated letters . . . suggests the primacy of pitch, tone, and duration to the work," Frost writes.[47] Sanchez's poemplays developed

Figure 12. Sonia Sanchez, 1990s. Photo by Marion Ettlinger. Courtesy of Sonia Sanchez.

out of this performance tradition, transforming dramatic play structure long before Ntozake Shange's experimental choreopoem.

Sanchez's writings express a womanist stance through the incorporation of chant. Her dramas explore the process of self-actualization and reveal the conditions that impede personal growth and collective empowerment. "I write to tell the truth about the Black condition as I see it. Therefore I write to offer a Black woman's view of the world. . . . I've always believed that the truth concealed or clouded is a partial lie," writes Sanchez.[48] Indeed, her revelatory writings expose how racism, sexism, poverty, domestic violence, polygamy, drug abuse, black-on-black crimes, and ineffectual leaders traumatize the black psyche and disempower the entire black community.

As an interpreter of life and revealer of truth, Sanchez uses chant in her poems and plays as a method to not only foretell the past, present, and future condition of blacks, but also inspire social change:

> I chant in many of my poems. That chanting calls up the history
> of Black chanters and simultaneously has the historical effect of old

chants: it inspires *action* and *harmony*. In . . . *Sister Son/ji*, Son/ji is at
a point of desperation or insanity or pretty close to it—which means
she is crying out in the night and no one listens or hears. . . . As she
moves towards the deep end, she chants something that is ancient and
religious. She chants her prayer. Her life. Her present. Her past. Her
future. And a breath force comes back into her and with this chanting
and on her knees she is reborn.[49]

Sanchez's plays depict imperfect men and women who struggle to find
meaning in their lives because their most basic physical and emotional needs—
including food, shelter, safety, and a sense of community—have not been met.
While some of Sanchez's female protagonists submit to their partners' physical or emotional abuse, others turn to chant for inner strength to resist the
oppressive forces in their lives. Chant provides the physical space necessary
for women such as Son/ji to voice their concerns, affirm their humanity, and
heal their emotional scars sustained in a racist and sexist society. Son/ji's
chant not only allows her to achieve spiritual enlightenment onstage, but also
promotes a sense of community among the audience and hopefully, liberatory action beyond the performance event itself.

Sanchez's poetry and experimentation with dramatic form garnered the
respect of her male peers within inner Black Arts circles. In fact, she was
often one of the few women whose works were included within seminal
Black Arts Movement collections. Jones/Baraka and Larry Neal's *Black Fire:
An Anthology of Afro-American Writing* (1968), for example, only features
eleven poems by women writers: Sanchez contributed four of them.[50] In addition, Sanchez's *The Bronx Is Next* provides the only female voice of "Black
Revolutionary Theatre" in *The Drama Review*'s 1968 "Black Theatre" issue.
Dudley Randall and Black Arts poet Haki Madhubuti (Don L. Lee) also
publicly celebrated Sanchez's visionary talent.[51] Randall published several of
Sanchez's works, including her first book of poetry, *Homecoming* (1969), and
considered her a "revolutionar[y]" on a par with prominent black intellectuals and activists such as Booker T. Washington, James Weldon Johnson, and
Malcolm X.[52] "This tiny woman with the infant's face attacks the demons of
this world with the fury of a sparrow defending her fledglings in the nest. She
hurls obscenities at things that are obscene," wrote Randall.[53] Madhubuti, in
turn, credited Sanchez for "legitimizing the use of urban Black English . . .
in the context of world literature" and similarly applauded her unyielding
spirit, proclaiming her a "first-rate playwright," "an accomplished children's
writer," and "a poet (and woman) of few but strong and decisive words."[54]

Having experienced support for her womanist thought by leading male
figures of the Black Arts Movement, Sanchez did not feel the need or desire
to join a feminist organization. She preferred working with Black Arts Movement compatriots because the intellectual community not only promoted the
liberation of black women, men, and children but also enabled her to engage

with the intersections of her identity. Sanchez continues to believe that the feminist movement essentially provided only a singular worldview. "There was not just one way of looking. I was not out there just saying, 'Women are going to be freed.' We were about the liberation of women, men, and children. . . . and I think that's important. . . . I would say that I am a womanist and my writing was about being involved with a black liberation movement," recalls Sanchez.[55] The Black Arts Movement provided an intellectual space wherein multiple viewpoints could coexist.

Sanchez remembers that motherhood, needing to earn a living, and "being in love" directly impacted her intellectual engagement with the Black Arts Movement. She recalls that although she and other women writers complicated Black Arts rhetoric by providing a black woman's perspective of black liberation, they never organized their efforts because they "were so busy trying to stay alive."[56] Sanchez explains:

> It was not a thing like: let us show up together and sit down and talk about how we as women playwrights survive. I taught school, I came home and fed my children. . . . If the Black Arts Movement did anything, it showed that you can be brilliant and a playwright and a poet but like everybody else, going through the same thing: having to get a babysitter, having to feed your children, having to bathe your children, having to cook. I would get standing ovations but I would come home and my children would say, "What do I have for dinner tonight mom?" And what that does is that it centers you. There's no place for ego there.[57]

While Sanchez did not join any exclusively feminist organizations during the Black Arts Movement, she did attend meetings with other women in black studies organizations. Despite her clear articulation of black feminist attitudes, Sanchez continues to not identify as a feminist. The term "womanist," however, grants her the intellectual space to simultaneously express her day-to-day struggles as a mother, her appreciation of black women's culture, and her concern for the survival of black men, women, and children. Equipped with the weapon of words, Sanchez continues to use her prophetic voice to issue a call to arms for black people to change the destructive patterns within their community.

The Warrior Mother: Creating New Values, Myths, and Herstory

Sanchez's first play, *The Bronx Is Next* (1968), investigates the role of poor black women within the black liberation movement. She originally envisioned *The Bronx Is Next* as the first in a trilogy of plays that would dramatize the Malcolm X Society and the Group on Advanced Leadership's mission to build an independent black nation, known as the Republic of New Afrika, within America. Supporters of the Republic of New Afrika advocated a reverse black migration from the inhumane conditions of Northern cities back to the agrarian lifestyle of the South. *The Bronx Is Next* opens with black nationalists Charles, Larry, Roland, and Jimmy executing a grassroots effort to burn down the tenement houses in Harlem. Major conflict arises when the black nationalists try to evacuate a prostitute named Black Bitch. Drunk with the fervor of black nationalist rhetoric, the male leaders quickly dismiss her plight and proceed to abuse her emotionally and sexually.[58] Black Bitch, however, refuses to join them because their plan does not include efforts to alleviate the problems of poor single mothers. *The Bronx Is Next* ends with the stage alight with the blaze of burning buildings as unknown persons move about.

At first glance Black Bitch appears to be a conglomeration of stereotypes and an impediment to the organized efforts of Charles, Larry, Roland, and Jimmy.[59] By providing specific names for the black male characters and only using the generic name of Black Bitch, Sanchez imparts a mythic quality to her female character. The black nationalist leaders, in fact, believe that Black Bitch embodies the aggressive Sapphire, promiscuous Jezebel, and emasculating black matriarch stereotypes. After forcibly removing Black Bitch from her home, they question her about her ideology and discover that she is a single mother who is critical of their revolution and who sells her body to a white police officer for money. This information allows the black nationalists to not only repudiate any moral obligation to help her, but also justifies their emotional and physical abuse of Black Bitch. After her explanation of how poverty and an unfaithful partner have left her vulnerable to the machinations of white and black men, the black nationalists mockingly refer to Black Bitch as a "[s]mart-assed-bitch" and "black matriarch."[60] Black Bitch's occasional bouts of defiance, attempts to explain her position, and seemingly unregulated sexuality only further alienate her from the black nationalists. "But you still a bitch. You know. None of this explaining to us keeps you from being a bitch," Charles reminds Black Bitch.[61] The male leaders then proceed to beat her and admonish her to remain silent. "I told you I only explain important things. There ain't nothing happening here yet that's important to me," says Black Bitch before exiting.[62] Black Bitch's articulation of "important things" includes her expressed concern for black women's labor, motherhood, sexual politics, and self-definition. These concerns reflect some of the core themes of black feminist thought.[63] Unfortunately, the black nationalists are unwilling or unable to account for them within their current understanding of black liberation.

Black Bitch's everyday conversation exposes the harsh realities of urban life and reveals how the intersections of her identity impede her pursuit of empowerment. Black Bitch's inability to acquire a living wage to support herself and her two sons forces her into a life of prostitution with White Cop and with black men. Sanchez remembers that during the 1960s, some black women who were not "making enough money to live anyplace" traded sexual favors with black and white men in order to supplement their income.[64] Sanchez describes Black Bitch as a "prototype" because her experiences represent "what was happening in many of the communities."[65] As a prototype, Black Bitch's plight provides an important glimpse into the everyday lives of black women. Black Bitch's struggles represent the unique challenges that urban black women face because they are poor, black, and female. White Cop, who represents white oppression, not only ignores vices within the Harlem community, but also contributes to street crime by exploiting black women's vulnerability.

Black Bitch reveals the irony of blaming black women for the deterioration of the Harlem community, rather than sex-seeking white men or the ineffectual New York Police Department. The play, in fact, reflects an actual shift that was occurring in New York City during the late 1960s. Police departments "'allowed' Black prostitutes to expand their base of operation," causing the "black ghettos of America" to become "a frequent haunt of sex-seeking white men," writes the sociologist Robert Staples.[66] As New York City experienced a major increase in black female prostitution, the Police Department did little to intervene in illegal activities. "Moreover, recent investigations of the police force in certain large cities have revealed a close collaboration between the men in blue and the peddlers of vice in ghetto communities," writes Staples.[67] Black Bitch exposes this situation for audiences. "I only explain the important things. He comes once a week. He fucks me. He puts his grayish dick in me and dreams his dreams. They ain't 'bout me. Explain him to my boys. *Laughs*. Man. I am surviving," says Black Bitch.[68] Survival and motherhood, rather than sexual deviance, force her into a life of prostitution. Her sexually explicit dialogue also suggest that White Cop's weekly visits offer little emotional connection and simply objectify her body. Referring to Black Bitch as a matriarch is a cruel affront because it belies the reality that she lives in a society that systematically disenfranchises her because she is both black and female. Her most basic needs have not been met and yet she somehow survives the psychological trauma of abuse, exploitation, objectification, and the threat of rape. As a prototype, she speaks to the resilience of black womanhood.

Black Bitch not only questions the motivations of the black nationalist leaders, but also challenges them to include black women's concerns within the framework of revolution. The male leaders carry out orders to burn down tenements in Harlem because they believe this will liberate blacks. In so doing, they hurt the very people whom they intend to help. Charles demonstrates a certain callousness to Black Bitch's resistance by reminding her that he "could fuck" her at any time on the streets "if [he] wanted to."[69] Charles's words suggest that (1) he has internalized the belief that black women are always sexually available, (2) the streets of Harlem are unsafe for black women, and (3) no one would come to a black woman's aid. With the threat of rape and death looming, Sanchez allows Black Bitch to issue a call to black men, similar to that of Abbey Lincoln, to protect and revere black womanhood. "Yeah. I know what I am. . . . But all you revolutionists or nationalists or whatever you call yourselves—do you know where you at? I am a black woman and I've had black men who could not love me or my black boys—where you gonna find black women to love you when this is over—when you need them?" asks Black Bitch.[70] By identifying herself as a black woman, mother, and helpmate to black men, Black Bitch asserts her humanity and disrupts demoralizing images of black womanhood. She, in fact, wants to work with black men to build strong, loving black families. Until the nationalists include her concerns within their vision of a liberated future, however, she will continue to survive on her own, just as her foremothers have done.

Black Bitch's interactions with the black nationalist men, therefore, provide the means for Sanchez to critique sexist discourse and express her vision of a truly liberated black America. Sanchez explains Black Bitch's purpose as follows:

> I don't think this Black Bitch was a person that was put in there to show how much black men hated black women. No, she was a person put in to remind them of their humanity. To remind them whatever you do, if you don't bring the family into it, it's not going to work. And she was a single black woman with children. She was a family. Whether you like the idea that she was single or not. And unless you remind yourself as to how you deal with family then you're doomed for failure. . . . The impetus for any kind of change has got to be: the betterment of your community, the betterment of women and children, the betterment of people, period.[71]

In so doing, Sanchez admonishes black men and women to unify and fight for the betterment of their *entire* people.

Rather than present the revolutionary men as simply malicious, Sanchez takes great care to humanize them by revealing how their lives are constantly threatened by daily interactions with white police officers. Jimmy relates the following experience to his comrades:

> Man. Do you know that jest yesterday I was running down my ghetto street and these two white dudes stopped me and asked what I was doing out so early in the morning—and cuz I was high off some smoke—I said man—it's my street—I can walk on it any time. And they grabbed me and told me where everything was.[72]

Jimmy's story implies that he has been socialized to behave in a submissive manner when confronted by white police in Harlem. Noncompliance, or simply asserting one's rights to run down one's own street in the neighborhood, routinely results in excessive police force. Jimmy's story also reveals that black men live in a state of fear that they can be assaulted or killed for simply existing in their own neighborhoods. In order to reclaim their sense of masculine pride, Charles suggests that the revolutionaries "change places" with White Cop and re-create Jimmy's experience.[73] White Cop initially refuses to play along, but acquiesces once Jimmy accuses him of cowardice. This deadly game of race reversal quickly reveals the perils of "running while black" and White Cop pleads for the game to end. Having proven their point about the dangers of racial profiling and corrupt law enforcement, the revolutionaries take White Cop back to the apartment complex, effectively condemning him to death. Again, White Cop pleads: "Holy Mother—you can't do this to me. *Screams*. But, I'm white! I'm white! No. This can't be happening—I'm white!"[74] Neither the Holy Virgin Mary nor his belief in his racial superiority will save him from this ritual cleansing.

Unfortunately, at the time Sanchez wrote *The Bronx Is Next*, the affirmation of the sanctity of black lives had not become a topic within mainstream academic discourse. The disconnect between the everyday experiences of black Americans and white perceptions of the world became more pronounced as Sanchez faced opposition for including the play in her tenure file at Temple University. She remembers a white male member of her tenure committee confronting her in a hallway about the improbability of a black man being seized and killed for simply running down a street in Harlem. Sanchez recalls responding to her colleague as follows:

> The next day I'm drinking my tea in the morning. I'm opening my *Times*. On the front page was [a story about] a young black man [who] had been killed running through the streets of Harlem. Two cops had killed him 'cause they told him to stop and he didn't stop. So I went into my office and I knocked on his door and I held [the *Times*] up and said, "Look." And he didn't say another word.[75]

Sanchez believes that her plays "were reflecting what was going on in the world but at the same time making a statement about it too."[76] Unfortunately, her statement about the extrajudicial killings of blacks, written more than fifty years ago, remains just as relevant today.

Sanchez's critique of racial profiling and corrupt law enforcement is part of a long tradition of black activism which continues strong with the Black Lives Matter movement of today. Just three years before the murder of seventeen-year-old Trayvon Martin, which served as a catalyst for the formation of Black Lives Matter, Sanchez made the following prophetic statement about the need to protect black youth:

> It's still happening today. Young blacks get killed constantly if they're out at a certain time of night. . . . If you're a black person—especially

a male—you cannot be out on the streets of any major city not knowing where you're going. If you do, you die. You're dead. If you're
outside [or] even if you're in the car at two and three o'clock. You
have got to know how to maneuver [in] the country and the world if
you're out there as a young man someplace. It becomes impossible to
stay alive even if you look respectable, you got a suit on. If a cop car
tags you, they're going to pull you over and ask you some questions.
Does it happen all the time? But it does happen because as Malcolm
said, "You might have a PhD but to some people you still a nigga."
That's very real.[77]

Needless to say, Sanchez continues to boldly state what she feels needs to be
addressed within the black community and America at large, regardless of
the consequences. *The Bronx Is Next* allowed Sanchez to bring these concerns to a much wider audience. More than anything, she wanted her very
real depictions of urban life to compel black audiences to *action*.

Sanchez uses the ritual of fire to symbolically destroy the past and embolden
audiences. With their mission accomplished, Charles informs the other men
that they need to move on to their next task: evacuating and burning down
the Bronx neighborhood. "You think this is the right strategy, burning out
the ghettos? Don't make much sense to me man. But orders is orders," states
Roland.[78] Charles's unyielding support and Roland's reluctance to burn
down ghettos represent the debates people had at the time to this actual idea.
Sanchez remembers that when she wrote *The Bronx Is Next*, blacks were
"placed" in Harlem ghettos, which consisted of brownstones that "were cut
up into apartment buildings." Some black nationalists believed that "the best
thing to happen to some of these so-called ghettos is to burn 'em down . . .
and take the people South where they were human beings."[79] Dramatizing
this debate allowed Sanchez to show the harsh realities of life in Harlem,
offering the final image of fire to inspire audiences to take immediate action
to better their own community.

In keeping with popular Black Arts imagery of the time, Sanchez uses the
image of fire to suggest the urgency of the artist's mission, as well as the death
of old ways of viewing the world. The Black Arts Movement poet Etheridge
Knight, who is Sanchez's former husband, writes: "The Black artist must create new forms and new values, sing new songs (or purify old ones); and along
with other Black authorities, he must create a new history, new symbols,
myths and legends (and purify old ones by fire)."[80] Sanchez actualizes this
rhetoric through an elderly black woman named Old Sister who appears
only briefly at the beginning of the play. When the so-called revolutionaries
attempt to take Old Sister with them on the trek, she insists on taking her
possessions (i.e., history) with her. The men ultimately decide that they cannot sacrifice the time needed to persuade her to leave her past behind. As
they take her back to her apartment, she thanks the Lord for sending her

these helpful men (who are ironically leading her to her death). As a nameless churchwoman who lives in the past, Old Sister takes on symbolic meaning. She represents the older generation of blacks who did not assert their rights against oppressive forces, but rather found comfort in the Bible. Her sacrificial death in this ritual of fire symbolizes a purification. Her death expunges old ways of living and creates an ontological space for new, more humane values to emerge.

Sanchez's application of black nationalist rhetoric proved both provocative and inspirational for audiences who witnessed *The Bronx Is Next*. The Black Theatre produced the premiere two years after *The Bronx Is Next*'s initial publication. While there are no reviews of the Black Theatre's premiere production, University of the Streets' subsequent New York production received favorable reviews for its brief performance run. In addition, Jacqueline Wood notes that Sanchez's depiction of violent grassroots activism "shocked many and emboldened the militant community."[81] Even though the trilogy remains incomplete, Mike Sell celebrates *The Bronx Is Next* as one of "the most acutely self-critical, resolutely revolutionary plays of the Black Arts era."[82] If Sanchez ever completes the trilogy, she intends for audiences to witness the harrowing journey south and conclude the trilogy with blacks arriving in the five states that the Republic of New Afrika has purchased: Louisiana, Mississippi, Alabama, Georgia, and South Carolina. Her second play, *Sister Son/ji* (1969), also responds to Knight's call to create new symbols, myths, and legends by creating a powerful warrior mother image.

Sister Son/ji uses innovative performance techniques to critique romanticized visions of black womanhood and to engage audiences. *Sister Son/ji* presents the life story of a black Mississippi woman through a series of poetic memory monologues delivered by a single actress in five vignettes. Son/ji remembers the four seasons of her life as a college student, emerging black nationalist, disillusioned young woman, and warrior mother. Once Son/ji abandons black men's visions of a submissive partner and dutiful follower, she finally finds empowerment by situating motherhood and black women's survival traditions within the framework of revolutionary action. As a warrior mother, Son/ji utilizes chant to create a sisterhood that allows other black women to voice their concerns as women, mothers, and lovers. Rather than use linear narrative, *Sister Son/ji* embraces fragmented notions of time and incorporates a (then-) novel use of music and movement to demonstrate shifts in scenes. These techniques draw audiences out of the action of the play, thereby inviting audiences to critically evaluate their own positionality.

Sister Son/ji unapologetically abandons Western dramatic structure and instead borrows from black women's literary traditions. Indeed, by deconstructing language—that is, condensing words, ignoring grammar rules, and incorporating Black English—*Sister Son/ji* follows a tradition of black women writers who presented the beauty of black vernacular and culture. Sanchez recalls that she wrote *Sister Son/ji* "in the spirit of the Black Arts" with the intention to "move away from a very staid way of looking at the stage," [83] as well as to reveal black women's daily struggles:

> We were moving on the level of Brecht. At least I was in terms of engaging an audience with theater to make them do something or think something or act or move. That's what that play [*Sister Son/ji*] was about. So I decided to [write *Sister Son/ji*] in the midst of all the crap that was happening to black women on college campuses, in their personal lives, in this movement. I don't care if you're a revolutionary or not revolutionary, black women were getting crap at some point. And so you can see . . . this woman, who then at the end [of the play], challenges that audience. [84]

Son/ji's memory monologues, much like the "dream landscapes" of playwright Adrienne Kennedy, invite audiences to hear black women's inner thoughts. *Sister Son/ji* remains unique, however, because the play uses agitation to challenge audiences to actualize the rhetoric of revolution by liberating black women and families.

While Sanchez and Son/ji share similar life experiences, Sanchez intended for Son/ji to represent a conglomeration of black women who seek wisdom and self-definition. The play is clearly autobiographical in nature, since both women were born in the South, share similar names, attended Hunter College, became political activists after encountering racism within academia, and briefly joined the Nation of Islam. Despite these similarities, Sanchez wanted Son/ji to hold greater meaning. Sanchez explains:

> Well, I think I made myself and a lot of women I knew in the movement that woman. All the things that happened to Son/ji didn't happen to me, but many of the things did. Some of the things happened to a group of women. At some point every woman I knew experienced everything. Every black woman I knew at the time had experienced everything that this young woman experienced and so I wanted it to be like a woman for all seasons.

The first season features the wakening of Son/ji's racial consciousness. When confronted by racism—her white political theory professor refuses to call the black female students by their individual names—Son/ji drops the course since "none of the negroes in the class was being respected as the individuals we are." [85] Son/ji explains to her lover Nesbitt that she must "stand up for herself just a little" and files a course appeal due to "discrimination." [86] Son/ji also makes the decision to abandon her "slave" name, adopt the name Son/ji, and become a black power activist. Her choice in name is significant because Son/ji derives from "Sonja," a variation of the name "Sophia" which means "wisdom" in Greek. Adopting a new name not only represents her need to define herself, but also symbolizes her quest to gain wisdom. Sanchez had become disillusioned with academia after encountering racially insensitive professors at Hunter College. She explains in an *Essence* magazine interview that after writing a story about her father's experiences as a black man in the United States, she received a mediocre grade with feedback from her professor that "things are not that terrible."[87] She later tested her professor by writing a creative story about a talking mirror. While the professor praised her new work, Sanchez dropped the course because this form of writing did not express her "reality."[88] Both Sanchez and Son/ji responded to racism by becoming black power activists within their communities. In contrast to Sanchez, however, Son/ji accepts prescribed gender roles without questioning the motivations of male leaders.

Son/ji initially embraces prescribed gender roles within the black power movement until she realizes that she is actively supporting her own disenfranchisement. The second season of Son/ji's life depicts her remembering her experience attending her first Black Power conference:

> i heard a sister talk about blk/women supporting their blk/men. Listening to their men, sacrificing, working while blk/men take care of bizness, having warriors and young sisters. . . . i will talk to sisters abt loving their blk/men and letting them move in tall straight/lines toward our freedom. Yes i will preach blk/love/respect between blk/men and women for that will be the core/basis of our future in white/America.[89]

The rhetoric at the Black Power conference uses prescribed gender roles to paint a romanticized vision of black America. This rhetoric suggests that complementary relationships between black men and women will lead to a liberated future. In this framework, however, black men lead the revolution while black women remain behind the scenes, offering support and bearing children. While problematic, the romantic sentiments expressed at this fictional conference capture the actual debate that occurred in the late 1960s regarding the term "revolutionary." "Did revolutionary black women work alongside men as equals in organizing for social change? Did they limit themselves to home, providing a domestic foundation and raising babies for the revolution? Did they follow or challenge existing leadership or establish their own?" writes scholar Michelle Nzadi Keita.[90] Similar to other women Sanchez knew at the time, Son/ji fully supports a revolutionary rhetoric that consigns her to the margins as a reproductive vessel. However, Son/ji quickly distinguishes the difference between romanticism and her reality.

As Son/ji matures, she begins to understand the paradoxes within her revolutionary community and becomes disillusioned. She remembers her partner leaving her with the sole responsibility of parenting while he attends meetings and stays out all night with his friends. As their sexual and emotional relationship deteriorates, Son/ji pleads with him to quit his destructive habits and build a strong family. Son/ji pleads:

> Don't go. Stay home with me and let us start building true/blk/ lives—let our family be a family built on mutual love and respect . . . Shouldn't we be getting ourselves together—strengthening our minds, bodies and souls away from drugs, weed, whiskey, and going out on Saturday nites. alone. what is it all about or is the rhetoric apart from the actual being/doing? What is it all about if the doings do not match the words?[91]

Her impassioned speech challenges her partner to actualize revolutionary rhetoric by establishing strong black families headed by parents who "love and respect" one another.[92] Perhaps more important, Son/ji's words reveal the irony that new ideologies do not necessarily mean any change when it comes to the oppressive forces within black women's lives.

In contrast to Black Bitch in *The Bronx Is Next*, however, Son/ji does not merely survive the harsh circumstances in her life. After an emotional break-down, Son/ji uses chant in order to harness her inner strength. Chant allows her to move beyond mere supplication to actively participate in her own liberation. Son/ji emerges as a warrior mother, fully capable of protecting black womanhood and leading black armies.

As a warrior mother, Son/ji utilizes the ritual of chant to empower other black women and lead them as an army against racist power structures. During her third season of life, Son/ji gathers her "sisters" and encourages them to "sing the killing/song for our men. let us scream the words of dying as we turn/move against the enemy."[93] As a drum beats Son/ji chants:

OOOOU—WAH

OOOOU—WAH

OOOU—OOOU—OOOU—WAH—WAH—WAH—

OOOU—OOOU—OOOU—WAH—WAH—WAH—

EEYE—YO

EEYE—YO

EEYE—EEYE—EEYE—YO—YO—

EEYE—EEYE—EEYE—YO—YO—[94]

The sacred action of chant allows Son/ji to break free from everyday speech and employ a repetition of sounds to create patterns, rhythm, and most important, meaning for other black women within their now war-torn environment. Her chant becomes the voice of the other women, strengthening and binding them together for the cause of black liberation.

As a warrior mother, Son/ji subverts the detrimental iconography of Aunt Jemima. After concluding her chant, she prepares to lead the army of black women by strapping on a gun, tying a handkerchief around her head, and fastening a baby carrier to her back. In contrast to the docile, bandana wearing icon of the past, this new kerchief-wearing warrior mother is fully prepared to engage in violent revolution. Much like Sanchez herself, Son/ji refuses to accept prescribed gender roles that would place her on the fringes of the war effort. Perhaps even more important, her own recognition of her inner strength reinforces black women's propensity to act as leaders.

Son/ji defines liberation in terms of building a black nation of strong black families. As a warrior mother, Son/ji openly confronts male leaders whose detrimental practices have harmed her children and community. For example, after the deaths of her older sons, she refuses to allow her partner Mume to send her remaining thirteen-year-old son Mungu into battle. "all the other warriors are fifteen. are we—do we need soldiers that badly. Mume. please send him back. he's just a boy. he's just my little boy," says Son/ji.[95] Instead of blindly following male leaders, Son/ji uses her position as a mother to question their ethics and motivations. Son/ji, in fact, believes that relationships between male leaders and their white allies have harmed the black revolution. Now a leader in her own right, Son/ji orders the removal of a "devil/woman," or a liberal white woman, and rallies support from her female compatriots.[96] Son/ji states: "can we trust the devils who have come to fight on our side? the women and i don't mind the male/devils here but the female/devils who have followed them. they shd not be allowed here. . . . It will become a problem if we don't send them packing. rt. Away."[97] While Son/ji does not necessarily hate white women, she does fear that their presence will weaken relationships between black women and men. Son/ji believes that strong black families provide the foundation for a liberated black America and she casts out anyone who might undermine this vision.

In the final season of her life, a now elderly Son/ji challenges the audience to likewise protect black children and families. Son/ji states:

> my son/our son did not die for integration. u must still remember those ago/yrs when we had our blk/white period. they died for the right of blk/children to run on their own land and let their bodies explode with the sheer joy of living. . . . i have my sweet/astringent memories becuz we dared to pick up the day and shake its tail until it became evening. A time for us. blk/ness. blk/people. Anybody can grab the day and make it stop. can u my friends? or may be it's better if I ask:
> will you?[98]

With this powerful speech Son/ji honors the memory of the dead and situates black liberation in terms of black children's bodies exploding with joy, rather than bullets. Rather than integrate into a country that does not recognize the humanity of black men, women, and children, Son/ji implores the audience to radically alter society in order to protect the sanctity of black families. Son/

ji remains an important Black Arts warrior figure because she not only represents the resilience of black motherhood and strong female leadership, but also challenges black men to actualize the rhetoric of black love.

While *Sister Son/ji* did not garner praise from white mainstream critics, the play remains Sanchez's most produced play. *Sister Son/ji* premiered in December 1970 at the Concept East theater in Detroit before the Negro Ensemble Company staged a brief Off-Broadway production at St. Mark's Playhouse. One year later, Joseph Papp's New York Shakespeare Festival (NYSF) Public Theatre produced the most notable production of *Sister Son/ji*. Working under the title of "Black Visions," the NYSF presented *Sister Son/ji* along with three other one-act plays at the Public Annex, a small theater typically used for experimental productions. In one of the few reviews of the production, the *New York Times* critic Clive Barnes erroneously dismisses Sanchez's experimental work, labeling it a "self-indulgent" play that merits "marginal literary interest."[99] He explains that "the monologue, despite the eloquence of Miss [Gloria] Foster, never becomes theater. . . . Had these been white visions rather than black, they might, I felt, have remained unproduced."[100] Despite Barnes's obvious cultural bias, his interpretation remains important because his reviews often influenced the success or failure of New York productions. To imply that Sanchez capitalized on her blackness and that her womanist vision was not worthy of the stage could have damaged her burgeoning career, had she chosen to pursue critical acclaim in mainstream theater.

The theater critic Clayton Riley of the *New York Amsterdam News*, a historically black newspaper, provided a more thoughtful critique that addressed the challenges of producing an experimental and woman-centered work. While he never specifically mentions Barnes's name, his closing remarks address the statement that *Sister Son/ji* "never becomes theatre." Riley writes:

> I have seen and worked with this piece [*Sister Son/ji*] before; the impossibility of doing it satisfactorily rests, I think, with the fact that contemporary forms in the theater do not provide a framework for it that serve well to project what Sister Sanchez has provided—an enormously personal examination of the life and times of a Black woman, her political and social growth, the processes of her coming to be who and what she is.[101]

Riley's comments suggest that any production of *Sister Son/ji* would encounter difficulty achieving mainstream success because the play thoughtfully examines black womanhood in an artistic medium that has historically excluded the stories of black women. *Sister Son/ji*'s success with black critics and audiences demonstrated that the stories of black women and men are, indeed, worthy of the stage. Sanchez's next play, *Dirty Hearts* (1971), continues the discussion of the suppression of black women's stories, but does so in terms of the world stage.

Dirty Hearts uses the trick-taking card game called Hearts, also known as the Dirty, Black Lady, Dark Lady, or Black Maria, as a metaphor for how global forces oppress women and men of color. Initially published in *Scripts 1* in 1971, *Dirty Hearts* premiered the same year at New York's Public Theatre. In contrast to her other plays, black women do not make a physical appearance in the play. Rather, *Dirty Hearts* focuses on the problems of a middle-class black man named Carl. The one-act play begins with a white conservative named First Man and his white liberal crony Second Man trying to convince Carl to play a game of Hearts. While a boastful Carl initially believes that he will win the game, he soon discovers that First Man controls the hands dealt so neither he, nor a scarred Hiroshima maiden named Shigeko, can possibly win. The card game symbolizes the world stage and each character's actions reflects his or her own position in global politics: white conservative males manipulate and dominate people of color; black men try to resist oppression, but ultimately remain subservient; Japanese women suffer in silence; and black women are not even allowed to play. Black women, however, are an absent presence within this game, only making a symbolic appearance as the Queen of Spades. Unfortunately, if players receive this card they gain thirteen points (an unlucky number) and lose the game. In other words, black women represent loss, or disempowerment. Furthermore, Wood writes that the "implications of the term *spade* as dirty or unwanted and its racialized use in reference to a black person should not be lost on the audience here."[102] Thus, within the innocuous realm of card-playing, Sanchez invites audiences to consider why representations of black womanhood continue to be associated with the filth of the world.

Sanchez intentionally excluded black women from the play in order to draw connections between their plight and that of Japanese women. In so doing, she hoped to critique the global oppression of women of color. "The point of that play was basically the nonappearance of a black woman other than the queen of spades, which means that her absence, I hope, was very pronounced. . . . And so in a sense the black woman became the Japanese woman. Scarred. Who wore a hat to hide her face, her color, the scars, and everything else," recalls Sanchez.[103] While Sanchez does not provide specific information about how Shigeko's disfigurement occurred, her description as a Hiroshima maiden suggests that her facial scars resulted from atomic radiation. Sanchez remembers that she based Shigeko on a Hiroshima maiden she met while on a hosting committee for atomic bomb victims of World War II. The Japanese woman wore a "white hat with a veil" to cover her scarred face.[104] Sanchez remembers finding the "attention" that the wealthy white liberals gave the Japanese woman and the "many . . . maidens who had come over and were scarred" quite troubling.[105] She recalls that rather than commit to never drop an atomic bomb again, white liberals simply offered "attention" and "help," enabling them to ignore the fact that the United States had committed crimes against humanity.[106] "The subtext is: well, why the hell did you drop the bomb in the first place? History and herstory has shown us that you didn't have to drop the bomb. The war was over. The Japanese were making appeals, trying to negotiate," recalls Sanchez.[107] Her penetrating question forces audiences to consider the possibility that perhaps a more insidious reason led to the decision to bomb a nation populated by a people of color. Furthermore, Shigeko's attempt to hide her "disfigured" face behind a "beach hat" and heavy makeup echoes black women's survival strategy of hiding their inner thoughts behind a culture of silence.[108] Shigeko's scars, then, testify to the domestic and global atrocities that the United States has committed against blacks and people of color.

Sanchez uses dramatic irony to condemn the United States's egregious actions during World War II, which she believes were racially motivated. In one of the most haunting moments of the play, Sanchez juxtaposes Shigeko's deformed face with her assertion that "america is kind."[109] History has shown, however, that the United States's bombing of Hiroshima and Nagasaki mutilated and killed hundreds of thousands of Japanese civilians. Ideologies of cultural superiority and perhaps a thirst for revenge allowed the United States to position Japanese people as *non-humans* and thus justify such atrocities. These racist ideologies can be traced back to the founding of the United States wherein white slavers placed blacks in the category of *non-humans* in order to justify chattel slavery. Shikego's ironic statement, therefore, not only encourages audiences to question the ethics of using atomic bombs against other human beings, but also how racial ideologies inform the United States's foreign and domestic policies. In so doing, *Dirty Hearts* rejects the racism of the past and calls for a new humanism that respects all of humanity.

Dirty Hearts marks an important moment when Sanchez became increasingly aware of world politics, developing a greater sense of the black diaspora and a humanistic vision of art. Her success as a poet resulted in many speaking engagements across the United States and abroad in countries such as Mexico, Jamaica, and China. These extensive travels throughout the 1970s resulted in greater knowledge of how racism disenfranchises people of color throughout the world. She developed a humanistic perspective of global suffering, which impacted her art. Sanchez recalls:

> The central theme of any of my plays and my poetry has always been: "What does it mean to be human?" Then I show you sometimes some very inhumane people populating those plays. At the core of that all is that we have got to as African Americans and as people on this earth try to figure out how can we act in a more humane fashion towards each other. I show you characters either doing that or attempting to do that. Doing it well and not doing it well.[110]

Her global perspective, coupled with reading Addison Gayle Jr.'s edited collection, *The Black Aesthetic* (1971), greatly influenced her conceptualization of the black aesthetic. Sanchez explains:

The black aesthetic meant . . . that you had black people beginning
to formulate ideas about a way to live in this country, a way to think
in this country, a way to teach in this country, a way to write in this
country. That would benefit first of all black people and eventually
would benefit the world. . . . That was what propelled me. This whole
idea that people began to add to it saying that there's a black way of
looking at the world. . . . But when I began to move in this world, I
realized that they had taken the African, meaning us, off the world
stage, period. As if we had not been a participant in the world. . . .
Our job was to put the African back on a world stage and to answer
the most important question that needed to be answered: What does
it mean to be human?[111]

Dirty Hearts departs from her previous plays by offering a black woman's
critique of global crimes against humanity. In so doing, she positions the
depiction of black women's humanity and experiences as vital to both black
art and the world at large.

Harkening back to the innovative performance techniques of *Sister Son/
ji*, Sanchez's fourth play, *Malcolm/Man Don't Live Here No Mo'* (1972),
uses the memory of Malcolm X's leadership to embolden audiences. *Mal-
colm/Man* utilizes song, movement, and brief poetic monologues delivered
by Brotha, Sistuh, and a Chorus of 3 Sistuhs to engage audiences. This process begins as the cast enters the stage snapping their fingers. Brotha, Sistuh,
and the Chorus form an "X" and then perform parts of Sanchez's poem "we
a baddDDD people" (1970) and Madhubuti's poem "A Message All Black-
people Can Dig: (& a few negroes too)" (1969). From this point onward,
the Chorus prompts onstage action by singing five questions to the tune of
the children's folk song, "blue/bird blue bird thru my window."[112] The Chorus asks Brotha (as Malcolm): "where did u come from?" "where did you
go?" "where did you go to?" "how u do/en?" and finally, "who killed u?"[113]
Brotha and Sistuh respond by moving in and out of the "X," portraying multiple characters in order to present key moments in Malcolm's life. Brotha
and Sistuh perform Malcolm's birth and early education, experiences as a
street hustler, spiritual conversion while imprisoned, initial encounter with
his future wife Betty Shabazz, and assassination.

In contrast to typical children's plays of the time, *Malcolm/Man* does not
shy away from difficult social issues. Rather, Sanchez uses Malcolm's life
experiences to raise awareness of how racism, drugs, and gun violence destroy
black children, families, and communities. "I [wrote *Malcolm/Man*] for children because there were not a lot of plays written for children to perform,"
recalls Sanchez.[114] Her interest in children's theater stemmed from her early
experiences working with BART/S artists to bring theater to children in the
Harlem community. In keeping with the greater Black Arts community, Sanchez valued young audiences and used children's theater as a teaching tool to

inspire social change. *Malcolm/Man* premiered at the Liberation School in Pittsburgh, Pennsylvania, and was subsequently performed in Philadelphia at the ASCOM Community Center's 1979 Kwanzaa celebration. Sanchez's admiration for the children at the Liberation School was so profound that when the New Lafayette Theatre's *Black Theatre* magazine published *Malcolm/Man* in 1972, she dedicated the play to them and her children Anita, Morani, and Mungy Weusi.

In contrast to masculinist depictions of Malcolm X's life that were prevalent at the time, *Malcolm/Man* creates a woman-centered history that celebrates his role as a son, husband, and father. Sanchez published *Malcolm/Man* seven years after the death of Malcolm, at a time when the memory of Malcolm's leadership had reached mythic proportions. Followers of Malcolm often portrayed him as a flawless saint, surrounded by a cadre of male compatriots. Sanchez's history, however, situates Betty Shabazz and Malcolm's mother Louise Norton Little as influential in his development as a strong leader. Sanchez, in fact, positions Malcolm within a matrilineal heritage. Sistuh answers the Chorus's question of "where did you come from?" by stepping out of the "X" as Little. Sistuh rocks an infant Malcolm and in direct address to the audience, tells them that she will nurture her son, teach him self-worth, and encourage him to become a lawyer if he so desires. When he reaches public school, however, his white teacher refers to him as an "uppity nigger" and discourages him from reaching his potential.[115] Brotha then reveals how Malcolm became imprisoned after becoming a victim of "White America['s]" temptations of "a gun, dope, high living . . . whiskey, reefers, wite women & hate."[116] Sanchez's woman-centered history continues as Malcolm discovers the teachings of Elijah Muhammad, joins the Nation of Islam, and meets his future wife. Rather than footnote his role as husband and father, Sanchez shows how Malcolm's decision to marry and raise a strong black family became integral to his leadership. "we'll have children who will live / who'll have lives that are positive / we'll raise them with love & care / they will be black muslims & aware," Malcolm promises Betty. In Sanchez's history, Malcolm values the sanctity of family and advocates healthy relationships between black men and women. Sanchez continues to emphasize the importance of strong black families during the final episode in the play: Malcolm's assassination. After the Chorus reveals that Malcolm has been shot and fatally wounded, Betty "runs" to him, "falls" at his feet, and "Screams & Cries over him."[117] Rather than depict Malcolm's assassination in terms of the loss of a public hero, Sanchez creates a touching scene wherein a family mourns the loss of their patriarch.

While *Malcolm/Man* privileges Malcolm's relationships with women, the play also avoids any criticism of his patriarchal rhetorical strategies. Malcolm's unwavering support of black women influenced his desire to include protecting black womanhood within his framework of black empowerment. In a well-known 1962 speech Malcolm publicly addressed the need for black men to "protect" black women. He declared:

> The most disrespected person in America is the black woman. The most unprotected person in America is the black woman. The most neglected person in America is the black woman. As Muslims, the Honorable Elijah Muhammed teaches us to respect our women and to protect our women. Then the only time a Muslim really gets real violent is when someone goes to molest his woman. We will kill you for our woman. I'm making it plain, yes. We will kill you for our woman. We believe that if the white man will do whatever is necessary to see that his woman gets respect and protection, then you and I will never be recognized as men until we stand up like men and place the same penalty over the head of anyone who puts his filthy hands out to put in the direction of our women.[118]

For Malcolm, protecting black womanhood was a distinguishing attribute of strong black manhood. His speech suggests that reaffirming black manhood provided a means to counteract oppressive forces within the lives of black Americans. In other words, he equated the acquisition of manhood with liberation for the entire black community. Malcolm understood that the de-feminization of black women perpetuated racist ideologies of blacks as non-human. The scholar Farah Jasmine Griffin notes that Malcolm's promise of protection also promoted a benevolent patriarchy which reinforced oppressive gender ideologies. "Malcolm's desire to 'protect' black women grew out of a sincere concern for their emotional, psychic, and physical safety; it was also reflective of the power struggle between black and white men and black men and women. Furthermore, the pure and protected black woman of his vision was also obligated to obey her protector—the black man," writes Griffin.[119] In other words, this benign patriarchy came with a cost: black women's continued subjugation. Malcolm's most famous speech, "The Ballot or the Bullet" (1964), continues this patriarchal rhetoric in his description of black nationalism. Malcolm stated: "The political philosophy of black nationalism means that the black man should control the politics and the politicians of his own community."[120] While idealizing black womanhood and excluding black women from active leadership roles is undoubtedly problematic, Malcolm's gender politics reflected a major tenet of black nationalist discourse of the time. Despite his failings, Malcolm's teachings have influenced scores of black women intellectuals and artists including Sanchez, Abbey Lincoln, Nina Simone, Angela Davis, and Alice Walker, to name just a few. Rather than critique Malcolm's gender politics, Sanchez treads on safer ground by focusing on his legacy of activism.

The Chorus of 3 Sistuhs encourages black audiences to preserve Malcolm's legacy by fostering strong black leadership in their own homes and communities. Similar to the classical Greek chorus, the 3 Sistuhs use song and dance to comment on the major themes of the play and guide the audience's interpretation of the dramatic action. Before the action begins, the young women sing the following prologue:

we be's hero/worshippers
we be's death/worshippers
we be's leader/worshippers
BUT: we should be blk/people worshippers
AND: some of us are leaderless toooooday
our homes are emptee cuz
MALCOLM/MAN DON'T LIVE HERE NO MO
MALCOLM/MAN DON'T LIVE HERE NO MO[121]

This song reveals the premise of the play: rather than idealizing Malcolm as a cultural hero, blacks need to do the more difficult work of continuing his efforts to strengthen families. The black community's stagnant activism has not only resulted in a loss of leadership, but also in a devaluation of family. Sanchez explains that she wrote *Malcolm/Man* "out of necessity" because others were ignoring problems that needed to be addressed. "*Malcolm/Man Don't Live Here No Mo'* meant that people were quoting Malcolm so many years after his death. And they hadn't moved beyond Malcolm. And Malcolm was dead. And he could no longer lead us. We can read him, we can understand him, we could internalize some of the things he said, but we need a live people leading us," remembers Sanchez.[122] The Chorus of 3 Sistuhs urges audiences to honor Malcolm's legacy by continuing to "unite" and "fight" under new leadership. Sanchez continued to incorporate a chorus of dancers to engage audiences with her call for strong black leadership in her next play, *Uh, Uh; But How Do It Free Us?* (1974).

Uh, Uh provides a scathing critique of the so-called revolutionary practices espoused by black nationalist leaders of the era. Sanchez's experimental drama provides a glimpse into the lives of four black women who struggle with the realities of revolution. The first episode, titled Group One, features a young black Muslim family in distress. Sister-wives Waleesha and Nefertia compete to win the affections of their "revolutionary" husband, Malik. Malik reigns as king of the castle, manipulating his "queens" for sex and money. Group Two examines the plight of a mother, drug addict, and prostitute named Black Whore.[123] Instead of offering her protection, the "revolutionary" leaders dismiss Black Whore's concerns and allow White Dude to beat her.[124] Group Three reveals the detrimental effects of prescribed gender roles. A young college student named Sister quickly learns that in order to adhere to the rhetoric of the "new Black woman," she must silently endure her lover's abuse and infidelity.[125] While the three groups tackle different issues within the black liberation movement, all share a core theme: black women suffering indignities as a direct result of negligent male leadership. Rather than romanticize or vilify black womanhood, Sanchez depicts a spectrum of black women who fight or simply survive the oppressive forces in their lives.

Group One reveals how the "revolutionary" practice of polygamy exploits black women and weakens black families. Sanchez uses comedy to emphasize the absurdity of polygamous lifestyles. The play begins with Malik, whose Arabic name translates to "king," lying across a bed with two pregnant women sitting on either side of him. His "queens" Nefertia and Waleesha are situated in such a way that they instantly appear as rivals for Malik's attention, thus foreshadowing the central conflict of the episode. Malik, meanwhile, insists that he sacrifices a great deal for the revolution. Indeed, his sacrifices include preening in front of a mirror, impregnating both women, and manipulating Nefertia into giving him her last two dollars. Malik never really has a meaningful conversation with either woman and quickly escapes their discontent by attending a play rehearsal. Clearly abandoned, both women struggle to unify their home and come to terms with their relationship with each other.

Group One provides an answer to the title of the play by demonstrating that the practice of polygamy does not, in fact, "free" black women or unify black families. For example, within the same conversation Nefertia and Waleesha refer to each other as both "sistuh" and "bitch."[126] They use motherhood as a status symbol and a means to compete with one another. Nefertia attempts to make Waleesha feel inferior by insisting that she shares Malik's ideology and will bear him a son. "He said you never read anything, not even a newspaper. We love each other becuz we have everything in common . . . Ours is not just physical love, he says. It's mental too. . . . I can have one too. Or even if I had a girl, Malik will love her just like he loves me now. Just like he loved me befo I came here to this house," says Nefertia.[127] Their polygamous lifestyle has essentially reduced Nefertia to her biological being, with her ability to breed future black warriors providing the means to legitimize her position as Malik's most beloved wife. However, by referencing Malik's emotional and physical love, Nefertia inadvertently reveals the absence of love and mutual respect within this polygamist relationship. Waleesha, in fact, does not agree with Malik's decision to practice polygamy, but follows his dictates out of a desire to prove her love for him. "Malik brought you here—you were his choice. His decision. And since I love him I have to abide by his choice, no matter how unwise it may be," Waleesha tells Nefertia.[128] Waleesha represents the old ways of living in that she blindly submits to the will of her patriarch and lacks any critical racial consciousness. Nefertia's passionate speech indicates that she embodies the ideals of the new so-called revolution. Both women, however, find themselves forfeiting their own desire to build strong black families by following Malik's unwise leadership. Their ridiculous plight responds to the actual conversations that the black militant community was having regarding the relationship between polygamy and the liberation movement. "[There] was a major discussion in the movement about polygamy. It was major. It was not minor. And so that play was somewhat controversial because a lot of people didn't want to be laughed at with the idea of being a polygamist," remembers Sanchez.[129]

Group Two demonstrates the dangers of using drug money to finance the
black revolution. As with Group One, Sanchez wrote this particular scene
as a response to the actual discussions that the black militant community
of Pittsburgh was having. "A lot of people were talking in Pittsburgh about
how they were going to make money off drugs to finance the so-called revolution," remembers Sanchez.[130] *Uh, Uh* dramatizes this "revolutionary"
practice through the unsavory exploits of Brother Man, First Brother, Second
Brother, and Third Brother. At first glance Brother Man displays the outward
markers of a typical black revolutionary: he wears an African hat and dashiki
with tiki. He and his cronies embody the street-hustler-turned-revolutionary-
hero image that was popular at the time. Sanchez disrupts this image by
depicting the black men, along with their drug supplier White Dude, on top
of white rocking horses. Black Whore and White Whore stand next to the
men with whips in their hands. By taking the slang term for cocaine (i.e.,
"white horse") literally, Sanchez creates a hilarious yet disturbing new image
that demonstrates the ridiculousness of allowing drug dealers and addicts to
lead the black revolution. As the men rock on their horses, they discuss their
recent release from prison and their plans to supply drugs to black communities across the United States. "I got the biggest hustle in the whole wide world
today. I found Blackness in the joint, you dig, and I wrote a book and everything I write is licked up by everyone. The Black/prison/writer is a hero. All
thanks is due to Malcolm/man, Eldridge/man for making this all so simple,"
proclaims Brother Man.[131] His disturbing words suggest that the hero worship of Malcolm has led to a lack of leadership within the black community.
Leaderless, the black community remains vulnerable to the machinations of
Eldridge Cleaver and other so-called revolutionaries. Rather than unify the
black community, the black men form alliances with White Dude, who symbolizes white America. This unholy union allows the black leaders to build
profitable drug empires at the expense of the most vulnerable people in society: poor black women.

Group Two demonstrates how the absence of strong leaders leaves poor
black women vulnerable to rape and emotional and physical abuse. After the
black leaders discuss their plans to control the black community, they direct
their attention toward Black Whore. They immediately disrespect her by calling her a "Black/bitch" and "broken down whore."[132] When Brother Man
eventually asks Black Whore for her name, she responds:

> Ain't got no name. Lost my name when I was eleven years old. I
> became just a body then so I forgot my name. Don't nobody know
> a black woman's name anyway. You gon' take me home with ya to
> keep? Put me in your pocket to hold/touch when you need some
> warmth? No? Well, since you ain't, then there ain't no reason to tell
> ya my name. All ya need to know is on my face and body. If you can
> read a map, you can read me.[133]

The chorus of dancers confirms that as a child, Black Whore was raped by an older man and then forced into a life of prostitution. Her speech suggests that her early victimization reduced her to her biological being and caused psychological trauma that led to a loss of identity. She understands that society has maligned black womanhood. While black women have been called every derogatory name, rarely have their identities or inner desires been so accurately represented. Black Whore, much like Abbey Lincoln and Malcolm X, wants black men to revere her and offer her protection against further assault. Until these men actualize this rhetoric, she will continue to survive by using the culture of dissemblance. While not a domestic worker, this strategy helps her to survive her hostile working conditions. Black Whore creates the appearance of openness by telling others that she can be "read" like a "map," while keeping her innermost self (i.e., her name) hidden. The black leaders are, in fact, too ignorant and consumed by their thirst for power to provide any help. "You are what you are cuz you wants to be. Don't go telling us nothing 'bout some dude turning you on when you was young. Every whore in the world says the same thing. Can't no dude in the world make you turn a trick unless you inclined to do so," says Brother Man.[134] His response suggests that he, too, has internalized the mythology of black women's supposed hypersexuality and he lacks a critical understanding of how oppressive forces operate in black women's lives.

As Black Whore's interactions with White Dude and the so-called black revolutionaries can attest, the current revolution has not altered the violent hierarchies that have existed since the dawn of the African slave trade. In reality, Black Whore does not happily seduce men for her own sexual gratification. Rather, discrimination and sexism have disenfranchised her to the point where she feels compelled to sell the only asset she has in order to feed her children. Brother Man, however, remains unmoved by her plight; he places a collar around her neck, and forces her to carry him on her back while on her hands and knees. This disturbing image powerfully resonates with one of the most iconic passages in Zora Neale Hurston's *Their Eyes Were Watching God* (1937). In this famous novel, former slave Nanny Crawford poignantly reveals how oppressive forces operate within the intersections of black women's identity. Nanny states, "Honey, de white man is de ruler of everything . . . de white man throw down de load and tell de nigger man tuh pick it up. He pick it up because he have to, but he don't tote it. He hand it to his womenfolks. De nigger woman is de mule uh de world so fur as Ah can see."[135] Following in the rich tradition of black women writers, Sanchez uses the image of black women as a pack mule to critique the interconnectedness of male privilege, sexism, misogyny, and racism. This moment reveals how male privilege fosters camaraderie among white and black men; sexism allows black men to dominate black women; and misogyny works to obscure racism, allowing black men to blame black women for all of the problems within the black community.

Group Two uses a violent beauty pageant to issue a call for black men to protect black women from white America's physical and ideological assault on black womanhood. During Brother Man's interrogation, Black Whore admits that a group of young black revolutionaries have attempted to help her by teaching her cultural pride. "Some of the younger dudes talk to me sometimes. Say I should stop this stuff. They say I'm a queen, the mother of the universe. A beautiful Blk/woman/queen," says Black Whore.[136] In contrast to the hustlers-turned-revolutionaries, these young men revere black womanhood. Their overzealous romanticism, however, conflicts with Black Whore's reality and she cannot accept their help. Brother Man finds humor in this contradiction and explores it further by gathering everyone together to witness her become a "queen." He supplies her with a fur coat and makeup and forces her to strut around the stage, even though "she's obviously scared."[137] As she gains confidence, White Dude becomes angry and insists that he represents ideal feminine beauty. Brother Man then forces Black Whore to compete with White Man (who now wears a coat, wig, earrings, and high heels) to "win the prize of 'queen of the universe.'"[138] As they promenade around the stage, Black Whore "becomes more regal."[139] Her ability to maintain her dignity, even within a hostile environment, further angers White Dude. He responds by punching and kicking Black Whore in the face and stomach, to the utter delight of Brother Man who declares, "The only queens in the world are white."[140] Black Whore's loss of the "queen of the universe" pageant signifies black women's inability to claim beauty and femininity.

Sanchez uses White Dude's physical attack and subsequent victory to suggest that white America maintains control through assaults on black beauty. Sanchez's argument reflects the teachings of Malcolm X, who not only acknowledged racist assaults on black womanhood, but also resisted such oppressive forces by affirming black feminine beauty. Malcolm validated this concern in a 1962 speech, asking:

> Who taught you to hate the texture of your hair? Who taught you to hate the color of your skin to such extent that you bleach to get like the white man? Who taught you to hate the shape of your nose and the shape of your lips? Who taught you to hate yourself from the top of your head to the soles of your feet? Who taught you to hate your own kind? Who taught you to hate the race that you belong to so much so that you don't want to be around each other? No, before you come around and ask, "Mr. Muhammed, does he teach hate?" you should ask yourself who taught you to hate being what God gave you![141]

While the black revolutionaries profess to follow the teachings of Malcolm, they simply maintain the status quo by mocking black women's beauty. In so doing, Sanchez credits drug abuse and misogyny as impairments to effective leadership. "Yeah, he hurts her . . . and those black men let that happen 'cause they're so high, they're amused by the whores. They don't like the whores, which means there was a core of perhaps not liking black women at all, period," remembers Sanchez.[142] The beauty pageant, therefore, provides a means for Sanchez to critique destructive practices within the black community and encourage black men to protect and revere the beauty of black womanhood.

Group Three reveals how idealized images and prescribed gender roles divide the black community and further oppress black women. The scene focuses on the unhealthy relationship of Brother and Sister. Sister's situation mirrors Nefertia's in that she is also a young, pregnant, naive college student in love with a manipulative so-called revolutionary leader. Brother maintains his black warrior public appearance by dating Sister, repeating popular black nationalist rhetoric, and mimicking the Cuban politician Fidel Castro's signature beard. Brother's militant appearance, however, belies his excessive lifestyle of drinking and smoking weed, as well as the financial and emotional support he receives from his secret lover, White Woman. Despite her mother's criticism that she is "a first-class fool" for allowing Brother to use her, Sister takes pride in her ability to actualize the rhetoric of complementary relationships.[143] "I told them that the new/Blk/woman didn't worry about a man taking care of her. She and her man work together. If he had no job she worked and let him do the work of organizing the people. Since the money came from the oppressor, it didn't matter who made it," says Sister.[144] Brother maintains the illusion of equality through emotional manipulation:

> We got a whole lot of work to do and to do it with someone like you should be a gasssss . . . so you close yo/eyes and continue to dream 'bout me. Us. Our future, just continue to dream 'bout us. Don't let nothing interfere with that . . . Don't ever forget you my woman. My Black woman. The woman I'm gonna show to the world. My choice for the world to see.[145]

While Brother creates an illusion of togetherness, he also inadvertently reveals that he selected Sister to fulfill a specific purpose. Indeed, Brother takes advantage of Sister's desire for sexual liberation and uses her popularity with other women to further his own career. Sister's mother, however, understands that Brother's "foreign talk" of the "new/Blk/woman" simply exploits her daughter.[146] "Blk/women been fighting a long time just to get Blk/men to take care of us now yo/kind gon' take us back," warns Sister's mother.[147] She worries that her daughter's illusion of liberation will undermine past societal gains and leave her more vulnerable as an unwed single mother. After discovering Brother's infidelity, Sister's illusion of complementary relationships dissolves and she packs her suitcase to leave him. "I am a Black woman, but

Figure 13. Sonia Sanchez, 2000s. Photo by Lynda Koolish. Courtesy of Sonia Sanchez.

that don't mean I should be a fool. To you being a Black woman means I should take all the crap you can think of and any extra crap just hanging loose. That ain't right, man, and you know it too," says Sister.[148] Brother responds to Sister's harsh reality check by slapping her repeatedly. He then reminds her that he loves her despite her "foolishness" and leaves the home to pursue his own interests.[149] In other words, the "new blk/woman" does not, in fact, free black women.

Finally, *Uh, Uh* exposes the all-too common practice of taking liberal white women as lovers to help finance the black revolution. Sanchez remembers that although "people didn't talk about [it]," black men involved in the liberation movement often had relationships with black and white women at the same time.[150] "[T]hey couldn't make a choice between the two of them. Someone questioned me and I said, 'It's not an anti-white woman statement. It was something that was happening,'" recalls Sanchez.[151] Brother's decision to leave Sister and most likely return to his white lover demonstrates the crushing blow that such relationships had on the black family. By the end of the play Sister appears as a shell of her former self, yet continues to take

Brother's abuse. *Uh, Uh*, therefore, reflects Sanchez's commitment to expose the "crap"—including polygamy, infidelity, drug abuse, domestic violence, corrupt leadership, and other destructive practices—that harm black women and families.

Sanchez used her prophetic voice to not only reveal the forces that oppress poor black women, but also question the ethics and motives of black revolutionary leaders. Sanchez's astute observations both supported and negated the masculinist rhetoric of the era. Yet it was her uncompromising strength that earned her respect from the majority of her peers. Womanist theology, as expressed by her grandmother, allowed Sanchez to appreciate the beauty and strength of black womanhood from an early age. Her plays, in turn, reflect this desire to disrupt controlling images and one-dimensional representations of black womanhood. As a womanist and Black Arts dramatist, Sanchez privileged the concerns of black women, recovered their silenced "herstory" in the United States, and created new images of black feminine strength, without compromising her commitment to the survival of all black peoples. All of Sanchez's female characters—regardless of their age, ideology, or lifestyle—desire healthy unions with black men and protection from the oppressive forces in their lives. Through her dramas Sanchez provides a necessary warning to the black community: in order for the black revolution to succeed, it must be built on a foundation of strong black families.

Chapter 4

✦

"Bring Your Wounded Hearts"

J.e. Franklin and the Art of Liberation

> She comes across as a militant crusader, championing reform
> and even revolution. J.E. [*sic*] does not languish in the skies
> dabbling in dreams, fancy and fantasy. . . . She communicates
> with people, addressing daily problems, provoking thought,
> educating, alerting, alarming, instructing, interpreting and
> entertaining. . . . J.E. Franklin is one of the foremost social
> commentators, critics and dramatists of our time.
>
> —Jerry Komia Domatob, 2003

J.e. Franklin holds the distinction of being the most prolific African American female dramatist of the Black Arts Movement, having written and adapted eleven plays for television, theater, and film. Her dramas were well received by both critics and audiences and garnered numerous awards, including a coveted New York Drama Desk Award for Most Promising Playwright. Despite her accomplishments, Franklin remains the least-discussed playwright within Black Arts Movement scholarship today. Sexism and racism within academic discourse, as well as Franklin's own negation of the popular rhetoric of the time, have contributed to the erasure of her important works within current narratives of the Black Arts Movement. Rather than subscribe to what she remembers as the "commandments" of the time (i.e., "The writer should be political," "All art should be political," and "Art should be revolutionary"),[1] Franklin used her own experiences as an educator, activist, and domestic worker to conceptualize art that reflected her own understanding of freedom, revolution, and liberation.

Franklin's refusal to adhere to the dominant set of standards or practices of the era positioned her as an outsider vis-à-vis the circle of Black Arts compatriots. Working with the belief that she was "called" to be a playwright, she was inspired by the works of Ed Bullins, Alice Childress, Langston Hughes, Anton Chekhov, and Eugene O'Neill.[2] Described as a "militant crusader," Franklin constructed plays that simultaneously educated, entertained, and edified audiences.[3] Careful negotiation allowed her to see her works produced for television and film, as well as in prominent Black Arts theaters. As a black woman intellectual, Franklin envisioned performance as a liberatory act that not only validates experiential knowledge but also fosters embodied learning. During the Black Arts Movement Franklin wrote *The In-Crowd: A Rock Opera in One Act* (1965), *Two Flowers* (1966), *Miss Honey's Young'uns* (1966 as *Mau Mau Room*), *The Prodigal Daughter* (before 1972), *Black Girl* (1969), *The Enemy* (1973), *Four Women* (1973), *MacPilate* (1974), *The Prodigal Sister* (1974) with Micki Grant, *The Creation* (1975), and *Another Morning Rising* (1976).[4]

This chapter critically examines Franklin's development as an artist and black woman intellectual, noting the ways in which her early upbringing, political activism, experiences as a domestic worker and educator, and interactions with other Black Arts intellectuals and artists shaped her playwriting career. This case study contends that Franklin's woman-centered dramas privilege black women's experiential knowledge and use catharsis to foster liberation and community. As a diverse and gifted writer, Franklin wrote "straight" plays, a children's rock opera, musicals, and works entirely in rhyming couplets. Regardless of the form, all of Franklin's works express human emotion through the experiences of black female protagonists who desire love and healthy relationships with black men and women. Franklin's dynamic works privilege black women's relationships with each other; reveal the emotional loss that black families experience as a result of absent husbands and fathers; and expose the impact that institutionalized white racism has on black women's psyches, educational prospects, and employment opportunities. Examining Franklin's dramas and theories of audience reception not only reveals the dynamic nature of Black Arts Movement debates, but also recovers an important moment within African American theater history.

Franklin negotiated a space for her works within black theaters by joining prominent workshops and forging creative relationships with influential black artists. The Harlem Writers Guild (1950–) in particular provided a space for Franklin to hone her craft, as well as connect with other artists in Harlem. Her plays were then produced by theaters and organizations with disparate ideologies, including Douglas Turner Ward and Robert Hooks's Negro Ensemble Company (1967–), Woodie King Jr.'s New Federal Theatre (1970–), New Feminists Theater, and the Mobilization for Youth. Franklin credits King, as well as the producer, playwright, and director George Houston Bass, as major influences on her development as a playwright. On multiple occasions King provided the means for her works to be produced, while Bass shaped her political consciousness and sharpened her writing skills. As her plays moved to the stage Franklin occasionally directed her own work, but more often she collaborated with the leading black female director Shauneille Perry. Franklin remembers requesting Perry to direct her works because of Perry's artistic sensibilities, incredible talent, and appreciation for black

Figure 14. J.e. Franklin at the Playwright's Studio in Harlem, 1990. Photo by Malika Nzinga. Courtesy of J.e. Franklin.

woman's culture. Despite their creative differences, Franklin also collaborated with the Tony-nominated writer and composer Micki Grant. Working with Grant, Franklin adapted her street-theater play *The Prodigal Daughter* into a full-length musical retitled *The Prodigal Sister*. Such collaborations fostered Franklin's creative spirit.

Franklin believes that performing her works not only provides an opportunity for actors to experience sensory learning, but also creates a space for audiences to *feel*. Franklin explains:

> I think that if you perform the word, you feel the word, you know the word, you have learned the word. Because maybe it's true [that] in the beginning there was the word, and the word made flesh. The word was made flesh, and so if you perform the word, you probably will not forget it in the same way that you will if you are introduced to the word in some non-sensory form, just through a textbook. I think that that's the one thing that we are up against and that we have to

confront. That is this non-sensory disembodied way of learning, that static mode of learning. I want people to see my work as dynamic, rooted in the human feelings, and liberated.[5]

Franklin believes that the process of shedding tears provides a liberatory release that allows audiences to resist disembodiment and embrace their own humanity. Long after the demise of the Black Arts Movement, she continues to foster a liberatory release for audiences. During her 2010 invocation to *Coming to the Mercy Seat* (2003), a collection of her ten-minute folk dramas, she invited audiences to "bring" their "wounded hearts" to the performance. Throughout the course of the evening, the majority of the predominately black audience responded to Franklin's invocation and the Legros Cultural Arts production by shedding tears. The impact of a hundred audience members experiencing an emotional release in such an intimate space created a sense of community and remains a powerful event to have witnessed.

Despite her prolific and award-winning playwriting career, Franklin's contribution to the Black Arts Movement remains underrepresented within contemporary narratives of the movement. Contributing to Franklin's erasure is the fact that critics of the 1960s and 1970s categorized her as a "Black playwright" rather than a "Revolutionary playwright." In his 1971 review of *Black Girl*, the critic and activist Carlos Russell echoed the popular rhetoric of the time; namely, that both "Black" and "Revolutionary" playwrights should serve the black community and express concern for and love of black people. Russell wrote:

> The Revolutionary playwright's mission graphically articulates the need for revolution, meaning by revolution the creation of new institutions, new forms, new values, a new order. The revolutionary playwright must help lead. His pace is quicker, deadlier, and non-compromising. Above all, he is a lover of his people. So is the Black playwright. . . . The Black playwright serves an invaluable purpose, for he makes possible the psychological and emotional transition from Negro-to-Black-to-revolutionary. He hastens the pace by accentuating our contradictions in a palpable manner. Miss Franklin is a Black playwright.[6]

While the "Negro-to-Black-to-Revolutionary" conversion rhetoric remains fraught with essentialist notions, Russell's comments are important because he validates the significance of "Black" playwrights such as Franklin. Contemporary scholars, however, tend to focus on "Revolutionary" playwrights of the era, the majority of whom were male. Franklin's works, however, greatly differ from those of her male peers. Rather than focus solely on the black revolution, Franklin's plays depict the day-to-day experiences of growing up black and female in the United States.

To date, only the scholars Beatrix Taumann and Rosemary K. Curb offer a discussion of Franklin's significance and provide insight into why her works have failed to gain representation within Black Arts narratives. In her brief discussion of women playwrights of the Black Arts Movement, Taumann writes:

> The plays by J.E. Franklin [sic] and Martie Evans-Charles differ greatly from those of their male counterparts by focusing on subjects which are of special interest for black women by portraying differentiating women characters who do not fit the usual stereotypes. These playwrights anticipate central themes of feminist theater which will emerge almost a decade later.[7]

Taumann suggests that Franklin's woman-centered dramas not only challenged stereotypes about black womanhood, but also contributed to the development of feminist theater. While her remarks imply that Franklin's dramas complicate contemporary masculinist narratives of the era, she does not offer further analysis beyond a two-sentence summary of the play *Black Girl*. Curb's article, "'Goin' Through Changes': Mother-Daughter Confrontations in Three Recent Plays by Young Black Women" (1979), offers the only substantial study of Franklin's work. In her article, Curb compares mother-daughter relationships in Franklin's *Black Girl* and dramas written by Martie Evans-Charles and Elaine Jackson. Curb finds that although the daughters in the plays do not mention feminism, each "has obviously been strengthened by the women's movement" and "struggles to break away from maternal values, prejudices, restrictions, fears, and ambitions."[8] Published during a flourishing of black feminist drama, Curb's article only hints at a desire to understand the relationship between the black feminist and Black Arts movements. While neither Taumann nor Curb fully explore Franklin's dramas, their studies provide a fruitful foundation for further study.

The devaluation of black women's writings has resulted in the exclusion of many of Franklin's works from publication and traditional archives. Less than half of Franklin's scripts written during the Black Arts Movement remain accessible today. The five complete scripts that survive are due in part to Franklin's own efforts to publish and maintain a personal collection. Franklin's "lost" plays are *Two Flowers* (1966), *The Prodigal Daughter* (before 1972), *The Enemy* (1973), *MacPilate* (1974), *The Creation* (1975), and *Another Morning Rising* (1976). Only traces remain of these works, since critics did not review these productions and Franklin herself offers only small clues to the plots of these works, which were written more than forty years ago. The New Feminists Theater, for example, performed *Two Flowers* and yet critics never reviewed the production. To exacerbate this problem, Franklin only remembers that the plot focuses on the lives of two females: one black and one white. While this book cannot offer close readings of these "lost" dramas, it attempts to fill the gaps and silences of history by utilizing an original interview with Franklin and her short story "The Enemy" (1972) as primary source material in order to offer an analysis of the traces of her works. Franklin's works, including her "lost" dramas, remain important because they express feminist attitudes within a Black Power milieu.

This chapter departs from previous studies by situating Franklin as a black woman intellectual who used her agency to create a *feeling* art based on her own concept of liberation. This study utilizes production reviews, previously published interviews and an original interview with Franklin, and close readings of Franklin's writings in order to understand her intellectual development and how she negotiated a space for her woman-centered dramas within Black Arts institutions. Recovering Franklin's legacy not only celebrates her contribution to the Black Arts Movement, but also furthers our understanding of the relationship between the Black Arts Movement and the origins of black feminist drama.

J.e. Franklin: Black Woman Intellectual

In the autobiographical portion of *Black Girl: From Genesis to Revelations* (1977), Franklin cites fairy tales and early experiential knowledge as foundational sources for her conception of drama. Franklin learned the importance of sound, conflict, and movement while growing up in a family of thirteen children in Houston, Texas. In order to provide for their large family, both parents worked; her father operated the family's store, while her mother worked as a maid in the homes of wealthy white families. Franklin's parents alternated work shifts, which made it necessary to enforce strict rules regarding noise in order to allow the parents undisturbed rest at home. Growing up in a silent house provided Franklin with a unique perspective and an appreciation for sound and movement. She recalls discovering the power of sound and conflict after nearly drowning in a gully at the tender age of three. She remembers an older sister confronting their brothers for their inattentive caregiving. Franklin writes:

> When the panic was over, they returned me to the world of silence and low murmurs. But it was different this time. This time I could bring sound and movement to my world as a result of the scene at the water. The sound of the scene—Conflict. Movement. Life. Over and over it repeated itself within me. . . . I held fast to the scene for some time, silently taking the parts of my siblings as if they were characters in the re-play. In the corner of the room where I usually played, I softly murmured their lines and kept the incident alive.[9]

As Franklin matured, her imaginative play fueled her love of writing. She remembers collecting discarded pencils and tablets of paper at every turn.

"The few sheets of paper in each tablet disappeared almost as fast as I got my hands on them. To put such a quantity of paper in a tablet is a cruel jest. And that is what I was now, a writer, and I had to find a way to keep myself in tools to record the many dramas I had collected over the years," writes Franklin.[10] Her mother fed her love of literature, often bringing home cast-off fairy-tale books from her employers' homes for Franklin to read. She would later incorporate elements of Cinderella into the premise of her best-known play, *Black Girl*, as well as her firm understanding of sound, movement, and conflict into all of her dramas.

Franklin's experiences as a domestic worker greatly shaped her conception and ultimate rejection of the feminist movement. She explains in a 2010 interview that she spent a great deal of time working alongside her mother in the homes of white families during her youth. She remembers observing the disrespectful words hurled at white women from their own family members while she performed mundane tasks such as making beds, ironing, and peeling potatoes. Franklin perceives these white women as having "a separate set of problems that did not involve us."[11] While black communities "needed economic resources," black women "were already liberated" and therefore not in "need" of a feminist movement, remembers Franklin.[12] She resolutely dismisses the fallacy that black and white women have a shared experience and instead stresses the importance of racial solidarity:

> I've never seen any instances where something impacts on black women that doesn't impact on black men. It impacts on us as a family. . . . So at one time there was this attempt to get black women to join the feminist movement. But that hasn't been our problem. Black women have always been involved in all aspects of community life. White women were fighting to get their liberty from white men, the kind of world they live in. They were the ones who were marginalized and denied equality. They weren't fighting for us. They were fighting for themselves. They were telling us about themselves. About what was going on in the white families, as if we didn't know. We knew [because] we worked in those homes. They don't know what goes on in our homes but we worked inside white homes as domestics. I was a domestic worker so I know what goes on.[13]

Similar to early black feminists, Franklin critiques the mainstream feminist movement for removing any racial context from their framework of "sisterhood." She understood that ignoring the implications of black women's intersectionality only reinforces white supremacy and suppresses black women's actual needs. Thus, she sees the feminist movement as not only divisive for black men and women but also harmful to black families. Yet Franklin's words also present concerns. Her romantic vision of a cooperative black community belies the intracultural contradictions and gender inequalities therein.

Despite Franklin's disdain for the feminist movement, her intellectual thought demonstrates a major tenet of womanist thought: concern for the survival of black men, women, and children. In so doing, she reaffirms black women's ongoing tradition of grassroots activism within their own communities. She herself remained actively involved in her own community, serving as an analyst for the U.S. Office of Economic Opportunity in New York City and volunteering at the Black Panther Party's soup kitchens. Finally, her plays also express her womanist thought, which is often articulated through black female characters who labor as domestic workers.

Franklin decided to pursue a career in playwriting after witnessing a production of Rosalyn Drexler's Obie Award-winning one-act musical *Home Movies* (1964). At the time of the production, Franklin had only recently moved to New York City after receiving her bachelor of arts degree in languages from the University of Texas. Her first encounter watching black actors onstage proved inspiring. "Barbara Ann Teer and James Anderson . . . were the first black actors that I had ever seen on the professional stage. . . . It was the first time that I started getting a passion [or] a spark that made me want to write for the stage. . . . What they were doing made me want to write something for people to be on the stage and be that happy, doing what they were doing. That's really what lured me into wanting to be a playwright," remembers Franklin.[14] During the summer of 1964, she combined her passion for teaching and her love of theater to create her first play, *A First Step to Freedom*.

A First Step to Freedom emerged from Franklin's experiences teaching black children at the Mississippi Freedom Democratic Party's (MFDP's) Freedom School in Harmony, Mississippi. After working as a youth director at the Neighborhood House in Buffalo, New York, Franklin felt that her "roots were dying."[15] She returned to her Southern roots and assisted the MFDP's efforts to increase literacy and voter registration in the South. Despite lacking basic resources such as textbooks and a classroom, Franklin taught middle and high school-aged black children how to read. She remembers this experience as both challenging and highly rewarding. "[These were] students who were just totally turned off, students who had been taken out of school, and sent to pick some white man's cotton, and who were marked 'present' and just passed on from one grade to the next. . . . I was heartbroken by what I saw and I didn't know how to fix it. We didn't have any books," recalls Franklin.[16] After being "chased out of every place we tried to set up a school in," Franklin decided to teach the children outside under the shade of a tree.[17] While sitting on the grass, she listened to the children of sharecroppers recount their memories of growing up in the South and wrote them down. "Based upon their memory of what they had said, they were able to match up the lines on the paper, in the script, with what they had said and they learned how to read that way. And it was indeed their first step to freedom. And in many ways it was my first step to freedom, too, because I hadn't written a play and

[I] wrote a play," recalls Franklin.[18] Creating and performing *A First Step to Freedom* gave Franklin, along with poor black children, an opportunity to experience "an interior spiritual quality" known as *freedom*.[19]

When *A First Step to Freedom* premiered at the Sharon Waite Community Center, the performance signified much more than mere entertainment. Franklin, along with other volunteers, built the community center over the course of a summer with their own hands. The Sharon Waite Community Center functioned as a haven for poor blacks to gather and discuss their concerns and celebrate the spirit of their community. Franklin's production of *A First Step to Freedom*, in fact, realized W. E. B. Du Bois's vision of black theater put forth more than a hundred years previously. She and her community created a performance piece about black experiences in the South, performed by black children, for the black community of Harmony. Chronicling the racial violence of night riders, and disputes with whites in the community, as well as moments of black resistance, *A First Step to Freedom* functioned as an oral history and provided opportunities for the children of sharecroppers to reach far beyond expectations. "It was the first play they'd seen. . . . The place was packed, and they really enjoyed it because it was real to them. There wasn't a youngster in that community who didn't want to be in that play. . . . Not only did they learn to read . . . but the play put them in contact with people outside their communities. Three students—all from one family— went to college," remembers Franklin.[20] The long-term impact of *A First Step to Freedom* can never be fully measured. Inspired by the power of education through performance, Franklin continued to craft plays for students while serving as a lecturer at Herbert H. Lehman College of the City University of New York. Regardless of the genre or form, all of Franklin's works stress the importance of literacy and education within black communities.

While occasionally fraught with friction, the prestigious Harlem Writers Guild provided a space for Franklin to hone her craft and draw inspiration from other black women writers. John Oliver Killens, Rosa Guy, John Henrik Clarke, Willard Moore, and Walter Christmas founded the Harlem Writers Guild as a response to the exclusion they had experienced from the white literary world of New York. They envisioned the Harlem Writers Guild as a forum for gifted black writers to develop their work. Franklin recalls interacting with prominent black women writers such as Maya Angelou, Rosa Guy, and Alice Childress, as well as finding inspiration in Childress's play *Wine in the Wilderness* (1969). Franklin remembers joining the workshop so she could "learn how to talk like a writer [and] get help [with her] work."[21] Unfortunately, she also learned that her naturally inquisitive mind and earnestness were not always welcome among a cadre of writers. Franklin remembers asking a series of dramaturgical questions following a reading of a new work. Only too late did she realize that she had inadvertently interrupted the "ritual" conversations that took place after each reading. Franklin recalls that when her turn came to read early iterations of *Black Girl*, an unnamed female "anointed one" skewered her work. Rather than retaliate in kind, Franklin chose to write down any feedback and proceed with caution in the future. "I made a rule to myself that night concerning whom I would let read or hear my work in its initial stage [of] development. Still, that night I discovered what I was made of and saw that I could, with ease, distinguish shit from sugar," writes Franklin.[22]

Despite this early experience with negative feedback, the Harlem Writers Guild provided the opportunity for Franklin to submit her work for a televised production. Franklin remembers that following Martin Luther King Jr.'s assassination, a white representative from Boston's public television channel, WGBH, visited a Harlem Writers Guild meeting and requested their participation in a new television series, *On Being Black*. While many of the members (including the more experienced writers) submitted proposals, only Franklin's three-page treatment was selected for production. WGBH hired Franklin and bought the rights to produce what would become her first major hit: *Black Girl*.

WGBH script consultant George Houston Bass not only taught Franklin the fundamentals of playwriting, but also influenced her political views on black art and theater. During their revision sessions, Bass used his years of experience as a successful producer, director, and playwright to teach Franklin how to apply her knowledge of movement to her plays.[23] Franklin writes about her discovery as follows: "If a creation does not move internally, it stagnates and dies. . . . In internal writing it seems that the story line is moving along, not by a chain of incidents which happen to or act upon the characters, but by the internal personality needs, motivations, and make-up of the characters themselves."[24] Critics, in turn, often praised Franklin for the careful detailing of her characters and her honest portrayal of black women and families. Bass's standards for selecting scripts for WGBH's *On Being Black* series "struck the politically underdeveloped part of me," writes Franklin.[25] Bass had specific criteria for selecting plays: those written by black writers for primarily black audiences; those that explore the "social conditions" that psychologically and physically oppress the black community; those that investigate the tactics used to economically disenfranchise blacks; and those that celebrate the "joy," resiliency, and "beauty" of black America.[26] While Franklin's works may not subscribe to the "Black Revolutionary Theatre" as envisioned by Baraka, her plays address the political, social, and economic concerns of black communities. Inspired by Bass, Franklin's plays not only reveal and critique the oppressive forces that demoralize and disenfranchise black families and larger black communities, but also encourage audiences to celebrate their own humanity.

While WGBH provided Franklin with an invaluable mentor, she remained dissatisfied with the production process. Throughout the production Franklin disagreed with producers and the director's "style" and "interpretation" of her script.[27] In addition, she was displeased with the actors' interpretations of

Netta and Earl. "I found its tone low-keyed, its pacing slow, its mood somber and melodramatic, its energy restrained," writes Franklin.[28] She did, however, convince producers to cast her younger sister Yvette Franklin, rather than a light-skinned actress, to star in the role of Billie Jean. This difficult experience taught her that despite her best efforts, she had little creative control over the finished product. Now, having received critical acclaim for a project she did not fully support, Franklin moved back to New York and reestablished her working relationship with Woodie King Jr.

Franklin credits producer King with launching her playwriting career. Prior to meeting King, Franklin had experienced marginalization within the male-dominated sphere of New York theater. Franklin remembers her white agent submitting her works "to theaters all across the country . . . [but] there were no women involved."[29] Following the advice of her agent, Franklin stopped submitting her work under her birth name, Jennie Elizabeth Franklin, and instead used the gender-neutral "J.e. Franklin." As a result, the same works that were once rejected were now accepted by theaters. Franklin views her previous rejection as indicative of sexism, rather than a result of racism or a combination of the two. "My name, Jennie, is not a black name. They didn't want women. If you talked to white women and Asian women who are playwrights, they'll tell you the same thing. They didn't want them neither. So there was a gender thing, but that wasn't a color thing," remembers Franklin.[30] King, however, took a chance on a heretofore unknown playwright and produced Franklin's second play, *The In-Crowd: A Rock Opera in One Act* for Mobilization for Youth in 1967. When King's New Federal Theatre emerged out of the Mobilization for Youth's theater program in 1970, he again turned to her dramas. King produced the 1971 theatrical premiere of *Black Girl*, despite Franklin's belief that the televised production had marked the end of the play. Franklin remembers that King's (then) wife and script reader, Willie Mae King, selected *Black Girl* for their first season after watching WGBH's televised production.

Given a second opportunity to see her vision fully realized, Franklin actively contributed to the New Federal Theatre's critically acclaimed production of *Black Girl*. After helplessly witnessing a television director misinterpret her play, Franklin believed that a female director could provide the necessary movement to the play. While King initially suggested male directors, she persuaded him to hire Shauneille Perry, who had previously directed the 1969 Negro Ensemble Company Workshop production of *Miss Honey's Young'uns*. Franklin and Perry agreed that while she would not attend rehearsals, Franklin would occasionally speak with actors and answer their questions. Franklin remembers that the production received standing ovations and played to full houses consisting of many teenagers and some elderly patrons. When an actor performing as Mr. Herbert played for a "cheap laugh" and undermined the integrity of the production, Franklin remembers speaking to Perry and King about the situation. While they all agreed that the actor should be replaced if he did not cease, King remained mindful of gender dynamics. "Woodie suggested that it would be easier if a man told him, and he offered to tell the player," writes Franklin.[31] Eventually the actor left the show, but his replacement also performed for easy laughs. "At first I thought the players did not respect the director because she was a woman. But when I talked to Woodie and Shauneille about replacing the player, the problem presented itself in a different light. Some of the actors found their freedom to do as they pleased in the knowledge that there was a scarcity of black actors and actresses between the ages of forty and sixty," writes Franklin.[32] Despite the selfish antics of individual actors, *Black Girl* received rave reviews from critics, earning Franklin a 1971 New York Drama Desk Most Promising Playwright Award. *Black Girl* then moved to an Off-Broadway production at Theatre DeLys for a record six-month run of 247 performances. King and Perry's production of *Black Girl* firmly established Franklin as a force to be reckoned with in the world of New York theater.

While the New Federal Theatre's award-winning production of *Black Girl* cemented Franklin's status as a local celebrity, the mainstream media remained unconvinced of her talent. Following the success of *Black Girl*, Franklin received invitations to speak at public events, including Barbara Ann Teer's Sunday Symposium Series at the National Black Theatre. Film producers also met with Franklin to discuss the possibility of hiring her to adapt the theatrical production into a feature-length film. When film producers offered her only a small advance, however, Franklin understood that regardless of her success, others still doubted her abilities. "As for the money, the advance was no earth-shaking figure; the amount aroused my suspicion that I was still viewed as a high-risk writer: young, black, Southern female, the kind they feel won't or can't deliver," writes Franklin.[33] Rather than view the intersections of her identity as a disadvantage, she used her experiences as a Southern black woman as the very foundation for her intellectual thought.

As a black woman intellectual, Franklin offers a humanist prospective of black art and black revolution. The black aesthetic, according to Franklin, simply means "human arts" that grow from a human "view of the world, a perception of the world, an experience of the world."[34] She further explains:

> I think that when people say, "The Black Aesthetic" or "The Black Arts Movement" . . . it's a way of saying "The Human Aesthetic," [or] the "Human Arts Movement." Simply that energy that gets left in a place where it was born, where it came into being. That energy, that human energy, as opposed to that energy that is a part of white society and white culture, that they deliberately designed to be antithetical to the human energy. They deliberately designed it to be non-sensory, disembodied, dissociated from human life. People who are caught up in that get shaped and fashioned in a way that's radically different

from the way people live and work within the human world and experience the human world in a natural universally human sense.[35]

Franklin views the black aesthetic as an energy associated with human life, a way of living in the world. She believes that the arts promote the change or spiritual revolution so desperately needed in the world. "If we get a dictionary definition of the word 'revolution.' *Revolve. Turning back.* Turning around and turning back. I would like to turn some things around. Everybody thinks that revolution [means] violence. You can have a spiritual revolution. I think that there does need to be a spiritual revolution. There needs to be a revolution, for example, in the way we define the word 'human,'" explains Franklin.[36] As a black woman intellectual, Franklin met the needs of the black community by constructing plays that privilege human emotion and promote spiritual revolution.

At times, Franklin's humanist vision ran afoul of the popular rhetoric espoused by leading male figures of the Black Arts Movement. Her complicated relationship with Black Arts rhetoric is perhaps best exemplified in a rare interview with the editor and novelist Fred Beauford. During this 1971 interview Franklin discusses the premise of *Black Girl*, as well as her thoughts on black struggle. Franklin explains that as a writer, she "center[s]" herself "around the ethics of black people" and that *Black Girl* investigates "one's immediate situation—which is freeing the self to be."[37] Beauford, however, interprets Franklin's stance as individualistic and identifies her position as "almost counter to . . . leading artistic spokesmen" who declare "'there are no individuals.'"[38] Franklin responds to Beauford's criticism with linguistic savvy:

> The word individual . . . means not divided. It means single. It means whole. It means integrity. I don't think that we can talk about group struggle until we talk about the struggle of that individual within that group to choose to struggle as part of that group. So that I don't see myself as a collective. No collective does. Collectives, if we are talking in political terms, still see each single person of that collective as a[n] individual. And if one is not being an individual in that particular struggle, then one loses one's integrity. . . . Once you violate the individual integrity there is little energy or freedom left in the group to move on to meet human and personal need—and to share that love and feeling that you have with another human being.[39]

Franklin uses the etymology of the word "individual" to emphasize the importance of individuality in the struggle against oppression. Her comments suggest that community empowerment begins with the humanity and integrity of each individual. Her interview also reveals engagement with and ultimate rejection of dominant conversations about the role of the black artist. "If you are equating blackness with humanness, then when we say the role of the black artist, the responsibility of the black artist, we are talking about the human artist. And the human artist always deals with human things. And one becomes an artist because one feels the need to. So one is doing what one needs to do. What more can be asked?" says Franklin.[40] She writes because she has a question that needs to be answered. Despite criticism, Franklin continued to construct didactic, entertaining, and candid plays that consciously provide opportunities for audiences to "touch down" or connect with their own humanity.[41]

Touching Down: Dramatizing the Spiritual Revolution

Franklin's second play, *The In-Crowd: A Rock Opera in One Act* (1965), dramatizes the emotional struggles of a group of black revolutionary children known as the In-Crowd Army. The children's musical features a masked figure named Solomon who attempts to complete the third phase of initiation into the In-Crowd Army. While Solomon attempts to gain the trust of their leader Top Cat, played by a young boy or girl, club members perform their own rituals of survival. Within the safety of their clubhouse, Lou Anne, Betty, Arnold, and Robert use song to express their innermost needs, including love from their parents and liberation from the oppressive forces in their lives. The prologue, in particular, utilizes popular music of the day to emphasize this important premise. *The In-Crowd* begins with a lone child walking to the apron of the stage singing "Stop! In the Name of the Law!" an adaptation of the Supremes' hit "Stop! In the Name of Love." As the child sings the third verse and chorus, they reveal the precarious state of black adolescence:

> But in reality,
> I'm as helpless as can be.
> And since my tears don't mean a thing.
> I won't cry no more
> From the things you do to me.
> Stop! in the name of the law!
> Please stop! in the name of the law!
> Stop! in the name of the law!
> Stop![42]

Whereas the Supremes' song focuses on black women's emotional pain caused by a cheating partner, Franklin's version stresses the emotional pain that children suffer due to indifferent or uncaring parents. "Stop! In the Name of the Law!" not only reveals emotional vulnerability, but also demands that parents cease their criminal behavior. Franklin seamlessly weaves nine such thought-provoking songs throughout the course of *The In-Crowd*. These narrative songs encourage the shedding of tears, offering opportunities for actors and audiences to "touch down." Thus, the musical numbers offer more than entertainment; they create a psychic space to heal wounded hearts.

Despite working within the conventions of musical theater, *The In-Crowd* embraces the revolutionary spirit of the 1960s. The In-Crowd Army, in fact, incorporates ritual, black power debates, and collective identity politics into their meetings in order to strategize ways to liberate their community from oppressive forces. Upon Top Cat's entrance, the In-Crowd Army demonstrates racial solidarity and respect for their leader by standing at attention with fists raised in a Black Power salute. After establishing order, Top Cat reminds the children of the clubhouse rules and the purpose of their initiation ritual. Top Cat also offers further insight into their revolutionary cause, stating:

> You're soldiers in this In-Crowd
> And you all took a vow
> To never commit any crimes and disgrace this clubhouse.
> To always be upright
> And keep the faith for the fight
> That's before us.
> . . .
> Will he [Solomon] be for the parents
> Or will he stand with us
> On the Day of Liberation
> When the In-Crowd Army takes over the nation?[43]

While the children clearly mimic the actions of adult revolutionaries, their clubhouse meetings represent much more than a game.

The In-Crowd Army's initiation ritual, in fact, provides a safe way to express and validate the everyday concerns of black youth. The audience, in turn, become honorary members of this insurgency as Top Cat reveals inside information about their plan to establish a new order known as "Children's Liberation."[44] Top Cat's speech indicates the importance of trust, solidarity, and resistance against adult tyranny. Establishing a loyal army, therefore, becomes a key element in Top Cat's plan. In order to determine his suitability, Top Cat tests Solomon's loyalty, which quickly leads to an ideological debate about the meaning of liberation. Solomon responds to Top Cat's queries by reading a "Children's Bill of Rights" that he wrote on behalf of children. The "Children's Bill of Rights" includes five articles that demand parents to love their children and prohibit favoritism, unfair practices, abuse, and using children as scapegoats. Top Cat, however, opposes Solomon's solution because he believes parents would continue to act as judges, forcing children to remain subservient. Rather than work within the corrupt system, Top Cat proposes a radical reordering of the law: arrest their parents, charge them with "child abuse and neglect," and hold them accountable for their actions in a "High Court" comprised of children.[45] The In-Crowd Army accepts Top Cat's solution, holds a court hearing, and find their parents guilty. The children experience a change of heart, however, once their parents express their love for them through song. In a somewhat abrupt reversal, the In-Crowd Army sings a rousing rendition of "We Didn't Understand" to the tune of "Stop in the Name of the Law" and forgive their parents. As with most musicals of the era, *The In-Crowd* concludes with a contrived happy ending in the form of a joyous reconciliation of parents and children.

While the children find resolution for their parental concerns, Franklin allows the broader problems that impact poor black children at a national level to remain unresolved. The audience discovers through song that Arnold's abusive father has never told him that he loves him; Lou Anne's mother yells and berates her, confines her to the house, and forces her to work endlessly; Robert's father discourages his dream of becoming a famous musician like "Bird and Satch and Trane"; and Betty's mother beats her and treats her as a domestic worker.[46] After condemning the actions of parents Solomon suggests building a "separate little nation" free from all oppression:

> Consider what our Uncle Sammy has willed to us already:
> Polluted air and water
> And all life dying steady.
> Littered streets and playgrounds
> Dope and alcohol
> Slums with rats and maggots
> Crawling from the walls.
> Let's save the children from these things
> That make their lives too hollow.[47]

Solomon's speech uses the plight of poor black children as a galvanizing force within the black community. In so doing, he reveals how the children's personal troubles are also political and he critiques black children's worthless inheritance. The United States not only exerts control over black children's impulses or actions, but also determines their future. Rather than inherit pollution, death, drugs, disease, cramped living conditions, and an empty future, Solomon suggests building a nation filled with "sun" and freedom.[48] Solomon's use of the collective "Let's" implies that members of the In-Crowd, as well as audiences, should take part in this revolution to make black lives matter.

Solomon's revolutionary sentiments provided special meaning for the original cast, all of whom came from impoverished communities. Franklin wrote *The In-Crowd* for the Mobilization for Youth, a social service agency designed to provide instruction, job training, counseling, and mental health services for delinquent youths in the Lower East Side of New York. "It was just my attempt to write something for some children who didn't have any material to get up on the stage and act," remembers Franklin.[49] King Jr., who worked with Mobilization for Youth's theater program, collaborated with Franklin on the production, adding music and dance before performing the piece at the International Youth Festival in Montreal, Canada, in 1967.[50] Franklin attended the festival and describes the production as "lovely."[51] The Mobilization for Youth's production of *The In-Crowd* thus educated, edified, and entertained audiences through politically charged speeches, emotionally gripping musical numbers, and aesthetically pleasing production values.

Similar to *The In-Crowd*, *Miss Honey's Young'uns* (1966 as *Mau Mau Room*) also privileges the revolutionary spirit of black youth. *Miss Honey's Young'uns* provides a fictitious representation of historical events surrounding the desegregation of Southern universities. The action takes place inside the dilapidated Jefferson Davis House, which now functions as a black-only girls' dormitory. As the plantation of the former Confederate president Jefferson Davis, the dormitory not only symbolizes an oppressive environment, but also connects the past trauma of enslavement with the present-day horrors of institutional white racism. Throughout the play, the black youth strategize different ways to resist white oppression, yet all approaches ultimately fail. Lloyd Richards's Negro Ensemble Company Advance Workshop produced the premiere of the *Mau Mau Room* at St. Mark's Playhouse in 1969. While Franklin herself directed a subsequent production of the play at Skidmore College, she remembers Shauneille Perry's direction as particularly powerful. "I remembered it because [Perry] has a kind of a kinetic energy that makes the play move. . . . [S]omething about the way she has the actors moving on the stage is almost like a film," remembers Franklin.[52] The cast included future *Shaft* (1971) star Richard Roundtree, who performed the role of Jimmy, a hypermasculine Korean War veteran. "[*Mau Mau Room*] gave Richard Roundtree his beginning in the theater. That was his first play. And someone saw him in the role of Jimmy . . . and next thing I know he's Shaft," remembers Franklin.[53] Perry's superior direction, coupled with a breakout star and topical source material, ensured the success of *Mau Mau Room/Miss Honey's Young'uns*.

Rather than structure *Miss Honey's Young'uns* in traditional scenes and acts, Franklin uses seven rituals to reveal the cyclical nature of white oppression and black resistance. The use of ritual suggests that the performance space itself functions as sacred ground, allowing audiences to witness a solemn ceremony or recurring pattern within the black community. "Ritual is transformative. It's known by the group. It's a practice. . . . All of these pieces of action are part of something that has happened in the past, has happened now, and it's going to continue to happen in the future unless someone comes in and breaks the ribbon of what that is. Someone has to move one action out of the way and replace it with another action. If that doesn't happen, then you've got a ritual," remembers Franklin.[54] The first ritual introduces Miss Honey, a black domestic worker who prepares the roach-infested plantation for the arrival of four incoming freshmen. Upon seeing the condition of their dormitory, Evelyn attempts to convince her fellow students Berna Mae, Janice, and Veena to picket in order to receive equal accommodations. This first ritual, therefore, reflects the tradition of black women activists such as Ida B. Wells who worked within the system of government to bring about social change. Ritual two reveals the backlash against such efforts, including the indignities and violence that young black women endure in pursuit of their education and political autonomy. After arriving home from their first day of school, the girls disclose their emotional and physical pain: white students accosted Veena and spit on her sweater, white students shoved Evelyn and called her a "nigger," and a local restaurateur refused to take Evelyn's order. The second ritual concludes with unseen whites firing shots through the dormitory and burning a cross on their lawn. Ritual two thus highlights the inhumanity of whites, the failings of the Civil Rights Act (1965), and the dangers of white vigilante justice.

Rituals three through five reveal the cyclical trauma that blacks have endured since the Middle Passage. The emotional stress of living in a state of terror and violence, as well as witnessing the death of a fellow student, finally takes its toll on Veena and she slips into a state of madness. Her plight harkens back to the trauma that Africans endured on the decks of slave ships and while enslaved on American soil. As the scholar of African American theater Beverly J. Robinson notes, ritual was created in order to provide the psychic space needed to survive the dehumanizing practice of transforming the free African into a slave.[55] *Miss Honey's Young'uns* suggests that the cycle of trauma will continue until another, more powerful action is taken.

The trauma and violence that Franklin's fictional black students experience resonates with the actual dangers James Meredith faced while desegregating the University of Mississippi. While Franklin does not mention a specific college campus, the action could very well occur in the same location of the actual Jefferson Davis plantation in Biloxi, Mississippi. Franklin wrote *Miss Honey's Young'uns* at a time when Southern universities, and the University of Mississippi in particular, faced public scrutiny for discriminatory practices. Just four years before Franklin wrote the play, Meredith sued the University of Mississippi when his initial acceptance by the university was withdrawn after administrators discovered his race. After he won his case in 1962, hostile white crowds greeted him when he arrived on campus. Despite constant threats against his life, Meredith graduated from the University of Mississippi with a degree in political science and continued his efforts to actively resist racism. During the summer of 1966, the same year Franklin wrote *Miss Honey's Young'uns*, Meredith organized his famous solo 220-mile March against Fear in order to encourage black voter registration in the South. Unfortunately, a white gunman shot Meredith on the second day of his march from Memphis, Tennessee, to Jackson, Mississippi. While he recovered in the hospital, several civil rights organizations, including the Student Nonviolent Coordinating Committee (SNCC), became involved and marched in his stead. Frustrated by white resistance and violence, SNCC chairman Stokely Carmichael delivered a fiery speech in Greenwood, Mississippi, to crowds of students who responded by chanting "Black Power," thus ushering a black nationalist thrust into SNCC's ideology. Having worked in the Freedom School in Mississippi and heard youth share their experiences of night riders terrorizing their communities, Franklin understood the dangers that awaited black youth who resisted racial oppression. *Miss Honey's Young'uns* dramatizes these dangers, as well as the broader impact of student activism on the black liberation movement.

Miss Honey's Young'uns provides a platform to debate possible solutions to racial violence and inequality. The black students, in fact, embody the historical and current ideological positions of prominent leaders such as Booker T. Washington, W. E. B. Du Bois, Malcolm X, Martin Luther King, Huey Newton, and Angela Davis. Franklin explains:

> [T]hese young children . . . were trying to find the answer to a question they had, which was "How do you deal with the oppressive forces that are upon you? How do you liberate yourself from white oppression?" . . . How do you respond to oppression? What methods do you come up with? We tried them all. Martin Luther King said, "Love will fix it." Malcolm X said basically, "Eye for eye, tooth for tooth. Kill your oppressor." W. [E.] B. Du Bois said, "Get your education." Booker T. Washington said, "Set down your buckets where you are." There've been a number of our leaders who had different takes on how to deal with this white man. To be honest, they were all wrong.[56]

The roach-infested, dilapidated state of the black-only dormitory represents oppression to the black students. Although Evelyn, Berna Mae, Veena, their housemother Mavis, and male cohort Cordell strategize different ways to gain equal accommodations, none of their approaches stops the cycle of death. Similar to King, Evelyn attempts to work within the system and uses activist traditions such as picketing, sit-ins, boycotts, lists of demands, interracial alliances, and diplomacy. While Evelyn desires to speak directly to the university president Mr. Wolfgang, Cordell proposes a strategy of armed defense. In keeping with Malcolm X and with Newton's newly formed Black Panther Party, Cordell declares: "Somebody gotta die. This cracker never conceded nothing unless we pay him with our blood, and he ain't about to change."[57] Berna Mae, however, eschews Cordell's violent approach to liberation and sees education as the key to liberation. Much like her predecessor W. E. B. Du Bois, Berna Mae values education and insists that she enrolled in an all-white university "to be a student" first and foremost.[58] Similar to Booker T. Washington, Veena compromises with white authority figures in order to secure her safety and education. "Whatever these white folks tell me to do, I'm doing it. If they say sit, I'm gonna sit . . . if they say stand, I'm gonna stand," Veena states after shots are fired and a cross is burned on their lawn.[59] Mavis, a political activist and law student, embodies the militancy of the black activist Angela Davis. Mavis sports an afro, lectures the girls about the beauty of natural hair, and becomes enraged when she discovers Evelyn happily eating watermelon to the delight of white students. "Where I come from, we'd just throw a croaker-sack over her head and beat her ass, and I ain't but two inches away from doing it," Mavis declares.[60] Mavis views Evelyn's actions as "dangerous," and yet she also works within the system by insisting that they all file a lawsuit against the university.[61] While their approaches vary, each student demonstrates a similar desire to resist white oppression. Their failure to find a viable solution, however, allows institutional white racism to remain intact.

Although *Miss Honey's Young'uns* does not provide solutions to the problems raised, the play powerfully demonstrates the devastation of institutional white racism. Franklin first heard the term "institutional white racism" from the *Report of the National Advisory Commission on Civil Disorders*, also known as the *Kerner Commission Report*, in 1967. U.S. President Lyndon B. Johnson selected Governor Otto Kerner, Jr. of Illinois to chair an eleven-member commission to investigate why race riots were sweeping American cities and provide recommendations for how the government could prevent future disturbances. The *Kerner Commission Report* states:

> This is our basic conclusion: Our nation is moving toward two societies, one black, one white—separate and unequal. . . .
>
> Segregation and poverty have created in the racial ghetto a destructive environment totally unknown to most white Americans.
>
> What white Americans have never fully understood but what the Negro can never forget—is that white society is deeply implicated in the ghetto. White institutions created it, white institutions maintain it, and white society condones it.[62]

The *Kerner Commission Report* explicitly condemns white institutions for creating, maintaining, and condoning poverty in black communities, and it implicitly rebukes white Americans for ignoring this problem that impacts the entire country. The report concludes that a "system of failure and frustration . . . dominates the ghetto and weakens our society," culminating in civil unrest across major U.S. cities.[63] *Miss Honey's Young'uns* simply dramatizes the violence needed to maintain such disparate societies.

The black students' college experience demonstrates the disconnect between black and white America and the destructiveness of institutional white racism. Even when given the rare opportunity to attend college, the black students remain at a disadvantage because they still cannot afford textbooks and they have to endure harassment by white students, poor living conditions, and death threats, all while trying to maintain decent grades. The students become victims of institutional white racism as the stress and violence contribute to Jimmy's death and Veena's madness. Franklin considers institutional white racism as the central problem within black communities:

> Look at how many warriors have just died from stress. Trying to deal with institutional white racism, which is over there in the white community. Look at how many warriors we have lost. People who have stretched themselves out and we turn on each other, we go around in circles. We fight one generation thinking that, "Oh, our children won't have to go through this." Then our children get grown and then we see them go and do the same thing. Then it keeps going on, and on, and on. We just keep dying so obviously we haven't really put our finger on what the problem is. Those of us who have put our finger over what the problem is . . . Well, is anybody listening?[64]

Franklin's frank comments suggest that those who have identified the problem of institutional white racism have either been ignored or died as a result of the emotional toll. Until blacks fully understand institutional white racism, the cycle of death and madness will continue to destroy the black community.

Miss Honey's Young'uns also broadens the discussion of the "black community" by considering the impact of the liberation movement throughout the black diaspora. Franklin originally titled the play *Mau Mau Room*, but changed it at the behest of her agent. The term "mau-mau," in fact, carried significant revolutionary meaning throughout the black diaspora in the 1950 and 1960s. Mau-Mau served as the name of a secret society of Kikuyu insurgents who led a rebellion against British colonial rule in Kenya. Although the Mau-Mau Uprisings (1952–60) resulted in thousands of Kikuyu casualties and ended in a British and loyalist military victory, the Mau-Mau's efforts to liberate Kenyans inspired the Civil Rights Movement in the United States. Franklin remembers the impact of the Mau-Mau Uprisings as follows:

> The name [mau-mau] means, "death to the whites." . . . Growing up in the system at that time, we had some pieces of history about what was going on in Africa, what nations were trying to gain their independence, and what nations were leading the resistance to the white colonists. We admired Jomo Kenyatta . . . these men who were fighting and how he aspired for his freedom. . . . The term mau-mau was associated with moving out of the past over to the Civil Rights Movement in America.[65]

Similar to the Kikuyu insurgents, the black male students in *Miss Honey's Young'uns* form a secret society of men, lead an armed resistance against oppressive white rule, and suffer devastating casualties. The black male students experience ultimate defeat, however, because they correlate freedom with manhood, rather than the liberation of black men, women, and children.

Miss Honey's Young'uns positions black macho mythology as not only dangerous, but also counterproductive to the black liberation movement. Despite their efforts to resist institutional white racism, the black male students have, in fact, internalized black macho mythology. The six black male students view freedom in terms of their virility, aggressiveness, and ability to protect black female students. For example, after hearing that white students accosted Veena, Cordell declares: "Nasty bastards! I wish I had-a seen 'em . . . the no-dick cowards!"[66] Cordell's bravado firmly links his sexual prowess with bravery and protection. When shots ring out through the women's dormitory, Cordell and his friends purchase guns in a vain attempt to protect the women. Cordell and Falvie boast:

> CORDELL: I'm gonna get me some power if it's the last thing I do!
> FALVIE: Umm-gowa! Black Power! St. George gonna kill some dragons!
> CORDELL: White blood! Ten for one, right fellows? If they kill one-a us, we gonna take off ten of them. Right fellows?[67]

Cordell and Falvie's conversation suggests that blood thirst and the acquisition of power are the true motivating factors behind their insurgency. After receiving the guns that Jimmy acquires for them, the men proceed to boast about their fighting skills. However, the stage directions suggest that none of the men are actually familiar with weapons. Falvie *"tries to twirl"* his loaded gun *"Wyatt Earp-style"* and attempts *"some trick he saw in the movies or on television,"*[68] while Winston likewise pretends to shoot his gun at a tapestry. Their play becomes dangerous when Evelyn challenges Cordell's masculinity. She mocks his poor athletic skills and declares, "All you old armchair warriors can kiss my behind!"[69] Enraged, Cordell proceeds to hold a gun to her head and slaps her before accidently shooting and killing Jimmy for trying to intervene. Paradoxically, the black men's attempts to gain power result in the further abuse of black women and the death of a comrade, and they do nothing to change Miss Honey's plight.

Miss Honey's Young'uns disrupts controlling images of blacks by presenting the lived experiences of Miss Honey. At first glance Miss Honey appears as a hybrid of a Mammy and Uncle Tom stereotype. She is an illiterate, mild-mannered, and God-fearing middle-aged domestic worker who takes pride in her familial relationship with white students. When white vigilantes terrorize the black students, she appears complacent, cautioning the black girls against rebellion. Janice, a black middle-class student, even refers to Miss Honey as an "Uncle Tom" and a "white-folks-nigger."[70] "They don't know what they're saying when they say 'Uncle Tom.' They [just] think they know what they're saying," remembers Franklin.[71] Janice's harsh criticism and quick dismissal of Miss Honey's tenuous position at the university belies the untold horrors black women of the previous generation have experienced. Miss Honey represents the countless number of black women who experienced white terrorism and were denied access to higher education. With limited options, Miss Honey found the only work available to black women: that of the domestic worker. Despite her illiteracy, Miss Honey functions as a fount of knowledge for the next generation of black women. She passes down an oral history of survival and resistance through seemingly inconsequential stories. When Miss Honey mentions that their new housemother Mavis attends the same law school as did the civil rights activist Heman Marion Sweatt, she also reveals the cyclical nature of oppression. "I 'members his name just as good 'cause folks joked about it so much, said when the white folks get holt of him, he shore will sweat. I heard tell he had to be put away, they done him so bad," says Miss Honey.[72] Her words suggest a devastating familiarity with white vigilante justice. Rather than view Miss Honey as a fount of knowledge, the black students quickly dismiss her as a politically passive, archetypal Uncle Tom.

Miss Honey uses her position as "mammy" to white students to assist, advise, and protect black students. Miss Honey embodies the culture of dissemblance: she creates the appearance of openness with her white employers while keeping her sense of self and inner thoughts hidden. While she appears to dote on white students, she eventually reveals that the black students are, in fact, her "young'uns." Her maternal affection motivates her to disclose confidential information revealed by white students and to provide used clothes to her young'uns so they can gain stronger ground at the university. Miss Honey also encourages the black girls' pursuit of education. Similar to Franklin's own mother, she gives the girls the white students' cast-off textbooks which they otherwise could not afford. When not in the presence of whites, Miss Honey uses the Bible to proclaim a more militant message to her young'uns. "Just leave these white folks to God, H'its something in store for 'em, something terrible! Just you watch!"[73] Miss Honey assures the girls. Miss Honey discourages violent retaliation, yet she does suggest that the black girls maintain their dignity and use education as a weapon against racial oppression. "Y'awl just hold your heads up"[74] and "Y'awl just git this book-larning. That's something they can't take away from you,"[75] advises Miss Honey. Franklin views Miss Honey as a woman who has "just about seen it all." The students "needed her wisdom in order to keep them balanced. They came there to learn. They came to school to be scholars. She was very proud of them," remembers Franklin.[76] The girls, however, disregard Miss Honey's maternal wisdom and leave the university in a worse emotional state than when they arrived. Franklin's next play, *Black Girl* (1969), continues to engage with the themes of black women's labor, motherhood, and the importance of education.

Black Girl reimagines the Cinderella fairy tale from the perspective of a poor black Southern girl named Billie Jean. Rather than attend a ball and marry a handsome prince, Billie Jean aspires to attend college and join a dance troupe. Billie Jean's bitter half-sisters Norma Faye and Ruth Ann conspire to humiliate and stifle her dreams. Their mother, Mama Rosie, discourages Billie Jean while encouraging her foster daughter Netta to pursue a college degree in education. Billie Jean's grandmother, Mu'Dear, acts as her fairy godmother, intervening on her behalf so she can audition for the dance company. *Black Girl* concludes with Billie Jean and Mama Rosie's reconciliation and Billie Jean's departure for college.

As with all of Franklin's works, *Black Girl* began with a probing question that functions as the premise of the play. "Her sisters had chosen not to become. Would Billie Jean make the same choice?" writes Franklin.[77] This question grants Billie Jean, and young black women like her, the agency they need to grow into black womanhood. "I feel that plays should not mirror the condition, but be presented in such a way that they leave you with choices. . . . *Black Girl* is a play about choices. And that's what black theater and the arts should be about," states Franklin.[78] How then, does Billie Jean's identity as a poor black Southern girl impact her choices?

Billie Jean's choices are greatly impacted by the oppressive forces that deny the expressive gifts of black artists. Franklin explains that Mama Rosie grew up in a culture that "don't value the artists, and certainly don't value the black artists in many ways."[79] Mama Rosie and her ex-husband Earl express these sentiments in the following exchange:

> EARL: Ain't no colored girls making nothing off-a that [dance]. The white chicks is even starving trying to do it.
> MAMA ROSIE: I told her that mess wasn't gonna buy her a pot to piss in or a window to throw it out of.[80]

Mama Rosie and Earl understand that the racist society in which they live will not allow Billie Jean to achieve financial success. Indeed, history has shown that many black artists, including Ira Aldridge, Josephine Baker, Richard Wright, and countless others, were forced to relocate to Europe in order to receive the recognition they deserved for their talent. Franklin further explains:

> What else is this woman [Mama Rosie] supposed to say to her child? . . . Based upon her own experience, that child is about to let herself in for a whole lot of heartache. A whole lot of pain. As the parent, it's your natural tendency to protect your child from that even if you have to get harsh. It's a credit to Billie Jean's resilience, her strength, her passion, and her determination to be who she is, to forge a way for her own self . . . in spite of her mother's negative comments. Her mother wasn't the only one making them. . . . So that's the tenor of the time.[81]

While her family and teacher's discouragement may appear cruel, their intentions are honorable: they want to prevent Billie Jean from experiencing the harsh sting of racism and rejection. Similar to Billie Jean, Franklin also remembers wanting to be an artist and ultimately having her elementary school teachers discourage her pursuit of drawing. "One day, my teacher said, 'Can't do that all your life.' Because they know what the society has in store for you. So on the one hand they're being truthful, but on the other hand, they're crushing dreams," remembers Franklin.[82] Against her family's wishes, Billie Jean holds on to her dream and continues to dance in the privacy of her bedroom, allowing the audience an opportunity to glimpse the black female body in motion. Billie Jean dances to Ahmad Jamal's jazz album *Poinciana* (1963) with passion and precision. The stage directions indicate that she "has a great deal of talent, and, with polish and training, it all could develop into something, though God only knows what the innovation would be called."[83] Despite her family's and teacher's warnings, Billie Jean makes the choice to *become*.

Black Girl uses black women's standpoint to provide an important critique of the American educational system and the lack of employment opportunities afforded black women. Exposition reveals that Billie Jean recently dropped out of high school because her teachers discouraged her dreams. Her half-sisters Norma Faye and Ruth Ann also dropped out of school because of their unplanned pregnancies. Mama Rosie places great value on education, despite the fact that none of her children have earned a high school diploma and she herself only has a fourth-grade education. Mamie Rosie lives vicariously through her foster daughter Netta, who is earning a bachelor's degree in education. Netta's situation reveals that even if a black child graduates high school and enrolls in college, institutional white racism will continue to hinder her progress. As students at a recently integrated Southern college, Netta and her fellow black classmates must endure the harassment of white students who spit and throw urine on them. Despite this reality, Mama Rosie continues to brag about Netta's future until Norma Faye offers a powerful critique of the oppressive forces in black women's lives. "What's so big about a teacher, Mama? You go in some white woman's kitchen and you liable to find one working there. What's the sense in wasting all that time at some fancy college just to work in a kitchen," says Norma Faye.[84] With these three simple sentences, Norma Faye reveals that blackness and femaleness preclude many employment opportunities. Regardless of their educational background or intelligence, black women of the early to mid-twentieth century had limited job prospects. The majority of black women who worked outside of the home labored as domestics in white homes or in fields as sharecroppers. Mama Rosie reflects this harsh truth since she herself works as a maid at Carver High School, despite her best efforts to describe herself as "staff." Norma Faye's worldview has been shaped by her traumatic experiences attending public school. "[Teachers] laugh at *all* of us. We a big joke to 'em. Ruth Ann, you know the teachers we had; what did they do?

Pass out them old raggedy-ass books the white schools didn't want no more, then mark us present if we was picking some white man's cotton . . . and pass us on. Hell, I don't need no diploma from Harvard to do that," says Norma Faye.[85] Her experience resonates with the oral histories that Franklin's students shared with her while she was working at the Freedom School in Harmony, Mississippi. Norma Faye's remarks imply that the Southern public school system not only fails black children, but also perpetuates poverty within black communities.

Black Girl critiques the myth of black matriarchy through its celebration of the strength and resilience of black warrior mothers. Franklin wrote *Black Girl* following the *Moynihan Report*'s damning conclusions that erroneously link so-called black matriarchy with black poverty. *Black Girl*, in fact, offers an alternative vision of female-headed households that is deeply rooted within African customs. The play takes place near and on Mother's Day and features three generations of black women who struggle to raise their children either by themselves or with minimum help from their husbands. All of the women became mothers as teens or young women, with anxieties over respectability motivating them to marry their babies' fathers.[86] These forced unions, however, result in strained marriages or divorce. Left with little financial or emotional support from men, the mothers turn to each other for advice, comfort, and validation. With Mu'Dear at the head, the women create a familial structure reminiscent of African societies, which Franklin describes as "matriachlinear," rather than matriarchal. Franklin believes matriarchy implies that "men do not stand on their own two feet, that they are somehow appendages to the women."[87]

Critics applauded Franklin's representation of strong warrior mothers and female-headed households. "The family is not, in my view, of the Moynihanesque matriarchy, but more like the Ashanti matrilineal family wherein males are not inferior in status, but rather their society consents to a relationship of heritage around its females. The grandmother in 'Black Girl' is the grand dame; strong, Black, together," wrote the *New York Amsterdam News* critic Carlos Russell.[88] Rather than depict black mothers as the source of the deterioration of the black family, Franklin illustrates how their feminine strength is vital to the survival of the black community. Franklin explains:

> [Mama Rosie and Mu'Dear are] keeping the family together. They bring food in the house [and] they bring money in. They're self-sufficient, they survive, [and] they work. These are strong women [and] they're not begging anybody for anything. They're right there in the house with her. Then she [Billy Jean] sees her teachers. . . . black women had role models in the community.[89]

As warrior mothers, Mama Rosie and Mu'Dear battle anyone who seeks to destroy their family. They somehow manage to maintain their pride while bearing the burden of providing basic necessities for their family's survival. Franklin's stage directions, in fact, describe Mama Rosie as a larger-than-life warrior mother. "*Mama Rosie's tall, powerful, attractive form looms in the doorway. The room shrinks before this big, black woman*," writes Franklin.[90] Her presence looms so large within the world of the play that the *New York Times* critic Walter Kerr suggested that Mama Rosie, as portrayed by Louise Stubbs, "deserves a play of her own."[91] The theater critic Elenore Lester likewise applauded Franklin's construction of Mu'Dear as "the very embodiment of Woman Power."[92] Despite their discouragement of her dreams, Mama Rosie and Mu'Dear provide the example of feminine strength that Billie Jean needs in order to forge her own path.

Billie Jean's decision to *become* represents a greater need for black girls to define themselves and break the vicious cycles of the past. Mama Rosie bears the scars of emotional trauma and inflicts similar pain on Billie Jean. When Billie Jean performs simple acts of defiance—such as humming while her mother speaks—Mama Rosie threatens to "beat all the black off-a" Billie Jean and hits her on the head with her fist.[93] At the end of the play, however, Franklin reveals the humanity of Mama Rosie by allowing her to express her wounded heart to her own mother. When Mu'Dear chastises Mama Rosie for saving strangers instead of her own family, Mama Rosie responds: "What about my own family? Who in this house ever helped me be something?"[94] With these two simple sentences Mama Rosie reveals the bitterness and sadness that black women experience when not given the opportunity to *become*. Institutional white racism, as well as an early pregnancy, prevented Mama Rosie from pursuing her dream of an education. Mama Rosie blames her mother and her own children for her failure and, as a result, she withholds the affection that Billie Jean so desperately needs. While Mama Rosie refuses to apologize for her behavior, she does eventually concede by asking Billie Jean to keep her informed of her dance career. After a painful goodbye to her daughter, Mama Rosie turns to her own mother for validation. "She know I didn't mean to hurt her, Deah. It just looked like all my children was gon' end up just like me . . . just like me," cries Mama Rosie.[95] Her shedding of tears connects her body and soul, as well as providing a liberating release that helps heal her wounded heart. Billie Jean also becomes liberated through her decision to not only break the cycle of teen pregnancy and abuse, but also defy society's expectations of a black female. *Black Girl* thus privileges black women's spirit, and in so doing disrupts mythologies of black womanhood.

Shauneille Perry's direction of *Black Girl* demonstrated a deep appreciation of Southern culture and a keen understanding of the oppressive forces that hinder black women artists. As a talented actress, director, and writer in her own right, Perry received a bachelor's degree in drama at Howard University, where she performed as a member of Owen Dodson's Howard Players. She then attended the Royal Academy of Dramatic Arts in London as a Fulbright scholar, but quickly transferred to the London Academy after she and other foreign students experienced racial harassment. Perry was among the first blacks to earn a master's degree in directing from the prestigious Goodman Arts Institute in Chicago. While clearly talented, Perry struggled to earn a living directing within mainstream theater. At the beginning of her career, only black and multiethnic theaters such as the Negro Ensemble Company, Rosetta LeNoire's AMAS Repertory Company, and the New Federal Theatre expressed interest in her talent. "For many years Blacks have not been accepted in the theatre. Now that we are doing our own thing—reacting to the rejection—we are being termed separatist. But who started the situation? . . . It's Woodie King and Douglas Turner Ward who call me," said Perry.[96] Her remarks suggest both an awareness of racism within the field of theater and gratitude for black producers who created a space for her to become one of the first black women to direct Off-Broadway.[97]

Perry's personal experiences of trying to succeed as a young black female artist within a white male-dominated theater milieu gave her an intuitive grasp of Billie Jean's predicament. Perry's direction of *Black Girl* included a simple and intimate set that emphasized the importance of religion within the lives of the Southern black women. While the original television version of the play omitted the religious aspects of the play (including Billie Jean at prayer), Perry's production featured a prominent photo of Christ in the home. Franklin remembers photos of Christ as commonplace within Southern homes. Franklin also recalls Perry blocking Mu'Dear to gesture toward the photo of Christ when she states the line, "Oh, my Father, Lord, show us the way."[98] Perry's attention to detail and grasp of character garnered the respect and admiration of Franklin, as well as theater critics. Perry, however, hoped that the success of *Black Girl* and the play's important theme of self-determination would have a more far-reaching effect. "I hope this makes people aware of what Black actresses can do. They can do more than 'Carmen Jones,' 'Anna Lucasta,' and the like," says Perry.[99] The three-dimensional characters created by Franklin allowed black actresses to display their talents (including the gift of dance) and move beyond stereotypical roles. Indeed, the critically acclaimed performances of Minnie Gentry and Esther Rolle as Mu'Dear and Louise Stubbs's performance as Mama Rosie attest to the creative talent of black women.[100] These powerful performances express life imitating art as Billie Jean also resists society's limitations of black women's creative talent. After the success of Perry's Off-Broadway production, *Black Girl* toured Baltimore, Washington, D.C., Chicago, and Detroit before finally becoming a major motion picture.

Despite the success of the theatrical production of *Black Girl*, the 1972 film adaptation received mixed reviews from critics, due in part to Ossie Davis's direction. Producers hired Davis, a well-known actor and civil rights activist, to direct the adaptation even though he had only directed one prior film. Davis explains that his involvement came from a personal need to offer positive representations of black girls. "There are a lot of Black girls out there, including two of my own who need something nice said about them," said Davis.[101] He argued that *Black Girl* represents a "serious film" that not only offers audiences "entertainment," but also "some real information about ourselves as a way of understanding who we are and to use that understanding to protect and defend ourselves as a community."[102] Davis wanted *Black Girl* to become a success that would inspire Hollywood producers to invest in "decent black films."[103] Despite his hopeful optimism, *Black Girl* received only mixed reviews from critics. While the *New York Amsterdam News* reported that the film provided "a faithful expansion of the play,"[104] the mainstream *New York Times* critic Roger Greenspun described the work as "a poor movie that makes it look as if there never had been a good play."[105] Greenspun attributed the failure of the film to Davis's "pedestrian to downright helpless" direction.[106] "Sloppy editing, awkward confrontations, dull and obvious camera technique—all are the director's responsibility," wrote Greenspun.[107] Yet the *New York Amsterdam News* insisted that the "non-exploitative" film warranted merit because it "depicts the uphill fight of a young black girl in the south" and does not rely on "drugs, violence, or frenzied criminality."[108] The reviewer's comments refer to the emergence of blaxploitation films such as Mario Van Peebles's *Sweet Sweetback's Baadasssss Song* and *Shaft*, released just months prior to *Black Girl*. These controversial films targeted black audiences and incited heated debate about whether or not they reflect sentiments of black empowerment or simply reinforce racist stereotypes. Despite Davis's intentions and favorable reviews from the *New York Amsterdam News*, Franklin perceived the film production as exploitative.

Franklin used her agency to resist directing and marketing *Black Girl* as a blaxploitation film. "Efforts were made early in the filming to exploit the material for sex and violence," writes Franklin.[109] She found Davis's decision to have Billie Jean disrobe in front of the camera particularly disheartening, considering the history of exploiting black women's bodies. While Franklin did not manage to have this scene removed from the film, she writes that she did convince producers to cast a dark-skinned actress rather than "a light-bright-damned-near-white actress" to play Billie Jean.[110] The marketing of *Black Girl* as a violent film, however, proved particularly difficult for Franklin to change. "The illustration that appeared in all the papers announcing the coming attraction showed a blow-up of Norma Faye's face, teeth snarling in a mad-dog fashion, threatening Billie Jean with a knife. A moment which had lasted only five seconds had been lifted from the film to represent the supposed essence of the entire play. . . . This was blatant misrepresentation," writes Franklin.[111] After contacting her agent, marketing executives responded by removing the image of the knife. A week later, marketing executives reversed their decision and returned to the original publicity poster. "To exploit or not to exploit, that was the question. Whether it would be more profitable to manipulate the audience's sensibilities so that it craved violence or to let the film speak for itself," writes Franklin.[112] Unfortunately, film executives chose to use the stereotypical image that had a proven track record of financial success: that of a violent, angry, animalistic black woman.

Similar to *Black Girl*, Franklin's next play, *The Enemy* (1973), focuses on the everyday experiences of a poor black girl and the community of black mothers that surrounds her. Franklin adapted *The Enemy* from her short story of the same title published in Woodie King's *Black Short Story Anthology* (1972). While *The Enemy* was never produced and no extant script remains, Franklin remembers that the play follows the basic premise of her short story. Franklin's short story is told from the perspective of a black girl named Addie, who witnesses her mother assault their neighbor, a young domestic worker named Miss Ella Greene. Addie mimics her mother's behavior by bullying Miss Ella's daughter, Dawn. *The Enemy* offers a critique of the emotional and physical cruelty that black women inflict upon one another. The only action that can possibly restore a semblance of sisterhood is Addie's shedding of tears.

Franklin's short story demonstrates that jealousy and hatred are learned behaviors, handed down from one generation of black women to another. Addie's story begins with her excitement at witnessing black women perform their ritual assault of Miss Ella. The black mothers in the rural community step off their porches, call Miss Ella a "witch" for her supposed promiscuity, and encourage their children to run from her and her family. Later, when Addie discovers that Miss Ella has been hiding a daughter in her shack, the women of the community use this information as further ammunition for another attack. As Miss Ella walks home from her labors, a "delegation" of black women confronts her on the street and threatens to burn her home and "bastard" daughter Dawn.[113] With the threat of harm to her daughter lingering in the air, Miss Ella finally asserts herself. "If you're trying to get to hell quick, you shore know what to do, 'cause I'll kill every last one-a you bitches before God get the news. I mean, you better not bother my child," threatens Miss Ella.[114] In complete defiance of the community, Miss Ella allows Dawn to attend school. Despite her ragged clothes and mother's poor position in the community, Dawn's intelligence allows her to gain the admiration of her peers. Addie, who has watched the behavior of the older women, becomes jealous of Dawn's success and views her as her "enemy."[115] From this point on, Addie makes it her mission to destroy Dawn's self-confidence by making her cry.

By the end of the short story, Addie learns the valuable lesson that the shedding of tears is restorative, not disempowering. Following in the footsteps of the adult women, Addie encourages the other students to torment Dawn. While Dawn silently endures their pranks and name-calling, the students eventually break her spirit. She begins to stutter, becomes introverted, and does "not display that love-of-knowledge."[116] After overhearing Dawn sing a haunting song about prayer, Addie is forced to consider her own un-Christian behavior and turns to her mother for advice. "God don't even listen to people like that, prayin' or not. He oughta strike 'em down for dirtyin' His book," Addie's mother responds.[117] Her mother's cruel words do not provide comfort. Rather, Addie continues to feel sick with guilt and shame over her behavior. She finally breaks down and cries, providing an important opportunity for her to reconnect with her own humanity. Her tears heal her wounded heart and empower her to break the cycle of jealousy and hatred toward other black girls. Addie's newfound confidence will perhaps allow her to form more genuine friendships with other black girls.

Four Women: A Play in One Act (1973) explores the black experience in the United States from the perspective of black female college students. Franklin wrote *Four Women* while teaching in the Education Department at Lehman College. "I had some students who wanted to do some plays and they couldn't find any material that they liked. I wrote *Four Women* based upon the Nina Simone song and the young women performed it there at Lehman College. They played the record and they performed their play," remembers Franklin.[118] Simone's "Four Women" (1966) conjures black women's history through Aunt Sarah's tale of labor and pain, mulatto Saffronia's experience of existing "between two worlds" as a product of rape, Sweet Thing's account of sexual trafficking, and Peaches's bitterness and anger over the injustice of it all.[119] Franklin adds a clever twist to Simone's song by reimagining Aunt Sarah, Saffronia, Sweet Thing, and Peaches as roommates attending an integrated college. Sarah now studies "Household Engineering" and refuses to act as a maid to the other girls. Sweet Thing takes "great care" with her appearance and dresses in the height of fashion.[120] Peaches demonstrates knowledge of her ancestry and a toughness that allows her to survive any challenge. While Franklin's Saffronia does not actually appear onstage, her friendship with a liberal white girl named Mae West incites a major conflict within the play. Mae, described as "a hippy-looking, Afro-wigged white girl [with] dashiki, beads, the whole bit," functions as a dramatic foil for Peaches, the leader of the group.[121] Franklin remembers constructing the character Mae and her dialogue based on the conversations her students were having with white female students of the time. *Four Women* privileges these everyday conversations, transforming them into the central conflict that educates and entertains audiences. Mae's insistence that she is the black women's "sister" provides the platform for a historical debate about blackness, enslavement, and the meaning of sisterhood.

Peaches and Sweet Thing use minstrelsy to reveal black women's history of exploitation in the United States and expose the absurdity of Mae's liberal politics. The minstrel mask allows Peaches and Sweet Thing to continue the tradition of using feminine wit and talent to disseminate knowledge about their subject position to black audiences while entertaining white audiences who willfully ignore their humanity.[122] While Peaches and Sweet Thing do not actually put burnt cork on their faces, they use similar performance practices of nineteenth-century black minstrel entertainers. Peaches and Sweet

Thing appear happy to perform their blackness for Mae. However, they perform their blackness in excess, complete with slave dialect, in a rendition of the popular minstrel song "Dixie" (1859). While Mae claps along to the upbeat song, the women deliver a powerful message for their actual intended audience: the black spectators attending *Four Women*. Peaches and Sweet Thing "spring into the room as if they had just received a curtain call" wearing bathing suits and "break out into song."[123] Caught up in the excitement of the musical number, Mae completely misses the satirical message behind their revised version of "Dixie." Daniel D. Emmett's original lyrics include: "In Dixieland where I was born / Early on one frosty mornin', / Look away! Look away! Look away! Dixie Land." Peaches and Sweet Thing reappropriate the anthem of the Confederate Army, changing the lyrics to: "In Dixieland where I was born / Babies die and mothers moan / Get away, get away, get away, Dixieland."[124] Peaches and Sweet Thing's upbeat performance revises the romantic image of the Old South by revealing the pain, sickness, and death associated with enslavement. Their revisionist history privileges black motherhood and the unique trauma they endured as a result of their blackness and femaleness.

Peaches and Sweet Thing's performance also challenges the minstrel-like antics of the actual Mae West, who positioned herself as an ally to black Americans. West was heralded by the black press for her financial contributions to anti-lynching campaigns and for including the talents of popular black entertainers in her films.[125] Yet contemporary scholars question the exploitative nature of West's films. The film scholar Pamela Robertson, for example, argues that West's appropriation of blues-like singing, her stereotypical representations of blacks as maids, and her consigning popular black entertainers to the background produced a "minstrelization" of blackness for white audiences.[126] Franklin's Peaches and Sweet Thing critique not only the motives of white liberal women but also their belief in a "shared" history of gender oppression. In so doing, they reveal an important absence within historical narratives of the United States.

Peaches and Sweet Thing signify to and educate black audiences about the horrors of enslavement by engaging Mae in the verbal game known as the Dozens, in which the players trade insults. Peaches begins their verbal battle by educating Mae about black women's history of rape while working in white homes. Mae distances herself from this history by informing them that she does not "consider" herself white.[127] This revelation provides an opportunity for audiences to consider the many nuances of blackness and its social construction. Peaches and Sweet Thing also consider the possibility that Mae simply "passes" for white until she corrects them. "I refuse to be this white woman you're trying to make me be. . . . I already know that being Black has nothing to do with skin color. No, I'm not passing but I'm just as Black on the inside as you are," says Mae.[128] As a college student, Mae has been taught to reject essentialist notions of blackness, yet she remains ignorant of black

women's experiences in America and how this has shaped the black consciousness. Playing the Dozens allows Sweet Thing and Peaches to express
their simmering anger in a language known only to them and black audiences familiar with the game. Each time Peaches or Sweet Thing offers a
particularly striking insult that disparages Mae's sexual purity, social status,
or ancestry, the girls snap their fingers in celebration. The women begin their
verbal acrobatics by suggesting that Mae "became Black" by getting "run
through by a Mandingo-train."[129] After Mae claims sexual purity and the
status of a lady, Peaches delivers a powerful speech that links their personal
dispute to the larger historical differences between black and white women:

> Black women ain't had time to be no goddamn ladies. We had to
> be WOMEN! . . . You old, white heifers are the biggest whores in the
> world . . . that's why Europe kicked you out. You think they put
> ladies on those ships with all those trashy convicts and puking bums?
> They kept their ladies in Europe . . . sister. If you learned to be a
> lady, *we* taught you, 'cause when you reached these shores those same
> white thighs that has spread syphillis [sic] all over Europe christened
> this country with the V-for-Victory![130]

Peaches takes pride in the labor performed by her ancestors and uses their
experiences to reject antiquated Victorian mores. She rejects a mythology
that positions black women as inherently sexual by creating a revised history
that focuses on the sexual deviancy of European women. In so doing, she
makes the bold claim that Mae descends from disease-ridden refuse. Unwilling to acknowledge this horrific history, Mae insists that black women were
not raped but rather were willing accomplices during enslavement.

No longer entertained by their charade, Peaches adopts black church worship practices and testifies to the humanity of black America. She takes on the
rhythms of a black preacher and asks her congregation, "But Aunt Jemima's
not the only one that's got sweet juice, old Moses is together, too. I wanna'
know have I got a witness?"[131] Sweet Thing responds, "You got a witness.
Uhm humn!"[132] With this exchange Peaches and Sweet Thing validate their
ancestors' humanity and grant them agency to feel sexual gratification. They
then proceed to taunt Mae, insisting that what she really desires is Moses's
"sweet juice," or sexual relationships with black men. Their game comes
to an abrupt end when Mae can no longer defend herself or her ancestors'
actions and leaves the dorm room in defeat. The women's debate remains
important, however, because it demonstrates how black women's history of
exploitation continues to inform present-day relations between black and
white women. Until Mae recognizes black humanity and attends to the intersections of identity, she will never experience sisterhood with black women.

Franklin's musical *The Prodigal Sister* (1974) returns to the theme of black
motherhood through a clever revisioning of the Prodigal Son parable. Franklin

used her "straight" ten-minute play, *The Prodigal Daughter*, which was performed for youth at New York's Lincoln Center and on Bronx street corners, as the basis for her new musical. While no extant script remains, Franklin remembers experimenting with rhymed couplets to tell the struggles of a young unwed mother. Like *The Prodigal Daughter*, *The Prodigal Sister* uses a similar premise for the book but incorporates additional music by Micki Grant.

The Prodigal Sister brings new substance to the parable through entertaining lyrics by Franklin and Grant, lively music that ranges from pop to gospel, and the DoWahs, a chorus of two black women and one man who offer commentary on the action of the play. With the help of the DoWahs, the audience learns that seventeen-year-old Jackie has become pregnant and would rather run away from home than face her father's wrath. After nearly falling victim to the dangers of the city (prostitution, drugs, jail, murder), she finds employment at a casket factory. Her coworker Lucille helps her return to her family by shipping her home in a casket. Once the casket is open and Dr. Patterson discovers her beating pulse, Mother declares Jackie's resurrection a "miracle," and the cast bursts into a spirited song praising the Lord for her safe return.[133] As with the original parable, the eldest child, Sissy, expresses bitterness over the parents' devotion to their lost daughter. Jackie responds to her sister's sadness by singing a poignant song about their childhood, which allows the sisters to reconcile their differences and make way for a contrived happy ending that features the show-stopping finale, "Celebratin." Despite adhering to the conventions of musical theater, *The Prodigal Sister* engages with topical issues of vital concern to the black community including marriage, abortion, teen pregnancy, unemployment, crime, poverty, and the detrimental effects of controlling images.

The Prodigal Sister presents marriage as an oppressive force within black women's lives. Jackie's decision not to marry her unborn baby's father stems from her experience observing her parents' marriage. She reveals her innermost thoughts about marriage through song. "Ain't gonna be nobody's wife 'cause / I ain't gonna be / nobody's . . . washer woman . . . pants patcher . . . maid . . . cleaning lady . . . slipper bringer . . . back scratcher . . . nobody's slave."[134] Jackie perceives marriage as an oppressive institution that reduces black women to black men's slaves. Mother, however, dismisses these concerns as mere "foolish talk" and warns Jackie that her actions will cause her father Jack to soundly "beat" her when he returns home.[135] Jack's behavior upon his arrival from work validates Jackie's concerns. Jack bellows:

> What you women doing freezing your asses for like you don't
> know what to do?
> Git here and git my hat and pail, Sissy, and tell Jackie to come
> take off my shoes.
> You got my bath water ready, Mama?
> (SISSY *and* MOTHER *are running in circles trying to do as papa says.*)[136]

Jack's demands, coupled with Mother's and Sissy's frenzied reactions to obey his orders, reinforces Jackie's critique of marriage. Unfortunately, Jack's word is law in their home, despite Mother's best efforts. For example, upon the discovery of Jackie's pregnancy and after hearing Mother's concern for the safety of their child, Jack harshly declares, "Better dead than unwed."[137] Mother first appeals to Jack's better nature, and then his desire to have a son (or in this case, grandson), before finally realizing that in order to get her daughter back, she must find a way to circumvent his rule. Concern for her daughter forces Mother, for perhaps only the second time in her marriage, to defy Jack and take matters into her own hands. Following the advice of her own mother, Mother confesses that she has squirreled away "a little running-money" so she could leave Jack should he beat or emotionally abuse her.[138] This secret stash of money allows her to hire a spiritualist to help locate Jackie. Mother's confession surprises Jack, who until now believed that he ruled every aspect of his home. While comical, Mother's revelation demonstrates how black women negotiate their interest within oppressive marriages, how motherhood can strengthen black women to take action in their own lives, and how black women pass down survival strategies from one generation to the next.

The Prodigal Sister takes a rather progressive position toward marriage and unwed teen pregnancy, yet retains a conservative view of abortion. When confronted by her gossiping neighbor about her daughter's illegitimate pregnancy, Mother initially denies the rumors because of her fear of what her community will think of her family. Privately, Mother initially condemns Jackie's actions and her refusal to identify and marry the baby's father. "Two months 'fore you due to graduate and you done ruint yourself! . . . They must'a gave me the wrong baby at that hospital where I got you. Cause ain't no way in the world I could'a birthed the likes of you!" Mother laments.[139] While Mother's initial concern centers on education and respectability, her feelings of dismay and disassociation quickly change upon the discovery of Jackie's flight. Mother exerts every effort to bring Jackie home, even convincing Jack to forgive their daughter for the sake of their potential grandson. Reverend Wynn, the spiritual leader of the black community, takes a practical stance toward Jackie's pregnancy, pronouncing "Better unwed than dead" to Jackie's family and neighbors.[140] Franklin explains that Reverend Wynn's pronouncement was not unusual because the black church "has always been very liberated."[141] The possibility of an abortion, however, never becomes a viable solution to Jackie's situation. Rather, abortion appears as an unwise, painful, and potentially deadly option. When Lucille offers to perform an abortion on Jackie, she describes the procedure as follows: "I can get you straight with a clean coathanger. It's gonna hurt like hell, though. And put your life in danger."[142] At the time Franklin wrote *The Prodigal Sister*, abortion in any form was prohibited in thirty U.S. states. Many women were forced to seek medical help from unskilled abortionists such as Lucille. Even when the U.S. Supreme Court struck down abortion restrictions in *Roe v.*

Wade (1973), poor women still could not afford professional medical attention and instead relied on local abortionists in their community. Jackie,
however, does not even consider Lucille's offer. Franklin explains that having
an abortion simply is not done in the black community. "So a girl . . . came
out pregnant, well, what are you gonna do? You better not get rid of no baby,
that's it. You bring that baby into the world and you bring it up," remembers
Franklin.[143] Jackie's decision not to have an abortion not only reflects the
religious underpinnings of the show, but also Franklin's own upbringing.

As an adaptation of a biblical tale, *The Prodigal Sister* offers a religious
message to help protect black girls and strengthen their communities. Jackie's flight to the city sparks conversations about the countless murders of
black women in urban centers. "Young girls [are] found in gulleys [*sic*] and
alleyways everywhere," says Mother.[144] Indeed, upon Jackie's arrival in Big
City she is bombarded with opportunities to pursue dangerous occupations,
including prostitution. Mother meanwhile prays that Jackie might "find
some kinda church" and rely on the Lord to protect her from danger.[145] Once
Jackie is returned home lifeless in a casket, Reverend Wynn delivers a stir-
ring sermon worthy of any church pulpit. "You done thou-shalt-notted one-a
your girls to death / About this motherhood situation. / I heard you practi-
cally had 'em in prison / And you been acting like the warden. / Why, girls
been getting in the family way ever' since / Adam ate that apple in the Garden. / . . . Better unwed than dead, Brother Jack," says Reverend Wynn.[146] His
words provide the chastisement that Jack, and perhaps some members of the
audience, also need to hear. The juxtaposition of Reverend Wynn's sermon of
loving, trusting, and gently guiding black girls and a community surrounding
Jackie's limp body offers a powerful critique to actualize principles taught
in the Bible. Rather than continue to gather in death, the black community
must proactively protect young black girls. This, in turn, will fortify the next
generation of black women and families.

The Prodigal Sister reveals the hidden depths of black womanhood, and
in so doing, disrupts the myth of the superwoman. *The Prodigal Sister* pre-
dates Michele Wallace's black feminist critique of superwoman mythology by
several years yet addresses those very concerns through Lucille's sorrowful
song "Superwoman." At the beginning of the play Lucille appears to embody
the myth of the superwoman: she labors in the cotton fields and kitchens to
support her children, receives a minuscule wage for her efforts, and silently
endures rape and the threat of rape by white employers. When she discovers
that she cannot find an honorable way to pay back her debt to boss Baltimore Bessie and will have to work as a prostitute, she admits that her "armor
must be slipping" and she sings "Superwoman." Theater critics hailed Saun-
dra McClain's performance of "Superwoman" as the highlight of the evening,
with *New York Amsterdam News* critic Jessica B. Harris noting that the song
"almost single-handedly destroys the myth of the strong Black woman."[147]
Through her song Lucille reveals her innermost thoughts as well as the most

painful experiences in her life. She tells of watching her father die due to injuries while working on a train and her inability to grieve after the loss of her newborn baby. She admits that even though she wanted to "scream," she had to remain "a tower of strength" for her children "to lean on."[148] Lucille's emotional song concludes with the final lines: "I'm no longer / Implacable, not unmovable, nor / undaunted. / I'm just a woman / who needs / A tower of strength to lean on."[149] This poignant song reveals the dangers of super-woman mythology. The notion that black women are somehow impervious to pain and suffering and are capable of withstanding arduous labor not only denies their humanity but also alienates them from black men. Lucille desires companionship and pleads for help, but does anyone listen?

The disparity between the critical reception and popularity of *The Prodigal Sister* with the Henry Street Settlement community demonstrated a disconnect between theater critics and everyday black audiences. The purpose of the initial production was to provide free live theater to the Henry Street Settlement, a black community that could otherwise not afford the price of a ticket. While critics described the production as "a slapdash cartoon," the plot as a "series of contrivances," and the dialogue as "sing-songy rhymed couplets," black audiences filled every available seat.[150] "At the performance I attended every seat was taken (with several infants in mothers' arms). The play indulged the audience, and the audience, readily, indulged the play. Its members were demonstrative and appreciative of the evening's entertainment to the point of freely making contributions at the door on their way home," wrote a *New York Times* critic.[151] Black critics also described *The Prodigal Sister* as a vastly entertaining play, yet erroneously found "no messages" about the "plight of black Americans."[152] When the play finally moved Off-Broadway to Theatre DeLys, the production failed to capture audiences, struggled financially, and never made the transition to Broadway as was originally planned. *The Prodigal Sister* remains important, however, because of the meaning it created for black audiences. Jessica B. Harris noted that Franklin's use of blues, gospel, and pop music "lends a kind of familiarity that gives the audience, and particularly the Black audience, easy accessibility to the material."[153] Thus *The Prodigal Sister* did not simply "indulge" the sensibilities of the Henry Street Settlement audience. Rather, the production used a combination of the familiar "black block party and a revival meeting" atmosphere to educate audiences about the need for the black community to protect young women from the dangers of urban living.[154]

The Creation (1975) and *Another Morning Rising* (1976), Franklin's final plays written during the Black Arts Movement, return to her earlier purpose of using drama to teach wisdom literature and literacy. While neither script remains extant, an interview with Franklin provides clues as to the content, form, and purpose of these works. Franklin remembers writing *The Creation* as a nontraditional way to "introduce material" to her students at Lehman College. She explains:

I was always searching for a form with which I could springboard off of into philosophical discussions to try and get the students to at least be introduced to wisdom literature and philosophy-based literature. I felt the only way to do it was to write a play. We were dealing with the origins of life and mythology: the fable story of the garden of Eden, where life came from, how old the earth was, and all these questions that I knew I felt would get people to engage in discussion. To talk about myth and what we believe and what we don't believe.[155]

With *The Creation* Franklin once again turned to the Bible for primary source material. She adapted the first three chapters of the book of Genesis, modernizing its language, in order to educate and engage audiences. Her search for a form led her to incorporate her unique rhyming couplets into the play. Franklin wrote the children's play *Another Morning Rising* while working as an artist-in-residence for the South Carolina Arts Commission. Founded in 1967, the South Carolina Arts Commission sought to make art accessible to all South Carolinians, regardless of their income or proximity to urban centers. Generous funding from the National Endowment for the Arts allowed Franklin to write a script that was used to teach reading fundamentals to children in grades K-12. Franklin remembers developing *Another Morning Rising* with The Company of Us, a theater troupe that then toured the play to children throughout South Carolina. These fragmented clues reveal that while Franklin worked outside of major Black Arts institutions, she continued to value the arts as an instrument for social change.

Franklin used her artistic agency to speak directly to the needs of the entire black community. Yet her plays also reflect particular concern for the survival of poor black women and children. In so doing, she reveals black women's standpoint and the detrimental effects institutional white racism has on black communities. All of her plays feature complex black female protagonists and determined youth who engage in dialogue with each other about issues that negatively impact their community. Central to these debates are concerns about motherhood, black women's silenced history, controlling images, high crime rates, lack of educational opportunities, and the struggles of young black artists. While Franklin does not always offer solutions to these problems, she does provide powerful representations of black women's intellectual thought and feminine strength without in any way reinforcing stereotypes of black womanhood. As a black woman intellectual, she redefined the meaning of liberation by examining the connection between the mind and body. Her emotionally gripping works foster liberatory releases, allowing actors and audiences to touch down and reconnect with their own humanity. From *A First Step to Freedom* to her more recent folk dramas, Franklin's works continue to educate, edify, and entertain audiences.

Epilogue

✦

Let the Search Continue

Sonia Sanchez! Sonia Sanchez! All I ever hear about is Sonia Sanchez!

—Piper McKay Forsgren, 2016

A former colleague of mine once expressed distaste for the methodology used in this book. "I prefer dead people," he quipped. *Why?* Because using written sources as evidence allowed him to avoid the interpersonal nature of oral history. Unfortunately, too many scholars prefer this disembodied approach to research. If anything, the writings of Patricia Hill Collins have taught me the value of conversations among black women. The process of listening to and recording the experiential knowledge of black warrior mothers has enriched my life. I feel both the privilege and responsibility to pass down this heretofore subjugated knowledge to my children, as well as the next genera- tion of artists and scholars. Just as Sonia Sanchez was allowed to overhear the womanist theology expressed by churchwomen of her youth, I look for opportunities for my nine-year-old daughter Piper to overhear me discuss these black women intellectuals. While she is sometimes exasperated by these teachable moments, I also believe that she has gained an appreciation of the tradition of black women writers, as evidenced by her desire to pen her own book. My hope is that one day she, along with the next generation of artists, activists, and intellectuals, will draw strength from these warrior mothers and actively participate in social change.

My conversations with Sanchez and J.e. Franklin, as well as the daughters of Martie Evans-Charles and Barbara Ann Teer, remain indelibly marked in my heart and mind. I now carry the memories of being in Sanchez's home, meeting her son, and watching her receive recognition and respect from the black community as we walked down the streets of Philadelphia. A mutual connection was forged at her local beauty salon as we discussed her efforts to bring black art to the black community. I feel privileged to have been able to laugh and cry in Teer's former office with her daughter Sade Lythcott as she expressed her love for her mother and admiration for her efforts to use art to transform the consciousness of blacks. I discovered Franklin's dynamic

Figure 15. Sonia Sanchez with the author in Philadelphia, 2010. Author collection.

manner of speaking and accepted her invitation to bring my "wounded heart" to the National Black Theatre's production of *Coming to the Mercy Seat: J.e. Franklin's 10 Minute Folk Dramas*. I rarely have a visceral response to productions, yet I found myself shedding actual tears of joy and sadness at her depiction of families in turmoil. I heard the pride in Adrienne Charles's voice as she discussed her mother's legacy and her own great sadness over her mother's passing. These conversations with living, breathing women increased my understanding of black feminist thought and forever changed my relationship with historiography.

I learned that the dramas of Evans-Charles, Franklin, Sanchez, and Teer express feminist attitudes and anticipated a wave of black feminist drama that is often attributed to Ntozake Shange's *for colored girls who have considered suicide/when the rainbow is enuf*. Collectively, their works privilege black motherhood; advocate female aspirations for autonomy; and demonstrate a deep commitment to the survival of black women, men, and children. Their careful negotiation within the male-dominated theatrical community of New York created an important ideological space for later self-identified black feminist dramatists. Readers should know, however, that the literary and artistic achievements of Franklin, Sanchez, Evans-Charles, and Teer did not cease with the decline of Black Arts Movement institutions in 1976.

Evans-Charles continued to enjoy critical success with her plays *African Interlude* (1978), *The Guest House* (c. 1981), *Daisy's Dilemma* (c. 1984), and *Meditation: A Family Affair* (2000). With *African Interlude*, she collaborated with producer Woodie King and director Shauneille Perry to tell the story of a lonely and plain young woman named Clara who must decide whether or not to risk her heart in pursuit of a relationship with an African businessman named Okala. In contrast to her previous works, *African Interlude* includes a controversial subplot about the merits of converting to the Nation of Islam and the efficacy of abortion. The theater critic Kannu praised *African Interlude*, describing the play as "a clash between womans [sic] lib and tradition, verses, the new direction within the Muslim communal system."[1] Despite Evans-Charles having discontinued her own membership with the Nation of Islam, the play remains sympathetic toward the anti-abortion stance of that religious organization and suspicious of sexual liberation as espoused by second wave feminists. She followed up this successful production with the gritty drama *The Guest House*, produced by the 18th Street Playhouse in New York. She then turned her attention back to youth, writing the children's play *Daisy's Dilemma*. While there are no extant manuscripts of this more obscure one-act play, the theater historians Anthony D. Hill and Douglas Q. Barnett describe *Daisy's Dilemma* as "a lighthearted story about how a daisy finds a home of her own."[2] Her next major production, *Meditation*, was produced during the summer of 2000 as a part of King's National Black Touring Circuit at the Henry Street Settlement's Abrons Art Center on the Lower East Side.

Meditation not only marks Evans-Charles's final major work, but also encapsulates her mission as a playwright: to validate the lived experiences of black women in the United States. Working under the title of "Great Black One-Act Plays," *Meditation* was produced alongside plays written by seventeen other legendary African American playwrights, including Langston Hughes, Alice Childress, Pearl Cleage, Amiri Baraka, Ben Caldwell, and Ed Bullins.[3] *Meditation* received positive reviews, with the *New York Amsterdam News* theater critic Eleanor Levine finding the play "quite humorous."[4] Levine writes:

> [Evans-Charles's] middle-class family characters meditate just before rush hour. The daughter is a young high school student who condescends to her mother, but eventually meditates as well. In due time, the entire family, including the bourgeois sister of the mother, is meditating in the living room. It is an amusing play that works with an unclouded idea—New Age comes to the middle class.[5]

Thus, *Meditation* uses comedy to both express black women's subjectivity and mediate intergenerational conflict among black women. In addition to this theatrical endeavor, Evans-Charles secured her legacy as an outstanding playwright and educator by nurturing the next generation of artists as an instructor of speech and drama at Medgar Evers College in Brooklyn. In her private time she continued to write poetry and screenplays, founded her own writing workshops, and worked as a "script doctor" in order to "help people develop their plays"[6] until her death in 2006.

Franklin's prolific playwriting career has continued into the twenty-first century, garnering numerous awards and honors for her experimental works. At last count, Franklin has written about a hundred plays, including *Christchild* (1981), her best-known post-Black Arts Movement drama. This allegorical play features an adolescent boy named Tom who believes he has been blessed with special gifts as a result of his being born on Christmas day. While Tom tries to come to terms with his special gifts, he meets opposition from his alcoholic father Benjamin, a physically abusive man who regularly beats him and his mother Katherine. After seeing the Holy Spirit, Tom decides that he must save his dysfunctional family from ruin by participating in a bear-fighting contest. King's New Federal Theatre mounted the first major production of *Christchild* in 1992 and received mixed reviews from theater critics. The critic Stephen Holden, for example, found little fault with Franklin's powerful depiction of "devastating scenes of family strife," yet he ultimately concluded that *Christchild* had "many flaws."[7] Holden writes:

> Important details of the story are not spelled out clearly enough, the crucial final scenes seem so hastily written that they barely register and the ending is too abrupt. But if "Christchild" finally lacks the polished eloquence of August Wilson's black history plays, it packs the same kind of emotional wallop.[8]

Despite Holden's unflattering dramaturgical comparison with Wilson's Pittsburgh Cycle, audiences and other critics enjoyed Franklin's work. In fact, she received the John F. Kennedy Center's New American Play Award for *Christchild*. In addition to this prestigious award, Franklin's post-Black Arts Movement efforts were rewarded with a National Endowment for the Arts Creative Writing Fellowship (1979) and a Rockefeller Fellowship (1980).

Franklin has begun publishing her works in anthologies and electronic databases. Her efforts to publish *Coming to the Mercy Seat: J.e. Franklin's 10 Minute Folks Dramas (the First Decatet)* (2003), *Precious Memories: The Second Decatet (10 Minute Black Historical Dramas)* (2004), and *To Break Every Yoke* (2013) have made her works much more accessible to a wider audience. More recently, the Alexander Street Press has increased its holdings of her works to a total of 49 plays, making 25 of her previously unpublished plays available in electronic format for millions of readers. Digitizing her works gives a new generation of artists the opportunity to appreciate them. For example, her previously unpublished play *Will the Real White Racism Please Die* will particularly resonate with young activists concerned with institutional white racism. This highly satirical play features Student White, a white student who petitions a university administrator to fire a black female teacher named Professor Terry for teaching the origins of institutional white racism. The administrator, Duke of Ed., responds to this concern by planting drugs in Professor Terry's office in order to get her fired. Black student activists, however, quickly find out about this plan and organize a rally to protest this blatant abuse of power. The one-act play closes with Student White and Duke of Ed. huddled in an office with their guns aimed at the door against student protesters. While amusing, the play also speaks to a growing concern about a lack of diversity in the curricula and faculty in higher education today. *Will the Real White Racism Please Die* is but one example of how Franklin's deeply critical plays continue to find meaning with today's audiences. She continues to teach young artists as an adjunct professor in the Department of Languages and Literature at Touro College, and she actively contributes to the proliferation of African American theater and performance as the founder and producing artistic director of the Blackgirl Theatre Company in New York.

Sanchez continued to teach, write books and plays, and garner critical success as a poet after the decline of the Black Arts Movement. She published one children's book, nearly a dozen books of poetry, and two plays: *I'm Black When I'm Singing, I'm Blue When I Ain't* (written 1982; published 2010) and *2 X 2* (written 2009; published 2010).[9] *I'm Black When I'm Singing*, a play about a mentally ill woman named Reena who uses the gift of song to find meaning in her life, premiered at the OIC Theatre in Atlanta, Georgia, in April 1982. The theater critic Helene C. Smith described *I'm Black When I'm Singing* as "a strong, somewhat oblique, heavy work [. . . that] is strongly worth seeing."[10] The scholar Jacqueline Wood credits this experimental work as an important predecessor to the black feminist works of Robbie McCauley. "[*I'm Black When I'm Singing* utilizes] nontraditional choral figures as devices of community service, anticipating performative communal interaction evident in experimental plays like Robbie McCauley's *Sally's Rape* (1992)," writes Wood.[11] As a performer of poetry, Sanchez is also credited as among the earliest poets and orators who contributed to the development of rap.[12] During the 1980s Sanchez formed a writer's workshop at the Afro-American Historical Museum, in her now hometown of Philadelphia. After a long career as an educator at various institutions, she finally retired from her position as a full professor in the Department of English at Temple University in 1999. Sanchez has received numerous awards and honors for her legacy as a skillful writer, performer, and teacher, including several honorary doctorate degrees, a National Endowment of the Arts Award (1978–79), a Pew Fellowship in the Arts (1993–94), and a lifetime membership in the NAACP (1994).

Sanchez would like readers to know that as with any artist, her work has evolved throughout the years. She continues to resist labels. During the course of our interview, I found that one of the most profound changes in her work is her thoughts on black queer identity. Now in her eighties, she no longer presents queerness as detrimental to the black community. Her more recent book of poetry, *Does Your House Have Lions?* (1997), which includes discussions of queer identity and the AIDS epidemic in the black community, reflects this change. "I've changed myself, and I know if I can change, anyone can. . . . The first time I heard Malcolm, I ducked. I had to learn then what he was saying and listen to him. When people talked about gay people years ago, I laughed like everybody else, right? And then I looked up, and my brother [Wilson Driver Jr.] was gay, and I grabbed his hand and loved him," remembers Sanchez.[13] Her brother's battle with AIDS and eventual death contributed to her personal and artistic growth as a writer. Sanchez is currently writing a memoir about her life and continues to develop her craft as a womanist dramatist and poet.

Teer continued to create ritualistic revivals, conceptualize theories of performance, and receive numerous awards for her artistic direction until her death in 2008. Her most notable theatrical works written after the Back Arts Movement include the ritualistic revival *Softly Comes a Whirlwind, Whispering in Your Ear* (1978), cowritten with Nabii Faison; the musical *Soul Fusion* (1980), also cowritten with Nabii Faison; and the ritualistic drama *The Legacy* (1988), which according to scholar Lundeana Thomas, "represents Teer's first attempts to adapt a traditional script to her vision."[14] Aptly named with the subtitle *A Love Story for the 80's, Softly Comes* tells the story of a talented singer named Isana who lets fear of failure hinder her musical career. Her lover, Ajire, encourages her to perform a benefit concert to raise the $30,000 needed to help free her father, who has been unjustly condemned to fifty years in prison for a shootout with the police during the Harlem Riots. Isana must now embrace her gift in order to liberate her father and metaphorically free herself from self-doubt. The National Black Theatre's production of *Softly Comes* received financial support from the National Endowment for the Arts and the New York State Council on the Arts. *Soul Fusion* and *The Legacy* also played to enthusiastic Harlem audiences, who by then were well-acquainted with Teer's holistic approach to theater. Mindful of the need to cultivate growth with her audiences, Teer continued to develop new approaches to performance, which resulted in her "Pyramid Process of Performing" or "God-Conscious Art." This acting technique involves "unlocking . . . the secret of soul in order to liberate creative energy. Improvisational techniques play heavily into these journeys of discovery," write theater historians Anne Fliotsos and Wendy Vierow.[15] Teer's efforts to celebrate black culture through "God-Conscious Art" received recognition on May 7, 1979, as Mayor Edward Koch declared "National Black Theatre Day" in New York state.

One of Teer's greatest legacies to the development of African American theater is the National Black Theatre Institute of Action Arts, now operated by its CEO, Sade Lythcott. Following Teer's return from Nigeria, a fire broke out and destroyed the building that housed the National Black Theatre. Company member Nabii Faison remembers 1983 as a difficult year for Teer because she was again denied loans because of her race and gender. He recalls Teer approaching fourteen banks with evidence that she could successfully implement her plan to build a cultural center and commercial real estate venture, but she was told, " 'Hell no, I don't want to be a part of it.' "[16] Despite this opposition, Teer persevered and successfully purchased property on 125th Street and Fifth Avenue and built a $10,000,000 theater arts complex known today as the National Black Theatre Institute. Teer's efforts to promote black art in the Harlem community resulted in many awards and honors, including the Monarch Merit Award from the National Council for Culture and Art (1983), AUDELCO Special Achievement Award (1989), "Barbara Ann Teer Day" in East St. Louis, Illinois (1991), commemoration as one of the "Legends of Our Time" in *Essence* magazine (1991), and several honorary doctorate degrees. While the National Black Theatre Institute has made no concrete plans to publish her ritualistic revivals, the theater continues to honor her legacy with images of her throughout the space and a lovely shrine dedicated to her remembrance. Teer's legacy lives on today as her daughter, a bright and savvy businesswoman in her own right, successfully brings her vision into the twenty-first century.

Recovering the works of Evans-Charles, Franklin, Sanchez, and Teer written during the Black Arts Movement is just the beginning. However useful, this book only investigates women playwrights of the Black Arts Movement who worked in Harlem. This book merely scratches the surface of black women's rich tradition of playwriting and theater production during the 1960s and 1970s. The works of Gertrude Greenidge, PJ Gibson, Elaine Jackson, Josephine Jackson, Micki Grant, Hazel Bryant, Aduke Aremu, Barbara Molette, Judi Ann Mason, Jackie Taylor, and Salamu, as well as Adrienne Kennedy, Pearl Cleage, and Alice Childress's relationship to the Black Arts Movement, need further attention. Black women also founded and cofounded successful Black Arts theaters outside of New York City; among them are Doris Derby's Free Southern Theatre, Val Gray Ward's Kuumba Workshop (now Kuumba Theatre), and Jackie Taylor's Black Ensemble Theater Company.

The efforts of black women directors and theater managers have also been excluded from narratives of the Black Arts Movement. While underrepresented in theater scholarship, today the efforts of black women directors such as Shauneille Perry, Gertrude Jeannette, Marjorie Moon, and Vinnette Carroll, as well as theater manger Stella Holt, paved the way for women artists. Carroll, for example, became the first black woman to direct on Broadway with Micki Grant's 1972 musical *Don't Bother Me, I Can't Cope.* Yet her endeavor to create a more inclusive theater community remains an obscure footnote in theater history. Collectively, these directors and managers demonstrate a rich history of black women artists whose efforts profoundly contributed to the development of theater in the United States.

The interdisciplinary nature and international reach of the Black Arts Movement also needs further investigation. While the revolutionary art, poetry, and theater of the era have received some critical attention, scholarship on the relationship between dance and the Black Arts Movement remains stagnant at best. Sustained critical investigations of the relationship between dance and the black aesthetic would provide much-needed information on the ways in which performers embodied (or contested) the varied sentiments of Black Arts ideology. This study merely acknowledges that Evans-Charles and Teer began their artistic careers as dancers, clearly noting that further study is needed. In addition, the Black Arts Movement had international implications. At different points in their careers, leading figures of the Black Arts Movement traveled to the African continent, Cuba, Mexico, and China, gaining further insight into the black diaspora and the global concerns of people of color. An artistic and intellectual exchange occurred and continued upon American soil as artists such as Teer worked with Nigerian artists, musicians, healers, and dancers. Yet few studies discuss the importance of this cultural exchange in one of the most influential American artistic movements of the twentieth century.

Barbara Christian's article "The Race for Theory" provides an important warning that is as relevant today as it was nearly thirty years ago. Black feminist critics must actively read and discuss the works of black women writers, continue to break the silences in historical narratives, and reclaim the works of black women writers or they will continue to be forgotten. Continuing black women's social activist traditions, after all, is an important legacy left behind by Evans-Charles, Sanchez, Franklin, and Teer. *In Search of Our Warrior Mothers: Women Dramatists of the Black Arts Movement* is an S.O.S.

Please reply soon.

Appendix A

✦

Chronology of Barbara Ann Teer

1937   Born Barbara Ann Teer on June 18 in East St. Louis, Illinois, to public school teacher Lila (née Benjamin) and Fred L. Teer, a civics teacher and assistant mayor. When she is a child, the musician Miles Davis occasionally serves as her babysitter. Graduates from Lincoln High School at the age of fifteen. Studies dance at Bennett College (North Carolina), Connecticut College, and University of Wisconsin.

1957   Graduates with a bachelor of arts degree in dance from the University of Illinois. Following graduation, studies drama with Sanford Meisner, Philip Burton, Paul Mann, and Lloyd Richards. She also tours Europe, studying pantomime with Elienne Decroux in Paris and dance with the Vigmont School of Dance in Paris and Berlin. Returns to the United States and performs with the Alvin Ailey and Louis Johnson dance companies.

1961   Dance captain on Broadway for Agnes DeMille in the musical *Kwamina*; knee injury ends her professional dance career; she teaches dance and drama at New York public schools.

1962   Performs in *Raisin' Hell in the Sun*; marries the comedian Godfrey Cambridge.

1963   Performs in *Living Premise*.

1964   Founds the Group Theatre Workshop with actor Robert Hooks; appears in the film *Gone Are the Days*, an adaptation of Ossie Davis's play *Purlie Victorious* (1961).

1965   Performs in *Prodigal Son* and Rosalyn Drexler's *Home Movies*; wins the Vernon Rice/Drama Desk Award for Best Actress for her performance in *Home Movies*; divorces Cambridge and marries Michael Adeyemi Lythcott. Later, her son Michael F. "Omi" Lythcott and her daughter Barbara Ann "Sade" Lythcott are born.

1966   Performs as original cast member of Ron Milner's *Who's Got His Own* and Douglas Turner Ward's *Day of Absence*.

1967   Performs in *The Experiment*, William Inge's *Where's Daddy?* and *Does a Tiger Wear a Necktie?*; directs *The Believers* Off-Broadway; serves as cultural director for the Harlem School of the Arts, a youth workshop.

1967   Leaves the Group Theatre Workshop, now renamed the Negro
        Ensemble Company.

1968   Founds the National Black Theatre; publishes "Needed: A New
        Image" in Floyd B. Barbour's *Black Power Revolt*; featured in "Me
        and My Song," a CBS-TV production; publishes "We Can Be What
        We Were Born to Be" in the *New York Times*.

1969   Appears in the film *Slaves*; directs *The Spook Who Sat by the Door*
        (Chicago); writes numerous articles for *Negro Digest/Black World*
        and the *New York Times*.

1970   Appears in the film *Angel Levine*; directs *The Beauty of Blackness*;
        directs *Five on the Black Hand Slide* Off-Broadway; National Black
        Theatre premieres *The Ritual: To Regain Our Strength and Reclaim
        Our Power*; New York's Channel 13 television station produces *The
        Ritual*.

1971   National Black Theatre tours *The Ritual* in Bermuda, the Apollo
        Theatre, the Association of Black Social Workers' Third Annual Con-
        ference, and numerous eastern colleges and universities, including
        Howard University.

1972   *A Revival: Change! Love Together! Organize!* premieres at the
        National Black Theatre; she receives a Ford Foundation Fellowship
        to travel and conduct research in Africa.

1973   Guest directs the *Black Heritage Series* on CBS-TV; receives first
        annual AUDELCO Recognition Award for Excellence in Theatre;
        travels to Nigeria for four months.

1974   Receives Internal Berlin Award and a Certificate of Achievement
        from the Harlem Chamber of Commerce; travels and conducts
        research in Haiti for two weeks; *Soljourney into Truth: A Ritualistic
        Revival* premieres at the National Black Theatre.

1975   Writes, directs, and coproduces film *Rise: A Love Song for a Love
        People*; serves on the Theatre Committee for the Second International
        Black and African Festival for the Arts (FESTAC); receives National
        Association of Media Women's Black Film Festival Award for Best
        Film, *Rise: A Love Song for a Love People*; *Soljourney* tours Guyana,
        South America, Trinidad, Barbados, and West Indies.

1976   Awarded a major grant from the Lilly Foundation; establishes a
        child-care program for employees of the National Black Theatre.

1977   *Soljourney* performs at the FESTAC in Nigeria.

1978   Creates ritualistic revival *Softly Comes a Whirlwind, Whispering in
        Your Ear* with Nabii Faison; receives Cultural Arts Service Award
        from the Black Spectrum Theatre Company.

1979   *Soljourney* produced at the Beacon Theatre in celebration of the
        tenth anniversary of the National Black Theatre; revivals of *Whirl-
        wind* and *The Ritual* at the National Black Theatre.

1980   Creates musical *Soul Fusion* with Nabii Faison; *Soul Fusion* pre-
            mieres at the Lincoln Center; speaks on Orisha tradition and culture
            at the First World Conference (University of Ife) in Nigeria.

1982   Revival of *Soul Fusion* produced by the National Black Theatre; *Soul
            Fusion* wins AUDELCO Award for Outstanding Musical Creator and
            Outstanding Male in a Musical.

1983   Receives Monarch Merit Award from Special Council for Culture
            and Art for contributions to the performing and visual arts; receives
            the National Black Treasure Award from the Hamilton Arts Center
            for outstanding contribution to African American theater.

1984   Publishes "Reinvention of the People" in the *New York Amster-
            dam News*.

1985   Featured in the publication of *Black Masks* and *The Gap*.

1988   Creates first ritualistic drama, *The Legacy*.

1989   Receives Kwanza Expo Award.

1979   Mayor Edward Koch declares May 7 to be "National Black Theatre
            Day" in New York state.

1980   Returns to Nigeria to share the National Black Theatre's cre-
            ative work.

1983   Purchases property on 125th Street and Fifth Avenue after a fire
            destroys theater space on 137th Street; builds $10,000,000 theater
            arts complex known today as the National Black Theatre Institute
            of Action Arts; receives Monarch Merit Award from the National
            Council for Culture and Art.

1984   Receives National Council for Culture and Art Award.

1987   Receives recognition from the Harlem Women's Committee/New
            Future Foundation, Inc.

1989   Receives Kwanza Expo Award and AUDELCO Special Achieve-
            ment Award.

1991   "Barbara Ann Teer Day" declared in East St. Louis, Illinois; honored
            in *Essence* magazine's "Legends of Our Time" issue.

c. 1995   Receives honorary doctorate degrees from the University of Roch-
            ester and University of Southern Illinois; henceforth refers to herself
            and is known by colleagues as "Dr. Teer."

2008   Continues to serve as executive director of the National Black The-
            atre until her death on July 21. The National Black Theatre continues
            to serve as a vital cultural institution for the black community of
            Harlem.

Appendix B

✦

Chronology of Martie Evans-Charles

1936	Born Martha Evans on July 30 in Harlem, New York City, to actress and public school teacher Estelle (née Rolle) and architect Walter Alexander Evans. Writes first play, *Every Inch a Lady*, while in junior high school. Graduates from George Washington High School.
c. 1957	Receives a bachelor of arts degree in speech from Fisk University (Nashville, Tennessee).
c. 1959	Receives a master's degree in speech pathology from Hunter College, her mother's alma mater; dances alongside her maternal aunt, Esther Rolle, in Asadata Dafora's African dance troupe Shogola Oloba; teaches at PS 156 in Harlem before becoming an assistant professor of theater and speech at Medgar Evers College in Brooklyn and the City College in Manhattan.
1960	Daughter Adrienne Charles born; Adrienne later performs as Ella during stage readings of *Job Security* and on New York's Channel 5 *Black News* television show; Adrienne attends rehearsals at the Negro Ensemble Company, observing her mother's acting.
1967–72	Attends New Lafayette Theatre rehearsals before becoming an actress, playwright, and audience developer for the theater.
1968–72	Participates in the New Lafayette Theatre's Black Theatre Workshop, headed by Ed Bullins.
1969	Writes *Where We At?*; George Lee Miles directs premiere of her play *Black Cycle* at the Black Theatre Workshop; enrolls daughter Adrienne in the Nation of Islam's Muhammad University Number 7; joins the Nation of Islam.
1970	Publishes *Job Security*; Black Magicians (an offshoot of the Black Theatre Workshop) premiere *Job Security* at the Third World Theatre; Black Theatre Workshop premieres *Jamimma*.
1970–71	Performs as "Eitram" in the New Lafayette Theatre's ritual, *The Devil Catchers*.
1971	Performs as "Toni" in Ed Bullins's *The Fabulous Miss Marie*; Black Theatre Workshop premieres *Black Cycle*; Black Magicians premiere *Job Security* at the Third World Theatre.

1972   Publishes *Black Cycle* in Woodie King and Ron Milner's *Black Drama Anthology*; participates in the Negro Ensemble Company's Playwright Workshop; Negro Ensemble Company's Playwright Workshop premieres *Where We At?* as a series of "Works in Progress"; cofounds the Black Playwright's Workshop with Richard Wesley; Shauneille Perry directs *Jamimma* at Henry Street Settlement's New Federal Theatre.

1973   Awarded a $9,500 playwriting grant (worth $54,750 in 2017 dollars) from the Rockefeller Foundation; joins the prestigious Frank Silvera Writers' Workshop; speaks at symposium, "The Dilemma of the Black Playwright," with Ed Bullins, Richard Wesley, and Charles Gordone; the Afro-American Studio Theatre Centre produces *Black Cycle*.

1973–74   Kuumba Workshop (Chicago) produces *Black Cycle*; Afro-American Studio for Acting and Speech produces *Black Cycle*.

1974   Writes musical *Asante*; publishes *Job Security* in James V. Hatch's edited anthology *Black Theatre U.S.A.: Forty-Five Plays by Black Americans 1847–1974* under the subheading "Modern Black Women."

c. 1975   Writes *Friends*, an adaptation of Rosa Guy's young adult novel *The Friends* (1973); leaves the Nation of Islam after the death of Elijah Muhammad; publishes "The Confrontation" in *Impressions: A Black Arts and Culture Magazine*; New Federal Theatre produces staged readings of *Friends*; Marjorie Moon's Billy Holiday Theatre produces *Jamimma*; University Players at Elizabeth City State University (North Carolina) produce *Job Security*.

1976   Harlem Performance Center stages *Jamimma*.

1978   Shauneille Perry directs *African Interlude* at Henry Street Settlement's New Federal Theatre.

1982   18th Street Playhouse premieres *The Guest House*.

c. 1984   Writes one-act children's play *Daisy's Dilemma*.

1992   Barbara Ann Teer's National Black Theatre produces staged reading of *Friends* as a part of "Women's Reading Series."

2000   Woodie King Jr.'s National Black Touring Circuit produces comedy *Meditation: A Family Affair* for the "Great Black One-Act Plays" festival at Henry Street Settlement's Abrons Art Center.

2006   Leads playwriting workshops and writes screenplays and poetry until her death on December 14.

Appendix C

✦

Chronology of Sonia Sanchez

1934   Born Wilsonia "Sonia" Benita Driver on September 9 in Birmingham, Alabama, to Lena and Wilson L. Driver. During her youth she marries Albert Sanchez, a Puerto Rican immigrant, and keeps his surname for her professional name.

1935   Mother dies; paternal grandmother, "Mama," raises her and sister, Anita Patricia.

1940   Mama dies.

1943   Moves to Harlem with father and stepmother.

1951   Graduates from high school.

1955   Receives a bachelor of arts degree in political science from Hunter College in New York.

1956   Studies poetry with Louise Bogan at New York University.

1957   Daughter Anita born in New York.

1962   Contributes to the literary magazine *Minnesota Review*.

1963–65 Teaches at the Downtown Community School; joins the New York branch of the Congress of Racial Equality (CORE).

1964   Works alongside community artists and adolescents at Harlem Youth Opportunities Unlimited.

1965   Joins Amiri Baraka's Black Arts Repertory Theatre/School.

1965–67 Teaches at the Downtown Community School (San Francisco).

1967–69 Joins Amiri Baraka, Ed Bullins, Marvin X, and Sarah Fabio at San Francisco State College to help found the first black studies program in the United States and teaches black literature and creative writing.

1968   Publishes *The Bronx Is Next*; marries the poet Etheridge Knight; sons Morani and Mungu are born in San Francisco.

1968–69 Staff worker at the Mission Rebels in Action (San Francisco).

1969   Publishes first book of poetry, *Homecoming*; travels to Bermuda.

1969–70 Teaches "The Black Woman" at the University of Pittsburgh.

1970   Publishes *Sister Son/ji*; *Sister Son/ji* premieres at Concept East (Detroit); Theatre Black (New York) premieres *The Bronx Is Next*; publishes book of poetry, *We a BaddDDD People*; contributes to *Black World*; divorces Etheridge Knight.

1970–71   Teaches at Rutgers University (New Jersey).
1971   Publishes *Dirty Hearts*; Negro Ensemble Company produces *Sister Son/ji* as a series of "Works in Progress"; New York's Public Theatre premieres *Dirty Hearts*; edits and publishes the poetry of Countee Cullen Workshop students in an anthology, *360 Degrees of Blackness Coming at You*; publishes two books of poetry, *Ima Talken bout the Nation of Islam* and *It's A New Day: Poems for Young Brothas and Sistuhs*; travels to Jamaica and meets Amy Garvey; records *A Sun Lady for All Seasons* with Smithsonian Folkways Recordings.
1971–73   Teaches at Manhattan Community College.
1972   Publishes *Malcolm/Man Don't Live Here No Mo'*; New York Shakespeare Festival produces *Sister Son/ji*.
1972–73   Teaches at Amherst College (Massachusetts).
1972–75   Teaches at Amherst College; joins the Nation of Islam and heads the Office of Human Development in Chicago.
1973   Publishes children's book *The Adventures of Fat Head, Small Head, and Square Head*; publishes two books of poetry, *A Blues Book for Blue Black Magical Women* and *Love Poems*; publishes a book of fiction, *We Be Word Sorcerers: 25 Stories by Black Americans*; travels to China.
1974   Publishes children's book, *The Adventures of Fathead and Squarehead*.
1975   Publishes *Uh, Uh; But How Do It Free Us?*; Northwestern University's Black Folk's Theatre premieres *Uh, Uh; But How Do It Free Us?*
1976   Teaches at the University of Pennsylvania; performs audio recording of her poetry on *Black Box 3*.
1977   Teaches in the English Department at Temple University (Philadelphia).
1977–78   Founds a poetry writer's workshop at YM/YWHA in Philadelphia.
1978   Publishes book of poetry, *I've Been a Woman*.
1978–79   Receives National Endowment of the Arts Award.
1979   Children perform *Malcolm/Man Don't Live Here No Mo'* at ASCOM Community Center (Philadelphia).
1982   Jomandi Productions stages *I'm Black When I'm Singing, I'm Blue When I Ain't* at OIC Theatre (Atlanta).
1983   Publishes book of poetry, *A Sound Investment*; publishes *Crisis in Culture: Two Speeches by Sonia Sanchez*.
1984   Publishes book of poetry, *Homegirls and Handgrenades*; promoted to full professor at Temple University.
1985   Stages *I'm Black When I'm Singing, I'm Blue When I Ain't* at Virginia Commonwealth University, produced as partial fulfillment of M.F.A thesis; awarded M.F.A. degree from Virginia Commonwealth University.
1986   Publishes *Generations, Selected Poetry: 1969–1985*.

1987 Publishes book of poetry, *Under a Soprano Sky*; receives honorary doctorate from Trinity College (New York); appointed Laura Carnell Professor at Trinity College.

1988 Receives the State of Pennsylvania Governor's Award for Excellence in the Humanities.

1989 Receives Peace and Freedom Award from Women's International League for Peace and Freedom; receives Paul Robeson Social Justice Award from Bread and Roses; travels to Norway with the writer James Baldwin; serves as distinguished poet in residence at Spelman College (Atlanta).

1993–94 Receives a Pew Fellowship in the Arts.

1994 Becomes a lifetime member of the National Association for the Advancement of Colored People.

1995 Writes *Black Cats Back and Uneasy Landings*; publishes book of poetry, *Wounded in the House of a Friend*; performs "Stay on the Battlefield" on compact disc *Sweet Honey in the Rock: Sacred Ground*; performs song/poem "Sometimes I Wonder" on the compact disc *All That and a Bag of Words* with D Knowledge; featured in the film *A Furious Flowering of African-American Poetry, 1994*.

1997 Publishes book of poetry, *Does Your House Have Lions?*; featured on Sinbad's *Vibe Show*.

1998 Publishes book of poetry, *Like the Singing Coming Off the Drums: Love Poems*; featured on *The Cosby Show*; receives honorary doctorate from Temple University.

1999 Publishes book of poetry, *Shake Loose My Skin: New and Selected Poems*; retires from Temple University.

2000 Performs poetry on Russell Simmons's *Def Poetry Jam*; performs "When URE Heart Turns Cold" on the compact disc *The Rose That Grew from Concrete*; performs "Wounded in the House of a Friend (Set No. 2)" on the compact disc *Our Souls Have Grown Deep like the Rivers: Black Poets Read Their Work*.

2001 Teaches as visiting professor at Howard University (Washington, D.C.).

2002 Receives honorary doctorate from Ursinus College (Pennsylvania).

2003 Teaches as visiting professor at Bucknell University (Pennsylvania).

2004 Receives the Harper Lee Award for Alabama Distinguished Writers; records poetry *Full Moon of Sonia Sanchez* on compact disc; receives honorary doctorate from Haverford College (Pennsylvania).

2005 Performs poetry at Russell Simmon's *Def Poetry Jam*; teaches as visiting professor at Columbia University (New York); featured in *A Furious Flower II*; performs poetry on compact disc *Monnette Sudler: Meeting the Spirits*.

2006 Performs "Humbled" with Ursula Rucker on the compact disc *Ursula Rucker: Māāt Mama*.

2009   Writes 2 X 2.
2010   Publishes 2 X 2.
2016   Writing an autobiography and speaking at conferences and public
         events.

Appendix D

✦

Chronology of J.e. Franklin

1937   Born Jennie Elizabeth Franklin on August 10 to domestic worker
        Mathie (née Randle) and small business owner Robert Franklin.
1964   Receives bachelor of arts degree from the University of Texas at
        Austin; moves to New York City, attends the Union Theological
        Seminary, and lives above Judson's Poet's Theatre; develops passion
        for the theater after witnessing Barbara Ann Teer and James Ander-
        son perform in *Home Movies*; during the summer works with the
        Mississippi Freedom Democratic Party and teaches at the Freedom
        School (Carthage, Mississippi); helps build the Sharon Waite Com-
        munity Center (Harmony, Mississippi); writes and directs *A First
        Step to Freedom* for the Sharon Waite Community Center; marries
        Lawrence Seigel, and later her son Malike and daughter N'Zinga
        are born.
1964–65 Youth director for the Neighborhood House (Buffalo, New York).
1965   Writes *The In-Crowd: A Rock Opera*.
1966   Writes *Two Flowers*; the New Feminist Theatre produces *Two
        Flowers*.
1967   Woodie King Jr. produces the premiere of *The In-Crowd: A Rock
        Opera* for the Mobilization for Youth theater division; King's
        production of *The In-Crowd: A Rock Opera* is presented at the Inter-
        national Youth Festival in Montreal, Canada.
1967–68 Works as an analyst in the U.S. Office of Economic Opportunity.
1969   Writes *Mau Mau Room*; Negro Ensemble Company Workshop
        produces the premiere of *Mau Mau Room* at St. Mark's Playhouse,
        Shauneille Perry directs; joins prestigious Harlem Writers Guild and
        writes *Black Girl*; script consultant George Houston Bass helps edit
        Black Girl for televised production on Boston's WGBH.
1969–75 Teaches at the CUNY-Lehman College as a lecturer in education and
        writes several plays for her students.
1970s   Director of the New Federal Theater's Zora Neale Hurston Writer's
        Workshop.
1970   Changes title of *Mau Mau Room* to *Throw Thunder at This House*.

1971   Woodie King Jr.'s New Federal Theatre produces *Black Girl* at St.
            Augustine Chapel, Shauneille Perry directs; King and Perry present
            Black Girl Off-Broadway at Theatre DeLys before touring the
            production in Baltimore, Washington, D.C., Chicago, and Detroit;
            receives Media Women Award; receives Drama Desk Award for Most
            Promising Playwright; Dramatist Play Service publishes *Black Girl*.

c. 1971   Writes *The Prodigal Daughter* for street theater project performed on
            Bronx street corners and at Lincoln Center; writes screenplay for film
            adaptation of *Black Girl*, Ossie Davis directs.

1972   World premiere of *Black Girl* (film) at the Cinerama Penthouse
            on Broadway; changes title of *Throw Thunder at This House* to
            Cut Out the Lights and Call the Law; publishes short story, "The
            Enemy," in Woodie King Jr.'s collection, *Black Short Story Anthology*.

1973   Adapts "The Enemy" for the stage; writes *Four Women* for students
            to perform at CUNY-Lehman College.

c. 1973   Writes book to *The Prodigal Sister* and collaborates with Micki
            Grant on music.

1974   Receives the Institute for the Arts and Humanities Dramatic Arts
            Award, Howard University; writes *MacPilate*; Woodie King Jr.'s New
            Federal Theater produces *The Prodigal Sister* at Henry Street Play-
            house and Off-Broadway at Theatre DeLys, Shauneille Perry directs.

1975   Writes *The Creation* for students at CUNY-Lehman College.

1976   Awarded funding from the National Endowment for the Arts to
            work with the South Carolina Arts Commission (uses theater to
            teach literacy to children grades K-12); writes *Another Morning Ris-
            ing* for the theater troupe, The Company of Us, to tour throughout
            South Carolina; Samuel French publishes *The Prodigal Sister*.

1977   Publishes *Black Girl: From Genesis to Revelations*.

1978   Receives the Better Boys Foundation Playwriting Award and Ajabei
            Children's Theater Annual Award; writes *The Hand-Me-Downs*.

1978–79   Teaches at Skidmore College (New York) and directs *Cut Out the
            Lights and Call the Law* for university season.

1979   Receives a National Endowment for the Arts Creative Writing
            Fellowship.

1980   Receives a Rockefeller Fellowship; writes *Guess What's Coming to
            Dinner* and *Will the Real South Please Rise?*

1981   Writes *Christchild*.

1982–89   Resident playwright at Brown University (Providence, R.I.).

1983   Writes *Where Dewdrops of Mercy Shine Bright*.

1984   Changes title of *Cut Out the Lights and Call the Law* to *Miss Hon-
            ey's Young'uns*; the McGinn-Cazale Second Stage Theater produces
            Black Girl as part of its "American Classics" series.

1985   Writes *Two Mens'es Daughter*.

1989   Revises *Christchild*; writes *Grey Panthers* and revises it three times.

1990s	Faculty member at the Harlem School of the Arts; founds and serves as producing artistic director of Blackgirl Ensemble Theatre, Inc.
1990	Visiting assistant professor in the Department of Theatre Arts at the University of Iowa.
1992	Woodie King Jr.'s New Federal Theatre produces *Christchild*; receives John F. Kennedy Center New American Play Award for *Christchild*.
1994	Publishes *Christchild* in Marisa Smith's edited anthology *Women Playwrights: The Best of 1993*.
2002	*Wonderland* premieres at the University of Iowa.
2003	Publishes *Coming to the Mercy Seat: J.e. Franklin's 10 Minute Folk Dramas (The First Decatet)*.
2004	Publishes *Precious Memories: The Second Decatet (10 Minute Black Historical Dramas)*.
2010	National Black Theatre produces *Coming to the Mercy Seat: J.e. Franklin's 10 Minute Folk Dramas* at Legros Cultural Arts, Chantal M. Legros and Charles Murray direct.
2013	Publishes *To Break Every Yoke*, a collection of four plays, including *Freedom Rider*.
2014	Performances of *Freedom Rider* play to sold-out houses at the Dwyer Cultural Center.
2015	Guest speaker, along with Ntozake Shange, at the Negro Ensemble Company's "Year of the Woman: Plays in Reading" series; Negro Ensemble Company produces *Miss N'Victas*.
2016	Adjunct professor in the Department of Languages and Literature at Touro College (New York); director of drama ministry at Harlem's St. James Presbyterian Church; edits forthcoming book, *Will the Real White Racism Please Die*; continues to serve as producing artistic director of Blackgirl Ensemble Theatre, Inc.
2017	Alexander Street Press makes twenty-five of her previously unpublished plays available in electronic format, including *Blackbird; Dice's Boys; The Eagle Flies on Friday; The Gift; I Reckon That's Why They Call Us Colored, Bless Their Hearts; Just like Some Kind'a Minstrel-Boy, King of Glory; A Lesson for Cameron; Library Lions; Little Jo; Mannish Boychild; Miss Hagar: The Oldest Living Relative; Miss N'Victas; The Onliest One That Can't Go Nowhere; The Parables of Jesus in Spirit-Rap; The Phoenix Alights; Racism 101; The Silent One; Slappy's Sweet Secret; Take the Case-a Sampson; Trial at Sayville; Visiting John Lee; Whistling Girls and Crowing Hens; Will the Real South Please Rise?; Will the Real White Racism Please Die.*

Preface

1. Sonia Sanchez, *We a BaddDDD People* (Detroit, Mich.: Broadside, 1970), 15–16.

Introduction

The epigraph is from Alice Walker, *In Search of Our Mothers' Gardens: Womanist Prose* (San Diego: Harcourt Brace Jovanovich, 1983), 9.

1. Barbara Christian, "The Race for Theory," *Cultural Critique* 6 (1987): 53, 62.

2. Melissa Chan, "Playwright Outraged after White Actor Cast as Martin Luther King in 'The Mountaintop,'" *New York Daily News*, November 11, 2015.

3. LeRoi Jones, "The Revolutionary Theatre," *Liberator* (July 1965): 4–5.

4. The term "intersectionality" was coined by Kimberle Crenshaw in her 1989 essay "Demarginializing the Intersection of Race and Sex: A Black Feminist Critique of Antidiscrimination Doctrine, Feminist Theory and Antiracist Politics." The essay identifies how interconnected social identities contribute to specific forms of discrimination. She then demonstrates how these discriminatory practices are ineffectually dealt with in antidiscrimination law in the United States.

5. Rebecca Daniels, *Women Stage Directors Speak: Exploring the Influence of Gender on Their Work* (Jefferson, N.C.: McFarland, 1996), 131–32.

6. Alice Walker, introduction to *In Search of Our Mothers' Gardens: Womanist Prose* (San Diego: Harcourt Brace Jovanovich, 1983), xi.

7. Despite the fact that Sonia Sanchez worked alongside Amiri Baraka to help found the first black studies program in the United States, Komozi Woodard's *A Nation within a Nation: Amiri Baraka (LeRoi Jones) and Black Power Politics* (1999) only references her one time in a book of over 300 pages.

8. James Edward Smethurst, *The Black Arts Movement: Literary Nationalism in the 1960s and 1970s* (Raleigh, N.C.: University of North Carolina Press, 2005), 85.

9. Kimberly Springer, *Living for the Revolution: Black Feminist Organizations, 1968–1980* (Durham, N.C.: Duke University Press, 2001), 106.

10. Springer, *Living for the Revolution*, 107.

11. Cheryl Clarke, *After Mecca: Women Poets and the Black Arts Movement* (New Brunswick, N.J.: Rutgers University Press, 2006), 93.

12. Clarke, *After Mecca*, 52.

13. Theoretical development of the Black Arts Movement began prior to Amiri Baraka's opening of the Black Arts Repertory Theatre/School in 1965. Theater historians such as Mike Sell credit the Umbra Poets Workshop (1962–65), a group of young black artists who met in the Lower East Side of New York, with being one of the more important artistic communities that spawned the theoretical development of the Black Arts Movement.

14. George Lee Miles, interview with author, July 12, 2010.

15. Nabii Faison, interview with author, July 13, 2010.

16. Kellie Jones, "Black West: Thoughts on Art in Los Angeles," in *New Thoughts on the Black Arts Movement*, ed. Lisa Gail Collins and Margo Crawford (New Brunswick, N.J.: Rutgers University Press, 2006), 65.

17. Sonia Sanchez, interview with author, June 30, 2010.

18. Patricia Hill Collins, *Black Feminist Thought: Knowledge, Consciousness, and the Politics of Empowerment* (Boston: Unwin Hyman, 1990), 30.

19. Collins, *Black Feminist Thought*, 5.

20. Collins, *Black Feminist Thought*, 13.

21. Mae Gwendolyn Henderson, "Speaking in Tongues: Dialogics, Dialectics, and the Black Woman Writer's Literary Tradition," in *African American Literary Theory: A Reader*, ed. Winston Napier (New York: New York University Press, 2000), 350.

22. Collins, *Black Feminist Thought*, 92.

23. Darlene Clark Hine, introduction to *The Face of Our Past: Images of Black Women from Colonial America to the Present*, ed. Kathleen Thompson and Hilary Mac Austin (Bloomington: University of Indiana Press, 1999), ix; emphasis in original.

24. While the content of the *Moynihan Report* (1965) was widely contested after its release, the report remains important because it reflects a moment when the United States federal government supported efforts to investigate and take action against poverty within urban black communities.

25. Daniel Patrick Moynihan et al., *The Negro Family: The Case for National Action* (Washington, D.C.: Government Printing Office, 1965), 30.

26. Moynihan, *The Negro Family*, 35.

27. Karla F. C. Holloway, *Moorings and Metaphors: Figures of Cultures and Gender in Black Women's Literature* (New Brunswick, N.J.: Rutgers University Press, 1992), 87.

28. Michele Wallace, *Black Macho and the Myth of the Superwoman* (New York: Dial, 1978), 107.

29. Smethurst, *Black Arts Movement*, 81.

30. Sanchez, interview with author, June 30, 2010.

31. LeRoi Jones, "Revolutionary Theatre," 4–5.

32. Joanne Veal Gabbin, "The Southern Imagination of Sonia Sanchez," in *Southern Women Writers: The New Generation*, ed. Tonette Bond Inge (Tuscaloosa: University of Alabama Press, 1990), 180.

Chapter 1

The title quotation, "Set Your Blackness Free," is from *The Ritual*, written and directed by Barbara Ann Teer, performed by the National Black Theatre, VHS, recorded by the New York City Public Broadcasting Company's *Soul* program, February 2, 1970. Thanks to the National Black Theatre Archives for access to this recording. The epigraph is from Sonia Sanchez, "Barbara Ann Teer: 1937–2008," *American Theatre*, October 2008, 20.

1. There are no extant scripts of Barbara Ann Teer's *A Ritual to Regain Our Strength and Reclaim Our Power* (1970). Special thanks to the National Black Theatre for providing a filmed recording of the production.

2. Smethurst, *Black Arts Movement*, 104.

3. Lundeana Thomas, "Barbara Ann Teer: From Holistic Training to Liberating Minds," in *Black Theatre: Ritual Performance in the African Diaspora*, ed. Paul Carter Harrison, Victor Leo Walker II, and Gus Edwards (Philadelphia: Temple University Press, 2002), 363–67.

4. Smethurst, *Black Arts Movement*, 15.

5. Paul Carter Harrison, *The Drama of Nommo* (New York: Grove, 1972), 85.

6. Harrison, *Drama of Nommo*, 85.

7. Teer, "Letter," undated press release, National Black Theatre Archives.

8. Thomas, "Barbara Ann Teer," 368.

9. Thomas, "Barbara Ann Teer," 368.

10. Barbara Ann Teer, "The Black Woman: She Does Exist," *New York Times*, May 14, 1967.

11. Teer, "Black Woman."

12. Teer, "Black Woman."

13. Barbara Ann Teer, "Needed: A New Image," in *The Black Power Revolt: A Collection of Essays*, ed. Floyd B. Barbour (Boston: Porter Sargent, 1968), 219.

14. Teer, "Needed," 219.

15. Barbara Ann Teer, "The Great White Way Is Not Our Way—Not Yet," *Negro Digest*, April 1968, 29.

16. Teer, "Great White Way," 29.

17. Barbara Ann Teer, "We Can Be What We Were Born to Be," *New York Times*, July 7, 1968.

18. Harold Cruse, *Rebellion or Revolution?* (New York: William Morrow, 1968), 112.

19. Teer, "We Can Be," emphasis added.

20. Barbara "Sade" Lythcott, interview with the author, July 13, 2010.

21. Lythcott, interview, July 13, 2010.

22. Lythcott, interview, July 13, 2010.

23. Charlie L. Russell and Barbara Ann Teer, "Barbara Ann Teer: We Are Liberators Not Actors," *Essence*, March 1971, 59.

24. Rebecca Daniels, *Women Stage Directors Speak: Exploring the Influence of Gender on Their Work* (Jefferson, N.C.: McFarland, 1996), 132.

25. Daniels, *Women Stage Directors Speak*, 132–33.

26. Daniels, *Women Stage Directors Speak*, 132.

27. Jessica B. Harris, "The Sun People of 125th Street: The National Black Theatre," *The Drama Review* 16, no. 4 (1972): 40.

28. Karen Malpede and Barbara Ann Teer, "Barbara Ann Teer," in *Women in Theatre*, ed. Karen Malpede (New York: Limelight Editions, 1985), 225.

29. Russell and Teer, "Barbara Ann Teer," 59.

30. Russell and Teer, "Barbara Ann Teer," 59.

31. Russell and Teer, "Barbara Ann Teer," 59.

32. Nabii Faison, interview with the author, July 13, 2010.

33. Faison, interview, July 13, 2010.

34. Malpede and Teer, "Barbara Ann Teer," 225.

35. Ted Wilson, "Woodie: The King Maker: A Conversation with Woodie King, Jr.," *Black Renaissance* 8, nos. 2–3 (Summer 2008): 110.

36. Tony Best, "Barbara Ann Teer and the Liberators," *New York Amsterdam News*, November 12, 1975.

37. Harris, "Sun People," 40.

38. Faison, interview, July 13, 2010.

39. Harris, "Sun People," 41.

40. Mance Williams, *Black Theatre in the 1960s and 1970s: A Historical-Critical Analysis of the Movement* (Westport, Conn.: Greenwood, 1985), 52.

41. Russell and Teer, "Barbara Ann Teer," 57, emphasis in original.

42. Barbara Ann Teer, "Ritual and the National Black Theatre," in *Women in American Theatre*, ed. Helen Krich Chinoy and Linda Walsh Jenkins (New York: Theatre Communications Group, 1987), 35.

43. Best, "Barbara Ann Teer and the Liberators."

44. Barbara Ann Teer, "A Standard of Criticism for Black Art," undated press release, National Black Theatre Archives.

45. Teer, "Standard of Criticism."

46. Peter A. Bailey, "Annual Round-Up: Black Theatre in America: Metropolitan New York," *Black World*, April 1971, 6.

47. P. Olisanwuche Esedebe, *Pan-Africanism: The Idea and Movement, 1776–1991* (Washington, D.C.: Howard University Press, 1994), 4.

48. Barbara Ann Teer, "Letter by Barbara Ann Teer, Founder/Producing Director, National Black Theatre," press release, n.d., National Black Theatre Archives.

49. Teer, "Letter."

50. Carlton W. Molette II, "The Way to Viable Theatre?: Afro-American Ritual Drama," *Black World*, April 1973, 7–8.

51. Molette, "Way to Viable Theatre," 7, emphasis added.

52. Russell and Teer, "Barbara Ann Teer," 58.

53. Thomas Johnson, review of *Soljourney into Truth*, by Barbara Ann Teer, dir. by Barbara Ann Teer, National Black Theatre, New York, *New York Times*, May 11, 1974.

54. Barbara Ann Teer, *Soljourney into Truth*, 1975, unpublished MS, National Black Theatre Archives, 1.

55. Teer, *Soljourney into Truth*, 1.

56. Teer, *Soljourney into Truth*, 1.

57. Teer, *Soljourney into Truth*, 1.

58. Teer, *Soljourney into Truth*, 2.

59. Malpede and Teer, "Barbara Ann Teer," 226.

60. Thomas, "Barbara Ann Teer," 362.

61. *The Ritual*, New York City Public Broadcasting Company, February 2, 1970.

62. *The Ritual*, February 2, 1970.

63. Faison, interview, July 13, 2010.

64. *The Ritual*, February 2, 1970.

65. *The Ritual*, February 2, 1970.

66. *The Ritual*, February 2, 1970.

67. *The Ritual*, February 2, 1970.

68. Teer, "Ritual and the National Black Theatre," 43.

69. Teer, "Ritual and the National Black Theatre," 35.

70. Barbara Ann Teer, "An Invitation: Official Grand Opening at National Black Theatre *Change/Love Together/Organize: A Revival*," press release, 1972, National Black Theatre Archives.

71. Charlie Russell and Barbara Ann Teer, *A Revival: Change! Love Together! Organize!* 1972, unpublished MS, National Black Theatre Archives, 58–59.

72. Russell and Teer, *Revival*, 60.

73. Russell and Teer, *Revival*, 50.

74. Harris, "Sun People," 44.

75. Russell and Teer, *Revival*, 70.

76. Russell and Teer, *Revival*, 6.

77. Russell and Teer, *Revival*, 61.

78. Carlton W. Molette II and Barbara J. Molette, *Black Theatre: Premise and Presentation*, 2nd ed. (Bristol, Ind.: Wyndham Hall, 1992), 129.

79. Cornelius O. Adepegba, "Osun and Brass: An Insight into Yoruba Religious Symbology," trans. C. L. Adeoye, in *Òsun across the Waters: A Yoruba Goddess in Africa and the Americas*, ed. Joseph M. Murphy and Mei-Mei Sanford (Bloomington: Indiana University Press, 2001), 107.

80. Esedebe, *Pan-Africanism*, 64.

81. Teer, *Soljourney into Truth*, 18.

82. Teer, *Soljourney into Truth*, 29.

83. Anne Fliotsos and Wendy Vierow, *American Women Stage Directors of the Twentieth Century* (Urbana: University of Illinois Press, 2008), 415.

84. Teer, *Soljourney into Truth*, 29.

85. Teer, *Soljourney into Truth*, 28.

86. Teer, *Soljourney into Truth*, 30.

87. Teer, *Soljourney into Truth*, 30.

88. Teer, *Soljourney into Truth*, 31.

89. Daniels, *Women Stage Directors Speak*, 260.

90. Daniels, *Women Stage Directors Speak*, 260.

91. Daniels, *Women Stage Directors Speak*, 131–32.

92. Sanchez, "Barbara Ann Teer," 20.

Chapter 2

The title quotation, "We Black Women," is from *Where We At?* (1969), written by Martie Evans-Charles. Thanks to the Schomburg Center for Research in Black Culture for access to this unpublished manuscript. The epigraph is from Martie Evans-Charles, "Playwright Defends *Jamimma*," *New York Amsterdam News*, June 24, 1972.

1. Larry Neal, "Toward a Relevant Black Theatre," *Black Theatre: A Periodical of the Black Theatre Movement*, 1970, 14.

2. Lisbeth Gant, "The New Lafayette Theatre: Anatomy of a Community Art Institution," *The Drama Review* 16, no. 4 (1972): 47.

3. Shauneille Perry, "Books Noted," *Black World*, April 1972, 52.

4. Martie Evans-Charles's maternal aunt, Esther Rolle, performed in Melvin Van Peebles's *Don't Play Us Cheap* (1973) before becoming a household name as Florida Evans on the sitcoms *Maude* and *Good Times*. Rolle received a 1975 Golden Globe nomination for best actress in a musical/comedy for her performance in *Good Times*.

5. During the Harlem Renaissance, Martie Evans-Charles's maternal aunt Rosanna Carter found success as a Lafayette Player at the Lafayette Theatre in Harlem. During the late 1960s Carter joined the New Lafayette Theatre and

performed as Miss Minny Garrison and Marie Horton in Ed Bullins's *Goin' a Buffalo* (1969) and *The Duplex: A Black Fable in Four Movements* (1970), respectively. Carter performed alongside Martie Evans-Charles in the New Lafayette Theatre's 1970 ritual *The Devil Catchers* (1970). After the closure of the New Lafayette Theatre, Carter later received an AUDELCO Supporting Actress award for her performance in the 1977 premiere of Aisha Rahman's play *Unfinished Women Cry in No Man's Land While a Bird Dies in a Gilded Cage.*

6. The Shogola Oloba dance troupe was later renamed the Federal Theatre African Dance Troupe. In 1960 Esther Rolle became the dance troupe's director.

7. All of the character names in the New Lafayette Theatre's ritual *The Devil Catchers* (1970) originate from the actual performers' names. Martie Evans-Charles's character, Eitram, is Martie spelled backward.

8. Beatrix Taumann, *Strange Orphans: Contemporary African American Women Playwrights* (Würzburg: Königshausen & Neumann, 1999), 47.

9. Elizabeth Brown, "Six Female Black Playwrights: Images of Blacks in Plays by Lorraine Hansberry, Alice Childress, Sonia Sanchez, Barbara Molette, Martie Charles, Ntozake Shange" (dissertation, Florida State University, 1980), 55.

10. Brown, "Six Female Black Playwrights," 106.

11. Collins, *Black Feminist Thought,* 97.

12. New Federal Theatre, *Jamimma* program note, unpublished, 1972, Schomburg Center for Research in Black Culture.

13. New Federal Theatre, *Jamimma* program note.

14. New Federal Theatre, *Jamimma* program note.

15. Richard W. Wesley, "Harlem's Black Theatre Workshop," *Black World,* April 1972, 47.

16. Wesley, "Harlem's Black Theatre Workshop," 47.

17. Wesley, "Harlem's Black Theatre Workshop," 73.

18. Mike Sell, "Introduction: A Literary Gangster from Those Primitive Times of the Twentieth Century," in *Ed Bullins: Twelve Plays and Selected Writings,* ed. Ed Bullins with Mike Sell (Ann Arbor: University of Michigan, 2006), 13.

19. George Lee Miles, interview with the author, July 12, 2010.

20. Adrienne Charles, interview with the author, January 15, 2011.

21. Gant, "New Lafayette Theatre," 52.

22. Peter A. Bailey, "Annual Round-Up: Black Theatre in America: New York City," *Black World,* 1972, 34.

23. James V. Hatch, "From Hansberry to Shange," in *A History of African American Theatre,* ed. Errol G. Hill and James V. Hatch (Cambridge: Cambridge University Press, 2003), 393–94.

24. Martie Evans-Charles, "The Confrontation," *Impressions: A Black Arts and Culture Magazine,* October 1975, 38.

25. Evans-Charles, "Confrontation," 38.

26. In 1976 the Frank Silvera Writers' Workshop held a three-part series entitled "Crisis in the American Black Theatre." Martie Evans-Charles, along with playwrights Ed Bullins, Richard Wesley, and Charles Gordone, participated in the second symposium, "The Dilemma of the Black Playwright."

27. Barbara Lewis, "The Dramatic Crisis . . . ," *New York Amsterdam News,* February 14, 1976.

28. For more information about the myth and legacy of Aunt Jemima, see Marquette 1967, Kern-Foxworth 1994, McElya 2007, Wallace-Sanders 2008, and Manring 1998.

29. Kushauri Kupa, "Closeup: The New York Scene. Black Theatre in New York: 1970–1971," *Black Theatre: A Periodical of the Black Theatre Movement*, 1971, 50.

30. According to the Gospel of Luke (10.29–37), a lawyer asks Jesus to clarify the meaning of "neighbor" in reference to Leviticus 19.18, which implores Christians to love their neighbors. Jesus answers by recounting the tale of a man who falls victim to thieves. As the man lies beaten, naked, and "half-dead" on the side of the road, a priest and Levite pass by him. A Samaritan, however, displays "compassion on him," binds his wounds, puts him "on his own beast," takes him to an inn, and gives the innkeeper money to pay for his expenses while he heals.

31. Martie Evans-Charles, *Where We At?* 4–5, unpublished MS, 1969, Schomburg Center for Research in Black Culture, emphasis in original.

32. Evans-Charles, *Where We At?* 8.

33. For more information about the contributions of early blues women, see L. Jones 1963 and Davis 1998.

34. Collins, *Black Feminist Thought*, 100.

35. The song "Four Women" appears on Nina Simone's album *Wild Is the Wind* (1966), released by Phillips Records.

36. Nina Simone, *Wild Is the Wind*, compact disc, 1966, Philips Music, Philips 196ADAD.

37. Evans-Charles, *Where We At?* 5.

38. For a complete list of major themes within black women's blues tradition, see Harrison 1988.

39. Angela Y. Davis, *Blues Legacy and Black Feminism: Gertrude "Ma" Rainey, Bessie Smith, and Billy Holiday* (New York: Pantheon Books, 1998), 70.

40. Davis, *Blues Legacy*, 67.

41. Evans-Charles, *Where We At?* 7.

42. Evans-Charles, *Where We At?* 7.

43. Evans-Charles, *Where We At?* 9.

44. See Nathan 2008.

45. Nina Simone with Stephen Cleary, *I Put a Spell on You: The Autobiography of Nina Simone* (New York: Da Capo, 1993), 89.

46. Simone, *I Put a Spell on You*, 90.

47. Simone, *I Put a Spell on You*, 91.

48. Stokely Carmichael also served as honorary prime minister of the Black Panther Party.

49. Randall Grass, *Great Spirits: Portraits of Life-Changing World Music Artists* (Jackson: University of Mississippi Press, 2009), 8.

50. Evans-Charles, *Where We At?* 5.

51. *Black Cycle* was subsequently produced in 1973 at the Afro-American Studio Theatre Centre in New York and during the 1973–74 season at the Kuumba Workshop in Chicago.

52. Unsigned review of *Jamimma* by Martie Evans-Charles, dir. Kris Keiser, Lenox Avenue Building, New York, *New York Amsterdam News*, November 21, 1970, 3.

53. Martie Evans-Charles, *Black Cycle*, in *Black Drama Anthology*, ed. Woodie King and Ron Milner (New York: Signet, 1972), 527.

54. Evans-Charles, *Black Cycle*, 526.

55. Evans-Charles, *Black Cycle*, 526.

56. bell hooks, *Ain't I a Woman: Black Women and Feminism* (Boston: South End, 1981), 24.

57. hooks, *Ain't I a Woman*, 20.

58. Angela Davis, "Reflections on the Black Woman's Role in the Community of Slaves" (1971), in *Words of Fire: An Anthology of Black Feminist Thought*, ed. Beverly Guy-Sheftall (New York: New, 1995), 212, emphasis in original.

59. Davis, "Reflections," 213.

60. Evans-Charles, *Black Cycle*, 526.

61. Evans-Charles, *Black Cycle*, 526.

62. hooks, *Ain't I a Woman*, 18–19.

63. For more information about enslaved women and infanticide, see Staples 1973.

64. Harriet A. Jacobs (Linda Brent), *Incidents in the Life of a Slave Girl: Written by Herself*, ed. L. Maria Child (1861), ed. with an introduction by Jean Fagan Yellin (Cambridge, Mass.: Harvard University Press, 1987), 62.

65. Evans-Charles, *Black Cycle*, 543.

66. Evans-Charles, *Black Cycle*, 551.

67. Evans-Charles, *Black Cycle*, 541.

68. Evans-Charles, *Black Cycle*, 531.

69. Leith Mullings, "Images, Ideology, and Women of Color," in *Women of Color in U.S. Society*, ed. Maxine Baca Zinn and Bonnie Thornton Dill (Philadelphia: Temple University Press, 1994), 273.

70. Evans-Charles, *Black Cycle*, 543.

71. Darlene Clark Hine, *Hine Sight: Black Women and the Re-Construction of American History* (New York: Carlson, 1994), 41.

72. Hine, *Hine Sight*, 41.

73. Evans-Charles, *Black Cycle*, 549.

74. Evans-Charles, *Black Cycle*, 549.

75. Evans-Charles, *Black Cycle*, 549.

76. Rosemary K. Curb, "'Goin' Through Changes': Mother-Daughter Confrontations in Three Recent Plays by Young Black Women," *Kentucky Folklore Record* 25, no. 3–4 (1979): 96.

77. Evans-Charles, *Black Cycle*, 533.

78. Evans-Charles, *Black Cycle*, 532.

79. Evans-Charles, *Black Cycle*, 539.

80. James V. Hatch and Ted Shine, "'Job Security' Introduction," in *Black Theatre, U.S.A.: Forty-Five Plays by Black Americans 1847–1974*, ed. James V. Hatch and Ted Shine (New York: Free, 1974), 765.

81. Lawrence W. Levine, *Black Culture and Black Consciousness: African-American Folk Thought from Slavery to Freedom* (New York: Oxford University Press, 1977), 103.

82. Levine, *Black Culture*, 105–6.

83. Levine, *Black Culture*, 116.

84. For an in-depth discussion on the roles female tricksters play in world mythology, see Jurich 1998.

85. Levine, *Black Culture*, 110.

86. Levine, *Black Culture*, 110–11.

87. Levine, *Black Culture*, 108, 109–10.

88. Martie Evans-Charles, "Job Security," in *Black Theatre, U.S.A.: Forty-Five Plays by Black Americans 1847–1974*, ed. James V. Hatch and Ted Shine (New York: Free, 1974), 768.

89. Evans-Charles, "Job Security," 768.

90. Evans-Charles, "Job Security," 768.

91. Evans-Charles, "Job Security," 768.

92. Evans-Charles, "Job Security," 770.

93. Evans-Charles, "Job Security," 771.

94. Paulette Perrier, "The Black Magicians" review of *Job Security* by Martie Evans-Charles, The Black Magicians, Third World Theatre, 1970, *Black Theatre: A Periodical of the Black Theatre Movement*, 1971, 52.

95. Evans-Charles, "Job Security," 766.

96. Evans-Charles, "Job Security," 768.

97. Evans-Charles, "Job Security," 768.

98. Evans-Charles, "Job Security," 768.

99. Martie Evans-Charles, *Jamimma*, unpublished MS, n.d., Schomburg Center for Research in Black Culture, Act 2, Scene 2, p. 30 (2-2-30).

100. Kimberly Wallace-Sanders, *Mammy: A Century of Race, Gender, and Southern Memory* (Ann Arbor: University of Michigan Press, 2008), 61.

101. The character Vivian first appears as Jeannie in Martie Evans-Charles's *Black Cycle*. Vivian reveals to Jameena that she changed her name as an adult so that her mother Vera could not locate her.

102. Evans-Charles, *Jamimma*, 1-1-6.

103. Collins, *Black Feminist Thought*, 106.

104. Evans-Charles, "Confrontation," 38.

105. Evans-Charles, "Confrontation," 39.

106. Evans-Charles, "Confrontation," 39.

107. Vivian Robinson, "'Jamimma' Is a Warm Experience," review of *Jamimma* by Martie Evans-Charles, dir. Kris Keiser, Lenox Avenue Building, New York, *New York Amsterdam News*, December 19, 1970. Robinson also notes that director Kris Keiser hand-selected several cast members from within the Harlem community and limited audience numbers to sixty in order to create an intimate environment for the character-driven drama.

108. Other notable productions of *Jamimma* include performances at the Billy Holiday Theatre in 1975 and the Harlem Performance Center in 1976.

109. Howard Thompson, "The Stage: 'Jamimma,'" review of *Jamimma* by Martie Evans-Charles, dir. Shauneille Perry, New Federal Theatre, New York, *New York Times*, March 18, 1972.

110. Walter Kerr, "Where Did They Put That Tree?" review of *Jamimma* by Martie Evans-Charles, dir. Shauneille Perry, New Federal Theatre, New York, *New York Times*, May 28, 1972.

111. Jean Carey Bond, "Love and the Black Woman Explored in 'Jamimma,'" review of *Jamimma* by Martie Evans-Charles, dir. Shauneille Perry, New Federal Theatre, New York, *New York Amsterdam News*, June 10, 1972.

112. Evans-Charles, "Playwright Defends *Jamimma*."

113. Evans-Charles, *Jamimma*.

114. Martie Evans-Charles, *Asante*, unpublished MS, 1974, Schomburg Center for Research in Black Culture, Act 1, p. 17 (1-17).

115. Allen Woll, *Black Musical Theatre: From Coontown to Dreamgirls* (Baton Rouge: Louisiana State University Press, 1989), 249.

116. Woll, *Black Musical Theatre*, 253.

117. Evans-Charles, *Asante*, 1-10, 1-11.

118. Evans-Charles, *Asante*, 1-12.

119. Evans-Charles, *Asante*, 1-17.

120. Evans-Charles, *Asante*, 1-17.

121. Evans-Charles, *Asante*, 1-19.

122. Evans-Charles, *Asante*, 1-19.

123. Evans-Charles, *Asante*, 1-19.

124. Collins, *Black Feminist Thought*, 94.

125. Evans-Charles, *Asante*, 1-20.

126. Evans-Charles, *Asante*, 1-42.

127. Evans-Charles, interview, January 15, 2011.

Chapter 3

The title quotation, "Armed Prophet," is from Joanne Veal Gabbin's "The Southern Imagination of Sonia Sanchez" in *Southern Women Writers: The New Generation*, ed. Tonette Bond Inge (Tuscaloosa: University of Alabama Press, 1990), 180. The epigraph is from Joyce A. Joyce, "Interview with Sonia Sanchez: Poet, Playwright, Teacher, and Intellectual Activist," in *Conversations with Sonia Sanchez*, ed. Joyce Ann Joyce (Jackson: University Press of Mississippi, 2007), 185.

1. Alice Walker first coined the term "womanist" in her short story "Coming Apart" (1979).

2. Gabbin, "Southern Imagination," 180.

3. Sonia Sanchez, "Ruminations/Reflections," in *Black Women Writers (1950–1980): A Critical Evaluation*, ed. Mari Evans (New York: Doubleday, 1984), 415, emphasis in original.

4. Sonia Sanchez published the following books of poetry during the Black Arts Movement: *Home Coming* (1969), *Liberation Poem* (1969), *We a BaddDDD People* (1970), *It's A New Day: Poems for Young Brothas and Sistuhs* (1971), *Ima Talken bout the Nation of Islam* (1971), *A Blues Book for Blue Black Magical Women* (1973), and *Love Poems* (1973).

5. Rosemary K. Curb, "Pre-Feminism in the Black Revolutionary Drama of Sonia Sanchez," in *The Many Forms of Drama*, ed. Karelisa Hatigan (Lanham, Md.: University Press of America, 1985), 19.

6. Curb, "Pre-Feminism," 19, 28.

7. Mike Sell, *Avant-Garde Performance and the Limits of Criticism: Approaching the Living Theatre, Happenings/Fluxus, and the Black Arts Movement* (Ann Arbor: University of Michigan Press, 2005), 250.

8. Jacqueline Wood, "'Shaking Loose': Sonia Sanchez's Militant Drama," in *Contemporary African American Women Playwrights*, ed. Philip Kolin (New York: Routledge, 2007), 50, 47.

9. Delores Williams, *Sisters in the Wilderness: The Challenge of Womanist God-Talk* (New York: Orbis Books, 1995), xiii–xiv.

10. Sanchez explained during her interview with the author that in the South, older first cousins are often referred to as "aunt" and "uncle" as a sign of respect. Sanchez's three "aunts" were actually her first cousins.

11. Sonia Sanchez, interview with the author, June 30, 2010.

12. Sanchez, interview, June 30, 2010.

13. Sanchez, interview, June 30, 2010.

14. Sanchez, interview, June 30, 2010.

15. Michelle Nzadi Keita, "Sonia Sanchez: 'Fearless about the World,'" in *Impossible to Hold: Women and Culture in the 1960s*, ed. Avita H. Bloch and Lauri Umansky (New York: New York University Press, 2005), 285.

16. Sanchez, interview, 2010.

17. Abbey Lincoln delivered a talk entitled "Who Will Revere the Black Woman?" at the Black Arts Repertory Theatre/School in 1965. The address was published in *Negro Digest* the following year.

18. Abbey Lincoln, "Who Will Revere the Black Woman?" (1966), in *The Black Woman Anthology*, ed. Toni Cade (New York: New American Library, 1970), 84.

19. Joyce, "Interview with Sonia Sanchez," 184.

20. "Sonia Sanchez Tells It Like It Is," *New York Amsterdam News*, December 19, 1970.

21. "Sonia Sanchez Tells."

22. Keita, "Sonia Sanchez," 282.

23. Sanchez, interview, June 30, 2010.

24. Sanchez, interview, June 30, 2010.

25. Susan Kelly, "Discipline and Craft: An Interview with Sonia Sanchez," *African American Review* 34, no. 4 (2000): 683.

26. Sonia Sanchez with Claudia Tate, "Sonia Sanchez," in *Black Women Writers at Work*, ed. Claudia Tate (New York: Continuum, 1983), 139.

27. Sanchez and Tate, "Sonia Sanchez," 139.

28. Sanchez and Tate, "Sonia Sanchez," 139.

29. Sanchez and Tate, "Sonia Sanchez," 139.

30. Davis Reich, "'As Poets, as Activists': An Interview with Sonia Sanchez," in *Conversations with Sonia Sanchez*, ed. Joyce Ann Joyce (Jackson: University Press of Mississippi, 2007), 80–81.

31. Sanchez, interview, June 30, 2010.

32. Sanchez, interview, June 30, 2010.

33. Sanchez and Tate, "Sonia Sanchez," 148.

34. Sanchez, interview, June 30, 2010.

35. Sanchez, interview, June 30, 2010.

36. Joyce, "Interview with Sonia Sanchez," 203.

37. Joyce, "Interview with Sonia Sanchez," 203.

38. Sanchez, interview, June 30, 2010.

39. Sonia Sanchez, *Sister Son/ji*, in *New Plays from the Black Theatre: An Anthology*, ed. Ed Bullins (New York: Bantam, 1969), 107.

40. Juanita Johnson-Bailey, "Sonia Sanchez: Telling What We Must Hear," in *Conversations with Sonia Sanchez*, ed. Joyce Ann Joyce (Jackson: University Press of Mississippi, 2007), 73.

41. Johnson-Bailey, "Sonia Sanchez," 73.

42. Johnson-Bailey, "Sonia Sanchez," 73.

43. Sanchez, interview, June 30, 2010.

44. Sanchez, interview, June 30, 2010.

45. Dudley Randall, introduction to *We a BaddDDD People*, by Sonia Sanchez (Detroit, Mich.: Broadside, 1970), 10.

46. Elizabeth A. Frost, *The Feminist Avant-Garde in American Poetry* (Iowa City: University of Iowa Press, 2003), 77.

47. Frost, *The Feminist*, 77.

48. Sanchez, "Ruminations/Reflections," 415.

49. Sanchez, "Ruminations/Reflections," 416, emphasis in original.

50. LeRoi Jones/Amiri Baraka and Larry Neal's *Black Fire: An Anthology of Afro-American Writing* (1968) includes poetry from over forty male poets and five female poets: Sonia Sanchez, Lethonia Gee, Barbara Simmons, Carol Freeman, and Odaro (Barbara Jones).

51. The 1968 special black theater edition of *The Drama Review* also features *Papa's Daughter* by Dorothy Ahmad, but under the heading of "Theatre of the Black Experience."

52. Randall, introduction, 9.

53. Randall, introduction, 9.

54. Haki Madhubuti, "Sonia Sanchez: The Bringer of Memories," in *Black Women Writers (1950–1980): A Critical Evaluation*, ed. Mari Evans (Garden City, N.Y.: Anchor Books, 1984), 419, 421.

55. Sanchez, interview, June 30, 2010.

56. Sanchez, interview, June 30, 2010.

57. Sanchez, interview, June 30, 2010.

58. Sonia Sanchez, *The Bronx Is Next*, in *The Drama Review* 12, no. 4 (1968): 82.

59. While the black nationalists depicted in *The Bronx Is Next* share the names of prominent Black Arts participants Charles Patterson, Larry Neal, Rolland Snellings (Askia Toure), and Jimmy Garrett, Sonia Sanchez continues to deny any connection between these fictional characters and actual people.

60. Sanchez, *The Bronx*, 81, 82.

61. Sanchez, *The Bronx*, 82.

62. Sanchez, *The Bronx*, 83.

63. See Patricia Hill Collins's *Black Feminist Thought*.

64. Sanchez, interview, June 30, 2010.

65. Sanchez, interview, June 30, 2010.

66. Robert Staples, *Black Woman in America: Sex, Marriage, and the Family* (Chicago: Nelson-Hall, 1973), 90.

67. Staples, *Black Woman*, 89.

68. Sanchez, *The Bronx*, 82.

69. Sanchez, *The Bronx*, 81.

70. Sanchez, *The Bronx*, 81.

71. Sanchez, interview, June 30, 2010.

72. Sanchez, *The Bronx*, 80.

73. Sanchez, *The Bronx*, 80.

74. Sanchez, *The Bronx*, 83.

75. Sanchez, interview, June 30, 2010.

76. Sanchez, interview, June 30, 2010.

77. Sanchez, interview, June 30, 2010.

78. Sanchez, *The Bronx*, 83.

79. Sanchez, interview, June 30, 2010.

80. Larry Neal, "The Black Arts Movement," *The Drama Review* 12, no. 4 (1968): 30.

81. Jacqueline Wood, "'This Thing Called Playwrighting' [*sic*]: An Interview with Sonia Sanchez on the Art of Her Drama," *African American Review* 39, no. 1/2 (2001): 120.

82. Mike Sell, "The Black Arts Movement: Performance, Neo-Orality, and the Destruction of the 'White Thing,'" in *African American Performance and Theater History: A Critical Reader*, ed. Harry J. Elam and David Krasner (New York: Oxford University Press, 2001), 71–72.

83. Sanchez, interview, June 30, 2010.

84. Sanchez, interview, June 30, 2010.

85. Sanchez, *Sister Son/ji*, 101.

86. Sanchez, *Sister Son/ji*, 101.

87. Anita Cornwell, "Attuned to the Energy: Sonia Sanchez," in *Conversations with Sonia Sanchez*, ed. Joyce Ann Joyce (Jackson: University Press of Mississippi, 2007), 4.

88. Cornwell, "Attuned to the Energy," 4.

89. Sanchez, *Sister Son/ji*, 102.

90. Keita, "Sonia Sanchez," 285.

91. Sanchez, *Sister Son/ji*, 102–3.

92. Sanchez, *Sister Son/ji*, 102.

93. Sanchez, *Sister Son/ji*, 105.

94. Sanchez, *Sister Son/ji*, 105.

95. Sanchez, *Sister Son/ji*, 105.

96. Sanchez, *Sister Son/ji*, 106.

97. Sanchez, *Sister Son/ji*, 106.

98. Sanchez, *Sister Son/ji*, 106–7.

99. Clive Barnes, "Theatre: 'Black Visions,'" review of *Sister Son/ji* by Sonia Sanchez, dir. Novella Nelson, New York Shakespeare Festival, Public Theatre Annex, New York, *New York Times,* April 5, 1972.

100. Barnes, "Theatre: 'Black Visions,'" 37.

101. Clayton Riley, "'Black Visions' Is a Supershow," review of *Sister Son/ji* by Sonia Sanchez, dir. Novella Nelson, New York Shakespeare Festival, Public Theatre Annex, New York, *New York Amsterdam News,* April 15, 1972.

102. Wood, "'Shaking Loose,'" 52.

103. Sanchez, interview, June 30, 2010.

104. Sanchez, interview, June 30, 2010.

105. Sanchez, interview, June 30, 2010.

106. Sanchez, interview, June 30, 2010.

107. Sanchez, interview, June 30, 2010.

108. Sonia Sanchez, *Dirty Hearts*, in *Scripts 1* (November 1971): 47.

109. Sanchez, *Dirty Hearts*, 47.

110. Sanchez, interview, June 30, 2010.

111. Sanchez, interview, June 30, 2010.

112. Sonia Sanchez, *Malcolm/Man Don't Live Here No Mo'*, in *Black Theatre* 6 (1972): 24–26.

113. Sanchez, *Malcolm/Man*, 24.

114. Sanchez, interview, June 30, 2010.

115. Sanchez, *Malcolm/Man*, 25.

116. Sanchez, *Malcolm/Man*, 25.

117. Sanchez, *Malcolm/Man*, 26.

118. Malcolm X, "On Protecting Black Women," filmed May 1962, posted April 20, 2008, https://www.youtube.com/watch?v=6EIEKe8fVmg.

119. Farah Jasmine Griffin, "'Ironies of the Saint': Malcolm X, Black Women, and the Price of Protection," in *Sisters in the Struggle: African American Women in the Civil Rights–Black Power Movement*, ed. Bettye Collier-Thomas and V.P. Franklin (New York: New York University Press, 2001), 216.

120. Malcolm X, "The Ballot or the Bullet" (1964), in *The Portable Sixties Reader*, ed. Ann Charters (London: Penguin Books, 2003), 73.

121. Sanchez, *Malcolm/Man*, 24.

122. Sanchez, interview, June 30, 2010.

123. The character listing uses the names "Black Whore" and "Sister Whore" interchangeably. Throughout the entire play, however, the script only uses the name "Black Whore." For the sake of clarity, the name "Black Whore" will be used throughout this chapter.

124. The character listing and a small portion of the script use the names "White Dude" and "White Man" interchangeably. Most of the play uses the name "White Dude." To avoid confusion, this chapter only uses the name "White Dude."

125. Sonia Sanchez, *Uh, Uh; But How Do It Free Us?*, in *The New LaFayette Theatre Presents: Plays with Aesthetic Comments by 6 Black Playwrights*, ed. Ed Bullins (New York: Anchor, 1974), 213.

126. Sanchez, *Uh, Uh*, 170.

127. Sanchez, *Uh, Uh*, 170.

128. Sanchez, *Uh, Uh*, 170.

129. Sanchez, interview, June 30, 2010.

130. Sanchez, interview, June 30, 2010.

131. Sanchez, *Uh, Uh*, 173.

132. Sanchez, *Uh, Uh*, 173.

133. Sanchez, *Uh, Uh*, 177.

134. Sanchez, *Uh, Uh*, 178.

135. Zora Neale Hurston, *Their Eyes Were Watching God* (1937; New York: Harper Perennial Classics, 2006), 14.

136. Sanchez, *Uh, Uh*, 182.

137. Sanchez, *Uh, Uh*, 184.

138. Sanchez, *Uh, Uh*, 185.

139. Sanchez, *Uh, Uh*, 185.

140. Sanchez, *Uh, Uh*, 185.

141. Malcolm X, "Who Taught You to Hate Yourself?," filmed May 1962, posted June 6, 2011, https://www.youtube.com/watch?v=TT96uYPQZ3g.

142. Sanchez, interview, June 30, 2010.

143. Sanchez, *Uh, Uh*, 188.

144. Sanchez, *Uh, Uh*, 188.

145. Sanchez, *Uh, Uh*, 192.

146. Sanchez, *Uh, Uh*, 188.

147. Sanchez, *Uh, Uh*, 188.

148. Sanchez, *Uh, Uh*, 208–9.

149. Sanchez, *Uh, Uh*, 212.

150. Sanchez, interview, June 30, 2010.

151. Sanchez, interview, June 30, 2010.

Chapter 4

The title quotation, "Bring Your Wounded Hearts," is from J.e. Franklin's invocation to *Coming to the Mercy Seat: J.e. Franklin's Ten Minute Folk Dramas* (2003), produced by the National Black Theatre Legros Cultural Arts, New York, directed by Chantal M. Legros and Charles Murray, June 12, 2010. The epigraph is from Jerry Komia Domatob, preface to *Coming to the Mercy Seat: J.e. Franklin's Ten Minute Folk Dramas* (New York: Blackgirl Ensemble Theatre, 2003), 10–11.

1. J.e. Franklin, *Black Girl: From Genesis to Revelations* (Washington, D.C.: Howard University Press, 1977), 129.

2. La Donna L. Forsgren, "The Black Arts Movement (1965–1976): An Interview with Playwright J.e. Franklin," *Callaloo* 37, no. 5 (2014): 1149.

3. Domatob, preface, 10–11.

4. J.e. Franklin explained during an interview with the author that her (then) agent requested that she change the title of *Mau Mau Room* (1966). Franklin revised the title to *Throw Thunder at This House* (1970), followed by *Cut Out the Lights and Call in the Law* (1972) before settling on *Miss Honey's Young 'Uns* (1989).

5. Forsgren, "Black Arts Movement," 1157.

6. Carlos Russell, " 'Black Girl' Is Hunk of Black Life," review of *Black Girl* by J.e. Franklin, dir. Shauneille Perry, Theater DeLys, New York, *New York Amsterdam News*, August 7, 1971.

7. Taumann, *Strange Orphans*, 47.

8. Rosemary K. Curb, " 'Goin' Through Changes': Mother-Daughter Confrontations in Three Recent Plays by Young Black Women," *Kentucky Folklore Record* 25, no. 3-4 (1979): 101.

9. Franklin, *Black Girl: From*, 4–5.

10. Franklin, *Black Girl: From*, 10.

11. Forsgren, "Black Arts Movement," 1142.

12. Forsgren, "Black Arts Movement," 1153.

13. Forsgren, "Black Arts Movement," 1139.

14. Forsgren, "Black Arts Movement," 1141.

15. Charlayne Hunter, "2 Black Women Combine Lives and Talent in Play," *New York Times*, July 13, 1971.

16. Forsgren, "Black Arts Movement," 1139.

17. Forsgren, "Black Arts Movement," 1139.

18. Forsgren, "Black Arts Movement," 1140.

19. Forsgren, "Black Arts Movement," 1153.

20. Hunter, "2 Black Women."

21. Franklin, *Black Girl: From*, 16.

22. Franklin, *Black Girl: From*, 22.

23. After working with J.e. Franklin, George Houston Bass (1938–1990) continued to produce the works of black playwrights. He founded the Rites and Reason Theatre at Brown University in 1970.

24. Franklin, *Black Girl: From*, 28.

25. Franklin, *Black Girl: From*, 27.

26. Franklin, *Black Girl: From*, 27.

27. Franklin, *Black Girl: From*, 30.

28. Franklin, *Black Girl: From*, 35.

29. Forsgren, "Black Arts Movement," 1148.

30. Forsgren, "Black Arts Movement," 1148.

31. Franklin, *Black Girl: From*, 43.

32. Franklin, *Black Girl: From*, 44.

33. Franklin, *Black Girl: From*, 48.

34. Forsgren, "Black Arts Movement," 1141.

35. Forsgren, "Black Arts Movement," 1141.

36. Forsgren, "Black Arts Movement," 1146.

37. Fred Beauford, "A Conversation with *Black Girls'* J.E. Franlin" [*sic*], *Black Creation* (fall 1971): 39.

38. Beauford, "A Conversation," 39.

39. Beauford, "A Conversation," 39–40.

40. Beauford, "A Conversation," 40.

41. Forsgren, "Black Arts Movement," 1147.

42. J.e. Franklin, *The In-Crowd: A Rock Opera in One Act*, 1965, unpublished MS, courtesy of J.e. Franklin, 2.

43. Franklin, *The In-Crowd*, 1–2.

44. Franklin, *The In-Crowd*, 3.

45. Franklin, *The In-Crowd*, 6.

46. Franklin, *The In-Crowd*, 10.

47. Franklin, *The In-Crowd*, 14.

48. Franklin, *The In-Crowd*, 14.

49. J.e. Franklin, interview with the author, July 12, 2010.

50. Woodie King Jr.'s New Federal Theatre eventually grew out of his work with Mobilization for Youth.

51. Franklin, interview, July 12, 2010.

52. Forsgren, "Black Arts Movement," 1151.

53. Forsgren, "Black Arts Movement," 1151.

54. Forsgren, "Black Arts Movement," 1151.

55. For more information on the importance of ritual during the Middle Passage, see Beverly J. Robinson's "The Sense of Self in Ritualizing New Performance Spaces for Survival," in *Black Theatre: Ritual Performance in the Black Diaspora*, ed. Paul Carter Harrison, Victor Leo Walker II, and Gus Edwards (Philadelphia: Temple University Press, 2002), 332–44.

56. Forsgren, "Black Arts Movement," 1143.

57. J.e. Franklin, *Miss Honey's Young'uns*, in *Black Drama in America: An Anthology*, ed. with an introduction by Darwin T. Turner (Washington, D.C.: Howard University Press, 1994), 629.

58. Franklin, *Miss Honey's Young'uns*, 630.

59. Franklin, *Miss Honey's Young'uns*, 640.

60. Franklin, *Miss Honey's Young'uns*, 653.

61. Franklin, *Miss Honey's Young'uns*, 657.

62. Otto Kerner et al., *Report of the National Advisory Commission on Civil Disorders* (Washington, D.C.: Government Printing Office, 1967), 1.

63. Kerner, *Report*, 2.

64. Forsgren, "Black Arts Movement," 1143–44.

65. Franklin, interview, July 12, 2010.

66. Franklin, *Miss Honey's Young'uns*, 631.

67. Franklin, *Miss Honey's Young'uns*, 646.

68. Franklin, *Miss Honey's Young'uns*, 645; emphasis in original.

69. Franklin, *Miss Honey's Young'uns*, 661.

70. Franklin, *Miss Honey's Young'uns*, 634, 658.

71. Forsgren, "Black Arts Movement," 1150.

72. Franklin, *Miss Honey's Young'uns*, 624.

73. Franklin, *Miss Honey's Young'uns*, 640.

74. Franklin, *Miss Honey's Young'uns*, 625.

75. Franklin, *Miss Honey's Young'uns*, 633.

76. Forsgren, "Black Arts Movement," 1149.

77. Franklin, *Black Girl: From*, 133.

78. Hunter, "2 Black Women."

79. Forsgren, "Black Arts Movement," 1152.

80. Franklin, *Black Girl: From*, 21.

81. Forsgren, "Black Arts Movement," 1152

82. Forsgren, "Black Arts Movement," 1152.

83. J.e. Franklin, *Black Girl: A Play in Two Acts* (New York: Dramatists Play Service, Inc., 1971), 8.

84. Franklin, *Black Girl: A Play*, 20.

85. Franklin, *Black Girl: A Play*, 28; emphasis in original.

86. Mu'Dear gave birth to Mama Rosie at the age of twenty-one; Mama Rosie became a mother at the tender age of thirteen; Norma Faye had her first child at seventeen, or possibly younger; and Ruth Ann delivered a son at the age of fifteen.

87. Beauford, "A Conversation," 40.

88. Russell, "'Black Girl.'"

89. Forsgren, "Black Arts Movement," 1153.

90. Franklin, *Black Girl: A Play*, 6.

91. Walter Kerr, "Basic Freud, Bad Bellow," review of *Black Girl* by J.e. Franklin, dir. Shauneille Perry, Theater DeLys, New York, *New York Amsterdam News*, July 4, 1971.

92. Elenore Lester, "Growing Up Black and Female," review of *Black Girl* by J.e. Franklin, dir. Shauneille Perry, New Federal Theatre's Henry Street Playhouse, New York, *New York Times*, July, 11, 1971.

93. Franklin, *Black Girl: A Play*, 11.

94. Franklin, *Black Girl: A Play*, 122.

95. Franklin, *Black Girl: A Play*, 43.

96. Clarence Allsopp, "Black Womanhood and 'Black Girl,'" review of *Black Girl* by J.e. Franklin, dir. Shauneille Perry, Theater DeLys, New York, *New York Amsterdam News*, October 23, 1971.

97. Vinnette Caroll (1922–2002) became the first African American woman to direct on Broadway with the 1972 musical *Don't Bother Me, I Can't Cope.*

98. Franklin, interview, July 12, 2010.

99. Allsopp, "Black Womanhood."

100. Martie Evans-Charles's maternal aunt Esther Rolle replaced actress Minnie Gentry as Mu'Dear for four weeks during the New Federal Theatre's 1971 production of *Black Girl.*

101. James P. Murray, "Ossie Davis Makes Strides after Image Maker Award," *New York Amsterdam News*, November 25, 1972.

102. Murray, "Ossie Davis."

103. Murray, "Ossie Davis."

104. "'Black Girl' Is a Serious Sensitive Movie Production," review of *Black Girl* adapted by J.e. Franklin, dir. Ossie Davis, *New York Amsterdam News*, November 11, 1972.

105. Roger Greenspun, "Film: 'Black Girl' Arrives on Screen," review of *Black Girl* adapted by J.e. Franklin, dir. Ossie Davis, *New York Amsterdam News*, November 10, 1972.

106. Greenspun, "Film: 'Black Girl.'"

107. Greenspun, "Film: 'Black Girl.'"

108. "'Black Girl' World Premiere to Benefit Sickle Cell Anemia," review of *Black Girl* adapted by J.e. Franklin, dir. Ossie Davis, *New York Amsterdam News*, October 21, 1972.

109. Franklin, *Black Girl: From*, 60.

110. Franklin, *Black Girl: From*, 51.

111. Franklin, *Black Girl: From*, 61.

112. Franklin, *Black Girl: From*, 62.

113. J.e. Franklin, "The Enemy," in *Black Short Story Anthology*, ed. by Woodie King (New York: Columbia University Press, 1972), 352.

114. Franklin, "The Enemy," 352.

115. Franklin, "The Enemy," 353.

116. Franklin, "The Enemy," 356–57.

117. Franklin, "The Enemy," 358.

118. Forsgren, "Black Arts Movement," 1154.

119. Nina Simone, *Wild Is the Wind*, 1966, compact disc, Philips Music, Philips 196ADAD.

120. J.e. Franklin, *Four Women: A Play in One Act*, 1973, unpublished MS, courtesy of Ms. J.e. Franklin, 2.

121. Franklin, *Four Women*, 5.

122. For more information about black female minstrel performers, see Anne Marie Bean, "Blackface Minstrelsy and Double Inversion circa 1890," in *African American Performance and Theatre History*, ed. Harry J. Elam and David Krasner (New York: Oxford University Press, 2001), 171–91.

123. Franklin, *Four Women*, 8.

124. Franklin, *Four Women*, 8.

125. Pamela Robertson, *Guilty Pleasures: Feminist Camp from Mae West to Madonna* (Durham, N.C.: Duke University Press, 1996), 34.

126. Robertson, *Guilty Pleasures*, 35.

127. Franklin, *Four Women*, 16.

128. Franklin, *Four Women*, 16.

129. Franklin, *Four Women*, 17.

130. Franklin, *Four Women*, 18.

131. Franklin, *Four Women*, 20.

132. Franklin, *Four Women*, 20.

133. J.e. Franklin, *The Prodigal Sister: A New Black Musical* (New York: Samuel French, 1974), 52.

134. Franklin, *The Prodigal Sister*, 12–13.

135. Franklin, *The Prodigal Sister*, 13.

136. Franklin, *The Prodigal Sister*, 15.

137. Franklin, *The Prodigal Sister*, 17.

138. Franklin, *The Prodigal Sister*, 23.

139. Franklin, *The Prodigal Sister*, 10.

140. Franklin, *The Prodigal Sister*, 47.

141. Forsgren, "Black Arts Movement," 1155.

142. Franklin, *The Prodigal Sister*, 37.

143. Forsgren, "Black Arts Movement," 1155.

144. Franklin, *The Prodigal Sister*, 17.

145. Franklin, *The Prodigal Sister*, 18.

146. Franklin, *The Prodigal Sister*, 47.

147. Jessica B. Harris, "'Prodigal Sister' Rises above Its Weaknesses," review of *The Prodigal Sister* by J.e. Franklin, dir. Shauneille Perry, Theater DeLys, New York, *New York Amsterdam News,* December 7, 1974.

148. Franklin, *The Prodigal Sister*, 36.

149. Franklin, *The Prodigal Sister*, 36.

150. "Stage: Prodigal Sister," review of *Prodigal Sister* by J.e. Franklin, dir. Shauneille Perry, New Federal Theatre's Henry Street Playhouse, New York, *New York Times,* July 16, 1974.

151. "Stage: Prodigal Sister."

152. Angela E. Smith, "Bright Cast, Lively Music in New Play," review of *The Prodigal Sister* by J.e. Franklin, dir. Shauneille Perry, New Federal Theatre's Henry Street Playhouse, New York, *New York Amsterdam News*, July 27, 1974.

153. Harris, "'Prodigal Sister' Rises above Its Weaknesses."

154. Clive Barnes, "Stage: An Engaging 'Prodigal Sister,' " review of *The Prodigal Sister* by J.e. Franklin, dir. Shauneille Perry, Theater DeLys, New York, *New York Times*, November 26, 1974.

155. Forsgren, "Black Arts Movement," 1156.

Epilogue

1. Kannu, review of *African Interlude* by Martie Evans-Charles, dir. Shauneille Perry, Henry Street Settlement's New Federal Theatre, New York. *The Paper,* March 11, 1978.

2. Anthony D. Hill and Douglas Q. Barnett, *Historical Dictionary of African American Theatre* (Lanham, Md.: Scarecrow, 2009), 178.

3. Don Thomas of the *New York Beacon* writes that producer Woodie King Jr.'s "Great Black One-Act Plays" festival included *Sugar Mouth Sam Don't Dance No More* by Don Evans, *Mojo* by Alice Childress, *First Militant Preacher* by Ben Caldwell, *Soul Gone Home* by Langston Hughes, *The Past Is the Past* by Richard

Wesley, *When the Chickens Came Home to Roost* by Laurence Holder, *Happy Endings* by Douglas Turner Ward, *Andrew* by Clay Goss, *Pain in My Heart* by Rob Penny, *Skin Trouble* by Amiri Baraka, *Chain* by Pearl Cleage, *Fallen Angels* by Elois Beasley, *Every Goodbye Ain't Gone* by Bill Harris, *A Son Come Home* by Ed Bullins, *A Message in Our Music* by James Gillard, *Sara Love* by Charles Fuller, and *Life Agony* by Ron Milner.

4. Eleanor Levine, review of *Meditation: A Family Affair* by Martie Evans-Charles, dir. Chuck Patterson, Henry Street Settlement's Abrons Art Center, New York, *New York Amsterdam News*, July 27, 2000.

5. Levine, review of *Meditation*.

6. Adrienne Charles, interview with the author, January 15, 2011.

7. Stephen Holden, review of *Christchild* by J.e. Franklin, dir. Irving Vincent, New Federal Theatre, New York, *New York Times*, December 2, 1992.

8. Holden, review of *Christchild*.

9. Sonia Sanchez's post–Black Arts Movement published books of poetry (unless otherwise noted) include *I've Been a Woman: New and Selected Poems* (1978), the children's book *A Sound Investment* (1979), *Crisis and Culture: Two Speeches by Sonia Sanchez* (1983), *Homegirls and Handgrenades* (1984), *Generations, Selected Poetry: 1969–1985* (1986), *Under a Soprano Sky* (1987), *Wounded in the House of a Friend* (1995), *Black Cats Back and Uneasy Landings* (1995), *Does Your House Have Lions?* (1997), *Like the Singing Coming off the Drums: Love Poems* (1998), *Shake Loose My Skin: New and Selected Poems* (1999), and *Morning Haiku* (2010).

10. Helene C. Smith, "Emotional Play Explores the Exploitation of Black Women," *Atlanta Constitution*, April 30, 1982.

11. Wood, "Shaking Loose," 48.

12. For more information about Sonia Sanchez's contribution to the development of rap, watch the engaging documentary *Hip Hop Evolution* (2016), directed by Darby Wheeler, screenplay by Rodrigo Bascuñán, cinematography by Martin Hawkes.

13. Cheo Tyehima, "Sonia Sanchez Speaks," in *Conversations with Sonia Sanchez*, ed. Joyce Ann Joyce (Jackson: University Press of Mississippi, 2007), 116.

14. Thomas, "Barbara Ann Teer," 361–62.

15. Fliotsos and Vierow, *American Women Stage Directors*, 416.

16. Nabii Faison, interview with the author, July 13, 2010.

BIBLIOGRAPHY

Archives

Evans-Charles, Martie. Manuscripts. Schomburg Center for Research in Black Culture, New York.

Franklin, J.e. Manuscripts. Ms. J.e. Franklin Private Collection.

National Black Theatre. Papers. National Black Theatre Archives, New York.

New Federal Theatre. Papers. Schomburg Center for Research in Black Culture, New York.

Teer, Barbara Ann. Manuscripts. National Black Theatre Archives, New York.

Periodicals

Allsopp, Clarence. Review of *Black Girl* by J.e. Franklin, dir. Shauneille Perry, Theater DeLys, New York. *New York Amsterdam News*, October 23, 1971.

Bailey, Peter A. "Annual Round-Up: Black Theatre in America: Metropolitan New York." *Black World*, April 1971.

———. "Annual Round-Up: Black Theatre in America: New York City." *Black World*, April 1972.

———. Review of *The Prodigal Sister* by J.e. Franklin, dir. Shauneille Perry, New Federal Theatre's Henry Street Playhouse, New York. *Black World*, April 1975.

Barnes, Clive. Review of *The Prodigal Sister* by J.e. Franklin, dir. Shauneille Perry, Theater DeLys, New York. *New York Times*, November 26, 1974.

———. Review of *Sister Son/ji* by Sonia Sanchez, dir. Novella Nelson, New York Shakespeare Festival, Public Theatre Annex, New York. *New York Times*, April 5, 1972.

Beauford, Fred. "A Conversation with Black Girls's J.E. Franlin" [*sic*]. *Black Creation*, Fall 1971.

Best, Tony. "Barbara Ann Teer and the Liberators." *New York Amsterdam News*, November 12, 1975.

Bond, Jean Carey. Review of *Jamimma* by Martie Evans-Charles, dir. Shauneille Perry, New Federal Theatre, New York. *New York Amsterdam News*, June 10, 1972.

Chan, Melissa. "Playwright Outraged after White Actor Cast as Martin Luther King in 'The Mountaintop.'" *New York Daily News*, November 11, 2015.

Christian, Barbara. "The Race for Theory." *Cultural Critique* 6 (1987): 51–63.

Curb, Rosemary K. "'Goin' Through Changes': Mother-Daughter Confrontations in Three Recent Plays by Young Black Women." *Kentucky Folklore Record* 25, no. 3–4 (1979): 96–102.

Crenshaw, Kimberle. "Demarginalizing the Intersection of Race and Sex: A Black Feminist Critique of Antidiscrimination Doctrine, Feminist Theory and Anti-racist Politics." *University of Chicago Legal Forum* 1 (1989): 139–67.

Evans-Charles, Martie. "The Confrontation." *Impressions: A Black Arts and Culture Magazine*, October 1975.

———. "Playwright Defends *Jamimma*." *New York Amsterdam News*, June 24, 1972.

Forsgren, La Donna L. "The Black Arts Movement (1965–1976): An Interview with Playwright J.e. Franklin." *Callaloo* 37, no. 5 (2014): 1139–57.

Gant, Lisbeth. "The New Lafayette Theatre: Anatomy of a Community Art Institution." *The Drama Review* 16, no. 4 (1972): 46–55.

Greenspun, Roger. Review of *Black Girl* adapted by J.e. Franklin, dir. Ossie Davis. *New York Amsterdam News*, November 10, 1972.

Harris, Jessica B. Review of *The Prodigal Sister* by J.e. Franklin, dir. Shauneille Perry, Theater DeLys, New York. *New York Amsterdam News*, December 7, 1974.

———. "The Sun People of 125th Street: The National Black Theatre." *The Drama Review* 16, no. 4 (1972): 39–45.

Holden, Stephen. Review of *Christchild* by J.e. Franklin, dir. Irving Vincent, New Federal Theatre, New York. *New York Times*, December 2, 1992.

Hunter, Charlayne, "2 Black Women Combine Lives and Talent in Play." *New York Times*, July 13, 1971.

Johnson, Thomas. Review of *Soljourney into Truth* by Barbara Ann Teer, dir. by Barbara Ann Teer, National Black Theatre, New York. *New York Times*, May 11, 1974.

Jones, LeRoi. "The Revolutionary Theatre." *Liberator*, July 1965.

Kannu. Review of *African Interlude* by Martie Evans-Charles, dir. Shauneille Perry, Henry Street Settlement's New Federal Theatre, New York. *The Paper*, March 11, 1978.

Kelly, Susan. "Discipline and Craft: An Interview with Sonia Sanchez." *African American Review* 34, no. 4 (2000): 679–87.

Kerr, Walter. Review of *Black Girl* by J.e. Franklin, dir. Shauneille Perry, Theater DeLys, New York. *New York Amsterdam News*, July 4, 1971.

———. Review of *Jamimma* by Martie Evans-Charles, dir. Shauneille Perry, New Federal Theatre, New York. *New York Times*, May 28, 1972.

Kupa, Kushauri. "Closeup: The New York Scene. Black Theatre in New York: 1970–1971." *Black Theatre: A Periodical of the Black Theatre Movement*, 1971.

Lester, Elenore. "Growing Up Black and Female." Review of *Black Girl* by J.e. Franklin, dir. Shauneille Perry, New Federal Theatre's Henry Street Playhouse, New York. *New York Times*, July, 11, 1971.

Levine, Eleanor. Review of *Meditation: A Family Affair* by Martie Evans-Charles, dir. Chuck Patterson, Henry Street Settlement's Abrons Art Center, New York. *New York Amsterdam News*, July 27, 2000.

Lewis, Barbara. "The Dramatic Crisis. . . ." *New York Amsterdam News*, February 14, 1976.

Molette II, Carlton W. "The Way to Viable Theatre?: Afro-American Ritual Drama." *Black World*, April 1973.

Morgan, Jo-Ann. "Mammy the Huckster: Selling the Old South for the New Century." *American Art* 9, no. 1 (1995): 87–109.

Murray, James P. "Ossie Davis Makes Strides after Image Maker Award." *New York Amsterdam News*, November 25, 1972.

Nathan, David. Track Annotations for "Four Women." *To Be Free: The Nina Simone Story*. RCA/Legacy, 2008. CD.

Neal, Larry. "The Black Arts Movement." *The Drama Review* 12, no. 4 (1968): 28–39.

———. "Toward a Relevant Black Theatre." *Black Theatre: A Periodical of the Black Theatre Movement*, 1970.

New York Amsterdam News. "Sonia Sanchez Tells It Like It Is." December 19, 1970.

———. Unsigned review of *Black Girl* adapted by J.e. Franklin, dir. Ossie Davis. October 21, 1972.

———. Unsigned review of *Black Girl* adapted by J.e. Franklin, dir. Ossie Davis. November 11, 1972.

———. Unsigned review of *Friends* adapted by Martie Evans-Charles, unknown director, National Black Theatre, New York. August 22, 1992.

———. Unsigned review of *Jamimma* by Martie Evans-Charles, dir. Kris Keiser, Lenox Avenue Building, New York. November 21, 1970.

New York Times. Unsigned review of *Prodigal Sister* by J.e. Franklin, dir. Shauneille Perry, New Federal Theatre's Henry Street Playhouse, New York. July 16, 1974.

Perrier, Paulette. Review of *Job Security* by Martie Evans-Charles, The Black Magicians, Third World Theatre, New York. *Black Theatre: A Periodical of the Black Theatre Movement*, 1971.

Perry, Shauneille. "Books Noted." *Black World*, April 1972.

Riley, Clayton. Review of *Sister Son/ji* by Sonia Sanchez, dir. Novella Nelson, New York Shakespeare Festival, Public Theatre Annex, New York. *New York Amsterdam News*, April 15, 1972.

Robinson, Vivian. Review of *Jamimma* by Martie Evans-Charles, dir. Kris Keiser, Lenox Avenue Building, New York. *New York Amsterdam News*, December 19, 1970.

Russell, Carlos. Review of *Black Girl* by J.e. Franklin, dir. Shauneille Perry, Theater DeLys, New York. *New York Amsterdam News*, August 7, 1971.

Russell, Charlie L., and Barbara Ann Teer. "Barbara Ann Teer: We Are Liberators Not Actors." *Essence*, March 1971.

Sanchez, Sonia. "Barbara Ann Teer: 1937–2008." *American Theatre*, October 2008.

———. *The Bronx Is Next. The Drama Review* 12, no. 4 (1968): 78–84.

———. *Dirty Hearts. Scripts 1*, November 1971.

———. *Malcolm/Man Don't Live Here No Mo'. Black Theatre: A Periodical of the Black Theatre Movement*, 1972.

Smith, Angela E. Review of *The Prodigal Sister* by J.e. Franklin, dir. Shauneille Perry, New Federal Theatre's Henry Street Playhouse, New York. *New York Amsterdam News*, July 27, 1974.

Smith, Helene C. "Emotional Play Explores the Exploitation of Black Women." *Atlanta Constitution*, April 30, 1982.

Teer, Barbara Ann. "The Black Woman: She Does Exist." *New York Times*, May 14, 1967.

———. "The Great White Way Is Not Our Way—Not Yet." *Negro Digest*, April 1968.

———. "We Can Be What We Were Born to Be." *New York Times*, July 7, 1968.

Thomas, Don. "Woodie King to Present 18 African American Playwrights." *New York Beacon*, July 12, 2000.

Thompson, Howard. Review of *Jamimma* by Martie Evans-Charles, dir. Shauneille Perry, New Federal Theatre, New York. *New York Times*, March 18, 1972.

Wesley, Richard W. "Harlem's Black Theatre Workshop." *Black World*, April 1972.

Wilson, Ted. "Woodie: The King Maker: A Conversation with Woodie King, Jr." *Black Renaissance* 8, no. 2–3 (2008): 89–111.

Wood, Jacqueline. "'This Thing Called Playwrighting' [*sic*]: An Interview with Sonia Sanchez on the Art of Her Drama." *African American Review* 39, no. 1/2 (2001): 119–32.

Books and Dissertations

Adepegba, Cornelius O. "Osun and Brass: An Insight into Yoruba Religious Symbology." In *Òsun across the Waters: A Yoruba Goddess in Africa and the Americas*, edited by Joseph M. Murphy and Mei-Mei Sanford, translated by C. L. Adeoye, 102–12. Bloomington: Indiana University Press, 2001.

Bean, Anne Marie. "Blackface Minstrelsy and Double Inversion circa 1890." In *African American Performance and Theatre History*, edited by Harry J. Elam and David Krasner, 171–91. New York: Oxford University Press, 2001.

Brown, Elizabeth. "Six Female Black Playwrights: Images of Blacks in Plays by Lorraine Hansberry, Alice Childress, Sonia Sanchez, Barbara Molette, Martie Evans-Charles, Ntozake Shange." Ph.D. dissertation, Florida State University, 1980.

Brown-Guillory, Elizabeth. "Sonia Sanchez (1934–)." In *Black Women in America: An Historical Encyclopedia*, vol. 2, edited by Darlene Clark Hine et al., 1003–05. Brooklyn, New York: Carlson, 1993.

Clarke, Cheryl. *After Mecca: Women Poets and the Black Arts Movement*. New Brunswick, N.J.: Rutgers University Press, 2006.

Collins, Patricia Hill. *Black Feminist Thought: Knowledge, Consciousness, and the Politics of Empowerment*. Boston: Unwin Hyman, 1990.

Cornwell, Anita. "Attuned to the Energy: Sonia Sanchez." In *Conversations with Sonia Sanchez*, edited by Joyce Ann Joyce, 3–5. Jackson: University Press of Mississippi, 2007.

Cruse, Harold. *Rebellion or Revolution?* New York: William Morrow, 1968.

Curb, Rosemary K. "Pre-Feminism in the Black Revolutionary Drama of Sonia Sanchez." In *The Many Forms of Drama*, edited by Karelisa Hatigan, 19–29. Lanham, Md.: University Press of America, 1985.

Daniels, Rebecca. *Women Stage Directors Speak: Exploring the Influence of Gender on Their Work*. Jefferson, N.C.: McFarland, 1996.

Davis, Angela Y. *Blues Legacy and Black Feminism: Gertrude "Ma" Rainey, Bessie Smith, and Billy Holiday*. New York: Pantheon Books, 1998.

———. "Reflections on the Black Woman's Role in the Community of Slaves." In *Words of Fire: An Anthology of Black Feminist Thought*, edited by Beverly Guy-Sheftall, 200–218. New York: New Press, 1995. First published in 1971 by *The Black Scholar*.

Domatob, Jerry Komia. Preface to *Coming to the Mercy Seat: J.e. Franklin's Ten Minute Folk Dramas*. Edited by Tehut-Nin, 10–11. New York: Blackgirl Ensemble Theatre, 2003.

Esedebe, P. Olisanwuche. *Pan-Africanism: The Idea and Movement, 1776–1991*. Washington, D.C.: Howard University Press, 1994.

Evans-Charles, Martie. *Black Cycle*. In *Black Drama Anthology*, edited by Woodie King and Ron Milner, 525–51. New York: Signet, 1972.

Fliotsos, Anne, and Wendy Vierow. *American Women Stage Directors of the Twentieth Century*. Urbana: University of Illinois Press, 2008.

Franklin, J.e. *Black Girl: A Play in Two Acts*. New York: Dramatists Play Service, 1971.

———. *Black Girl: From Genesis to Revelations*. Washington, D.C.: Howard University Press, 1977.

———. "The Enemy." In *Black Short Story Anthology*, edited by Woodie King, 349–59. New York: Columbia University Press, 1972.

———. *Miss Honey's Young'uns*. In *Black Drama in America: An Anthology*, edited with an introduction by Darwin T. Turner, 615–65. Washington, D.C.: Howard University Press, 1994.

———. *The Prodigal Sister: A New Black Musical*. New York: Samuel French, 1974.

Frost, Elizabeth A. *The Feminist Avant-Garde in American Poetry*. Iowa City: University of Iowa Press, 2003.

Gabbin, Joanne Veal. "The Southern Imagination of Sonia Sanchez." In *Southern Women Writers: The New Generation*, edited by Tonette Bond Inge, 180–202. Tuscaloosa: University of Alabama Press, 1990.

Grass, Randall. *Great Spirits: Portraits of Life-Changing World Music Artists*. Jackson: University of Mississippi Press, 2009.

Griffin, Farah Jasmine. "'Ironies of the Saint': Malcolm X, Black Women, and the Price of Protection." In *Sisters in the Struggle: African-American Women in the Civil Rights–Black Power Movement*, edited by Bettye Collier-Thomas and V. P. Franklin, 214–29. New York: New York University Press, 2001.

Harrison, Daphne Duval. *Black Pearls: Blues Queens of the 1920s*. New Brunswick, N.J.: Rutgers University Press, 1988.

Harrison, Paul Carter. *The Drama of Nommo*. New York: Grove, 1972.

Hatch, James V. "From Hansberry to Shange." In *A History of African American Theatre*, edited by Errol G. Hill and James V. Hatch, 375–429. Cambridge: Cambridge University Press, 2003.

Hatch, James V., and Ted Shine. "'Job Security' Introduction." In *Black Theatre, U.S.A.: Forty-Five Plays by Black Americans 1847–1974*, edited by James V. Hatch and Ted Shine, 765. New York: Free, 1974.

Henderson, Mae Gwendolyn. "Speaking in Tongues: Dialogics, Dialectics, and the Black Woman Writer's Literary Tradition." In *African American Literary Theory: A Reader*, edited by Winston Napier, 348–68. New York: New York University Press, 2000.

Hill, Anthony D., and Douglas Q. Barnett. *Historical Dictionary of African American Theatre*. Lanham, Md.: Scarecrow, 2009.

Hine, Darlene Clark. *Hine Sight: Black Women and the Re-Construction of American History*. New York: Carlson, 1994.

———. Introduction to *The Face of Our Past: Images of Black Women from Colonial America to the Present*, edited by Kathleen Thompson and Hilary Mac Austin, ix–xiii. Bloomington: University of Indiana Press, 1999.

Holloway, Karla F. C. *Moorings and Metaphors: Figures of Cultures and Gender in Black Women's Literature.* New Brunswick, N.J.: Rutgers University Press, 1992.

hooks, bell. *Ain't I a Woman: Black Women and Feminism.* Boston: South End, 1981.

Hurston, Zora Neale. *Their Eyes Were Watching God.* New York: Harper Perennial Classics, 2006. First published in 1937 by J.B. Lippincott.

Jacobs, Harriet A. (Linda Brent). *Incidents in the Life of a Slave Girl: Written by Herself,* edited by L. Maria Child with an introduction by Jean Fagan Yellin. Cambridge, Mass.: Harvard University Press, 1987. First published in 1861 by Thayer and Eldridge.

Johnson-Bailey, Juanita. "Sonia Sanchez: Telling What We Must Hear." In *Conversations with Sonia Sanchez,* edited by Joyce Ann Joyce, 70–79. Jackson: University Press of Mississippi, 2007.

Jones, Kellie. "Black West: Thoughts on Art in Los Angeles." In *New Thoughts on the Black Arts Movement,* edited by Lisa Gail Collins and Margo Crawford, 43–74. New Brunswick, N.J.: Rutgers University Press, 2006.

Jones, LeRoi. *Blues People: Negro Music in White America.* New York: William Morrow, 1963.

Joyce, Joyce A. "Interview with Sonia Sanchez: Poet, Playwright, Teacher, and Intellectual Activist." In *Conversations with Sonia Sanchez,* edited by Joyce Ann Joyce, 177–205. Jackson: University Press of Mississippi, 2007.

Jurich, Marilyn. *Scheherazade's Sisters: Trickster Heroines and Their Stories in World Literature.* Westport, Conn.: Greenwood, 1998.

Keita, Michelle Nzadi. "Sonia Sanchez: 'Fearless about the World.'" In *Impossible to Hold: Women and Culture in the 1960s,* edited by Avita H. Bloch and Lauri Umansky, 279–91. New York: New York University Press, 2005.

Kern-Foxworth, Marilyn. *Aunt Jemima, Uncle Ben, and Rastus: Blacks in Advertising, Yesterday, Today, and Tomorrow.* Westport, Conn.: Greenwood, 1994.

Kerner, Otto, et al. *Report of the National Advisory Commission on Civil Disorders.* Washington, D.C.: Government Printing Office, 1967.

Levine, Lawrence W. *Black Culture and Black Consciousness: African-American Folk Thought from Slavery to Freedom.* New York: Oxford University Press, 1977.

Lincoln, Abbey. "Who Will Revere the Black Woman?" In *The Black Woman Anthology,* edited by Toni Cade, 80–84. New York: New American Library, 1970. First published in 1966 by *Negro Digest.*

Madhubuti, Haki. "Sonia Sanchez: The Bringer of Memories." In *Black Women Writers (1950–1980): A Critical Evaluation,* edited by Mari Evans, 419–32. Garden City, N.Y.: Anchor Books, 1984.

Malpede, Karen, and Barbara Ann Teer. "Barbara Ann Teer." In *Women in Theatre,* edited by Karen Malpede, 220–30. New York: Limelight Editions, 1985.

Manring, M. M. *Slave in a Box: The Strange Career of Aunt Jemima.* Charlottesville: University Press of Virginia, 1998.

Marquette, Arthur F. *Brands, Trademarks, and Good Will: The Story of the Quaker Oats Company.* New York: McGraw-Hill, 1967.

McElya, Micki. *Clinging to Mammy: The Faithful Slave in Twentieth-Century America.* Cambridge, Mass.: Harvard University Press, 2007.

Molette II, Carlton W., and Barbara J. Molette. *Black Theatre: Premise and Presentation.* 2nd ed. Bristol, Ind.: Wyndham Hall, 1992.

Moynihan, Daniel Patrick, et al., *The Negro Family: The Case for National Action.* Washington, D.C.: Government Printing Office, 1965.

Mullen, Harryette. "The Black Arts Movement." In *African American Writers,* vol. 1, edited by Valerie Smith, 57–58. 2nd ed. New York: Charles Scribner's Sons, 2001.

Mullings, Leith. "Images, Ideology, and Women of Color." In *Women of Color in U.S. Society,* edited by Maxine Baca Zinn and Bonnie Thornton Dill, 265–89. Philadelphia: Temple University Press, 1994.

Randall, Dudley. Introduction to *We a BaddDDD People,* by Sonia Sanchez, 9–11. Detroit, Mich.: Broadside, 1970.

Reich, Davis. "'As Poets, As Activists': An Interview with Sonia Sanchez." In *Conversations with Sonia Sanchez,* edited by Joyce Ann Joyce, 80–93. Jackson: University Press of Mississippi, 2007.

Robertson, Pamela. *Guilty Pleasures: Feminist Camp from Mae West to Madonna.* Durham, N.C.: Duke University Press, 1996.

Robinson, Beverly J. "The Sense of Self in Ritualizing New Performance Spaces for Survival." In *Black Theatre: Ritual Performance in the Black Diaspora,* edited by Paul Carter Harrison, Victor Leo Walker II., and Gus Edwards, 332–44. Philadelphia: Temple University Press, 2002.

Sanchez, Sonia. "Ruminations/Reflections." In *Black Women Writers (1950–1980): A Critical Evaluation,* edited by Mari Evans, 415–18. New York: Doubleday, 1984.

———. *Sister Son/ji.* In *New Plays from the Black Theatre: An Anthology,* edited by Ed Bullins, 9–107. New York: Bantam, 1969.

———. *Uh, Uh; But How Do It Free Us?* In *The New LaFayette Theatre Presents: Plays with Aesthetic Comments by 6 Black Playwrights,* edited by Ed Bullins, 165–215. New York: Anchor, 1974.

———. *We a BaddDDD People.* Detroit, Mich.: Broadside, 1970.

Sanchez, Sonia, with Claudia Tate. "Sonia Sanchez." In *Black Women Writers at Work,* edited by Claudia Tate, 132–48. New York: Continuum, 1983.

Sell, Mike. *Avant-Garde Performance and the Limits of Criticism: Approaching the Living Theatre, Happenings/Fluxus, and the Black Arts Movement.* Ann Arbor: University of Michigan Press, 2005.

———. "The Black Arts Movement: Performance, Neo-Orality, and the Destruction of the 'White Thing.'" In *African American Performance and Theater History: A Critical Reader,* edited by Harry J. Elam and David Krasner, 56–80. New York: Oxford University Press, 2001.

———. "Introduction: A Literary Gangster from Those Primitive Times of the Twentieth Century." In *Ed Bullins: Twelve Plays and Selected Writings,* edited by Ed Bullins with Mike Sell, 1–20. Ann Arbor: University of Michigan Press, 2006.

Simone, Nina, with Stephen Cleary. *I Put a Spell on You: The Autobiography of Nina Simone.* New York: Da Capo, 1993.

Smethurst, James Edward. *The Black Arts Movement: Literary Nationalism in the 1960s and 1970s.* Raleigh: University of North Carolina Press, 2005.

Springer, Kimberly. *Living for the Revolution: Black Feminist Organizations, 1968–1980.* Durham, N.C.: Duke University Press, 2001.

Staples, Robert. *The Black Woman in America: Sex, Marriage, and the Family.* Chicago: Nelson-Hall, 1973.

Taumann, Beatrix. *Strange Orphans: Contemporary African American Women Playwrights.* Würzburg: Königshausen & Neumann, 1999.

Teer, Barbara Ann. "Needed: A New Image." In *The Black Power Revolt: A Collection of Essays*, edited by Floyd B. Barbour. Boston: Porter Sargent, 1968.

———. "Ritual and the National Black Theatre." In *Women in American Theatre*, edited by Helen Krich Chinoy and Linda Walsh Jenkins, 34. New York: Theatre Communications Group, 1987.

Thomas, Lundeana. "Barbara Ann Teer: From Holistic Training to Liberating Rituals." In *Black Theatre: Ritual Performance in the African Diaspora*, edited by Paul Carter Harrison, Victor Leo Walker II, and Gus Edwards, 435–77. Philadelphia: Temple University Press, 2002.

Tyehima, Cheo. "Sonia Sanchez Speaks." In *Conversations with Sonia Sanchez*, edited by Joyce Ann Joyce, 111–16. Jackson: University Press of Mississippi, 2007.

Walker, Alice. *In Search of Our Mothers' Gardens: Womanist Prose.* San Diego: Harcourt Brace Jovanovich, 1983.

Wallace, Michele. *Black Macho and the Myth of the Superwoman.* New York: Dial, 1978.

Wallace-Sanders, Kimberly. *Mammy: A Century of Race, Gender, and Southern Memory.* Ann Arbor: University of Michigan Press, 2008.

Williams, Delores. *Sisters in the Wilderness: The Challenge of Womanist God-Talk.* New York: Orbis Books, 1995.

Williams, Mance. *Black Theatre in the 1960s and 1970s: A Historical-Critical Analysis of the Movement.* Westport, Conn.: Greenwood, 1985.

Woll, Allen. *Black Musical Theatre: From "Coontown" to "Dreamgirls."* Baton Rouge: Louisiana State University Press, 1989.

Wood, Jacqueline. "'Shaking Loose': Sonia Sanchez's Militant Drama." In *Contemporary African American Women Playwrights*, edited by Philip Kolin, 47–61. New York: Routledge, 2007.

X, Malcolm. "The Ballot or the Bullet." In *The Portable Sixties Reader*, edited by Ann Charters, 70–79. London: Penguin Books, 2003. First published in 1965 by Merit.

abortion, 141–42, 147
Adepegba, Cornelius O., 33
African heritage and aesthetics, 14;
    Evans-Charles and, 37, 38, 42, 43–44,
    55, 56, 62, 65–66; Franklin and, 132;
    pan-Africanism defined, 27; Teer and,
    17, 18, 20–21, 22, 27, 29, 33–34. *See
    also* Yoruba religion
Aldridge, Ira, 130
AMAS Repertory Theatre Company, 36,
    134
Anderson, James, 114
Angelou, Maya, 8, 115
Azular, Kwame, 29

Bailey, Peter, 26, 44
Baker, Josephine, 130
Bambara, Toni Cade, 49
Baraka, Amiri (LeRoi Jones), 6, 8,
    67, 72, 74, 77, 81, 147; "The
    Revolutionary Theatre," xi, 4, 13, 116
Barnes, Clive, 93
Barnett, Douglas Q., 147
Bass, George Houston, 8, 15, 108, 116,
    182n23
Beauford, Fred, 119–20
beauty, standards of, 21–22, 55, 62,
    64–65; Sanchez and, 103–4, 106
Belgrave, Cynthia, 36
Best, Tony, 26
Black Arts Movement, 3–4, 6–8, 10–15,
    152; early history of, 167n13;
    Franklin and, 15, 107–8, 110, 112,
    118–19; Sanchez and, 8, 68, 75,
    81–82
Black Arts Repertory Theatre/School
    (BART/S), 7, 72–74, 96
black Broadway musicals, 63
black church practices, 70–71, 139,
    141–42; Teer and, 14, 20, 25, 27, 28,
    29, 50

black female subjectivity, 4, 10, 11, 44,
    63, 65, 148
black feminist attitudes, 4–5, 7, 12;
    Franklin and, 113–14; Sanchez and,
    81–82
Blackgirl Theatre Company, 149
Black Lives Matter movement, 86
black macho mythology, 12, 47, 128
Black Magicians (theater troupe), 58
black matriarchy myth, 11–12, 51,
    54–55, 83, 132
blackness, 5; Teer and, 19, 26, 30
Black Panther Party, 76, 114, 125
Black Power Movement, 4, 6, 11–12;
    Sanchez and, 67, 90; Teer and, 19, 36
black queer identity, 150
black sisterhood, 48–49
Black Theatre Workshop, 7, 8, 14;
    Evans-Charles and, 37, 39, 42–43, 51,
    61; Sanchez and, 77, 78, 88
black women, images and stereotypes
    of, 10–12, 21–22, 128–29; Aunt
    Jemima, 47, 59–60, 91–92, 139;
    Evans-Charles and, 45–48, 59–62;
    Sanchez and, 74, 83. *See also* warrior
    mother persona
blaxploitation films, 135
blues, black women's contribution to
    the, 49–50
Bogan, Louise, 71
Bond, Jean Carey, 61–62
Brecht, Bertolt, 67, 78, 89
Brer Rabbit tales, 56, 57
Bridges, Ruby, 58
Brown, H. Rap, 26, 31
Brown, John, 58
Brown-Guillory, Elizabeth, 39–40, 69
Bryant, Hazel, 36
Bullins, Ed, 7, 8, 14, 20, 37, 42–43,
    147; *Clara's Ole' Man*, 13; *The Devil
    Catchers*, 39, 172n7; *The Fabulous*

Bullins, Ed, *continued*
    Miss Marie, 39; Franklin and, 107;
    Sanchez and, 75, 77–78
Burton, Philip, 21

Caldwell, Ben, 147
Carmichael, Stokely, 26, 31, 50, 125
Carroll, Vinnette, 36, 151–52, 184n97
Carter, Roseanna, 39, 171n5
Castro, Fidel, 104
Charles, Adrienne, 39, 40, 41, 43, 44,
    62, 145–46; photographs of, 45,
    51
Chekhov, Anton, 107
Childress, Alice, 8, 107, 115, 147
Christian, Barbara, 3, 152
Christmas, Walter, 115
Civil Rights Act, 124
Civil Rights Movement, 50, 115, 124–
    25, 127
Clarke, Cheryl, 7, 69
Clarke, John Henrik, 115
Cleage, Pearl, 147
Cleaver, Eldridge, 76–77, 101
Collins, Patricia Hill, 9–10, 19, 40, 49,
    64, 145
Congress of Racial Equality, 72
Crenshaw, Kimberle, 167n4
Cruse, Harold, 22
Cullen, Countee, 71
Curb, Rosemary K., 39, 69, 111

Dafora, Asdata, 39
Daniels, Rebecca, 24
Davis, Angela, 49, 52, 98, 125, 126
Davis, Ossie, 134–35
Dee, Ruby, 26
"Dixie" (song), 138
Domatob, Jerry Komia, 107
domestic service, 54, 60, 113, 123,
    128–29
Drexler, Rosalyn, 114
Du Bois, W. E. B., 115, 125
Dunbar, Paul Laurence, 71

Epic theater aesthetics, 70, 78
Esedebe, P. Olisanwuche, 27, 34
Evans, Charles, 42
Evans, Ronald, 42
Evans, Walter, 42

Evans-Charles, Martie, 3–15, 37–66,
    111, 152; "The Confrontation,"
    44–46; on education, 46–47, 56,
    57–59; on feminist movement, 5;
    later career of, 147–48; mother's
    and aunts' influence on, 14, 39, 40;
    Nation of Islam and, 44–46, 157;
    photographs of, 38, 41, 45, 51, 66;
    rituals and spiritual practices in,
    14, 43–44, 48, 51–52, 63, 64–65;
    scholarship on, 39–40. *See also* New
    Lafayette Theatre
    PLAYS: *African Interlude*, 147; *Asante*,
        14, 38, 44, 63–65; *Black Cycle*,
        14, 38, 39, 40, 47, 51–55, 173n51,
        175n101; *Daisy's Dilemma*, 147;
        Every Inch a Lady, 40; *Friends*,
        38, 62–63; *The Guest House*, 147;
        Jamimma, 5, 14, 38, 41, 42, 47–48,
        59–62, 175nn107–8; *Job Security*,
        14, 38, 47, 55–59; *Meditation*,
        147–48; *Where We At?*, 14, 38, 43,
        48–50, 64
Evers, Medgar, 50

Fabio, Sarah Webster, 75
Faison, Nabii, 9, 23, 24, 25, 29–30, 150,
    151
Fliotsos, Anne, 150
Foreman, James, 26
Forsgren, Piper McKay, 145
Foster, Gloria, 93
Franklin, J.e., 3–15, 107–44, 145–46,
    152; on actor–audience relationship,
    109–10; awards, 107, 118, 148; on
    black aesthetic, 118–19; Black Arts
    Movement and, 15, 107–8, 110, 112,
    118–19; on individuality, 119–20;
    influences on, 8, 15, 107–8, 112, 115;
    later career of, 148–49; liberation
    and, 107, 108, 112, 119, 133; name
    change, 117; photograph of, 109;
    ritual in, 121, 123–24; scholarly
    neglect of, 107, 111; teaching career,
    114–15, 132, 137, 143–44, 149
    WORKS: *Another Morning Rising*, 15,
        108, 111, 143–44; *Black Girl* (film
        and play), 15, 39, 108, 110, 111,
        112, 113, 115–18, 119, 129–36;
        Christchild, 148; *Coming to the*

Mercy Seat, 110, 146, 148; *The Creation*, 15, 108, 111, 143–44; *The Enemy*, 15, 108, 111, 136–37; "The Enemy" (story), 112, 137; *A First Step to Freedom*, 114–15; *Four Women*, 15, 108, 137–39; *The In-Crowd*, 15, 108, 117, 120–23; *MacPilate*, 15, 108, 111; *Miss Honey's Young'uns* (aka *Mau Mau Room*), 15, 108, 117, 123–29, 181n4; *Precious Memories*, 148; *The Prodigal Daughter*, 15, 108, 109, 111, 140; *The Prodigal Sister*, 15, 108, 109, 139–43; *To Break Every Yoke*, 148; *Two Flowers*, 15, 108, 111; *Will the Real White Racism Please Die*, 149
Franklin, Yvette, 117
Frank Silvera Writers' Workshop, 46, 172n26
Frost, Elizabeth A., 69, 79

Gabbin, Joanne Veal, 14
Gaines, J. E. "Sonny Jim," 39
Gant, Lisbeth, 37, 44
Garvey, Marcus, 33–34
Gayle, Addison, Jr., 95
Gentry, Minnie, 134
Giovanni, Nikki, 26
Grant, Micki, 15, 109, 140, 151
Green, Nancy, 47
Greenspun, Roger, 135
Griffin, Farah Jasmine, 98
Group on Advanced Leadership, 82–83
Guy, Rosa, 8, 62, 115

Hall, Katori, 3, 15
Hansberry, Lorraine, 50
Hare, Nathan, 75
Harlem, 7–8; Evans-Charles and, 42, 43, 47, 51, 62; Franklin and, 108; Sanchez and, 68, 71–72, 84–85, 87; Teer and, 19–20, 22, 26, 32, 34, 36, 151
Harlem Writers Guild, 7, 8, 15, 108, 115–16
Harlem Youth Opportunities Unlimited, 72
Harris, Jessica B., 25, 32, 142, 143
Harrison, Paul Carter, 20

Hatch, James V., 56
Hazlip, Ellis, 29
Henry Street Settlement, 143, 147
Hill, Anthony D., 147
Hill, Errol G., 44
Hine, Darlene Clark, 11, 54
Holden, Steven, 148
hooks, bell, 52
Hughes, Langston, 71, 107, 147
Hurston, Zora Neale, 3, 102

intersectionality, 5, 113, 167n4

Jackson, Elaine, 39, 111
Jacobs, Harriet, 53
Jamal, Ahmad, 131
Johnson, Lyndon B., 126
Jones, Gayle, 49
Jones, LeRoi. *See* Baraka, Amiri
Joyce, Joyce Ann, 69

Kannu, 147
Karenga, Maulana (Ron Everett), 42, 75
Keita, Michelle Nzadi, 69, 90
Kennedy, Adrienne, 89
Kerner Commission Report, 126
Kerr, Walter, 61, 133
Killens, John Oliver, 115
King, Martin Luther, Jr., 3, 72, 116, 117, 125
King, Willie Mae, 117
King, Woodie, Jr., 7, 8, 15, 25, 42, 108, 118, 122–23, 134, 147
Knight, Etheridge, 87, 88
Kupa, Kushauri, 48

Legros Cultural Arts, 110
LeNoire, Rosetta, 36, 134
lesbian subtexts, 13
Lester, Elenore, 133
Levine, Eleanor, 147
Levine, Lawrence, 56, 57
Lincoln, Abbey, 7–8, 67, 73–74, 85, 98, 102, 177n17
Little, Louise Norton, 97
Lythcott, Barbara "Sade," 8, 23, 145, 151

Macbeth, Robert, 7, 8, 19–20, 39, 42
Madhubuti, Haki (Don L. Lee), 81, 96

Madison, Yvonne (Lubaba Lateef), 36
Malcolm X, 29, 31, 50, 125; Sanchez
    and, 67, 72, 73, 81, 87, 96–99, 101,
    102, 103, 150
Malcolm X Society, 82
Malpede, Karen, 29
Mann, Paul, 21
Martin, Trayvon, 86
Marvin X (Marvin Jackmon), 75
Mau-Mau, 127
McCauley, Robbie, 149
Meisner, Sanford, 21
Meredith, James, 124
Miles, George Lee, 43, 51
minstrelsy, 137–38
Mississippi Freedom Democratic Party,
    114
Mobilization for Youth, 15, 108, 117,
    122–23
Molette, Carlton W., 27–28
Moon, Marjorie, 36
Moore, Willard, 115
Moynihan Report (The Negro Family:
    The Case for National Action), 11–12,
    75, 132, 168n24
Muhammad, Elijah, 44, 97–98, 103
Muhammad, Wallace D., 44–45
Mullings, Leith, 54

National Association for the
    Advancement of Colored People
    (NAACP), 50, 149
National Black Theatre (NBT), 7–9,
    18–19, 23–27, 62, 118, 150; actor
    and audience ("liberator" and
    "participant") relationship at, 17–18,
    25–26, 28–29, 30; Sanchez and, 79;
    Teer's management style at, 24
National Black Theatre Institute of
    Action Arts, 151
Nation of Islam, 44–46, 75–76, 89,
    97–98, 147
Neal, Larry, 37, 81
Negro Ensemble Company, 48, 93, 108,
    117, 123, 134
New Federal Theatre, 7, 8, 42, 61, 62,
    108, 117, 134
New Feminists Theater, 108, 111
New Lafayette Theatre, 7, 14, 19–20,
    37, 38–39, 42–44; "New Lafayette

school of playwriting," 43; rituals at,
    43–44, 51; Sanchez and, 77, 78, 97
Newton, Huey, 50, 125
New York Shakespeare Festival, 93
Nikolais, Alwin, 21

On Being Black (TV series), 116
O'Neill, Eugene, 107
oral history, 8–9, 129, 145

Perrier, Paulette, 58–59
Perry, Shauneille, 15, 38, 61, 108–9,
    117–18, 123, 147, 151; background,
    133–34
prostitution in plays, 11, 83–84, 99,
    102, 137

racism: in academia, 6, 89–90, 107; in
    American theater, 21–22; in feminist
    movement, 5, 113; institutionalized,
    11, 52, 91, 108, 127, 133, 149; racial
    profiling, 86–87; World War II and,
    95
Randall, Dudley, 79, 81
Rangel, Charles, 25
Republic of New Afrika, 83, 88
"revolutionary" theater, xi, 4, 13, 17;
    Evans-Charles and, 39, 40, 66, 69;
    Franklin and, 110, 116; Sanchez and,
    69–70, 81, 88; Teer and, 27, 32
Richards, Lloyd, 21, 123
Riley, Clayton, 93
ritual drama theory, 27–28
Robertson, Pamela, 138
Robinson, Beverly J., 124
Robinson, Vivian, 61
Rockwell, Norman, 58
Rolle, Estelle, 39, 40
Rolle, Esther, 39, 40, 134, 171n3,
    172n6, 184n100
Roundtree, Richard, 123
Russell, Carlos, 110, 132
Russell, Charlie L., 18, 21, 25, 30–31

Sanchez, Sonia, 3–15, 17, 67–106,
    145, 152; awards, 149; Black Arts
    Movement and, 8, 68, 75, 81–82;
    chant in, 68, 80–81, 88, 91; influences
    on, 7–8, 67, 70–72, 77–78, 95–96;
    later career of, 149–50, 186n9;

Nation of Islam and, 44, 76, 89; photographs of, 71, 73, 74, 80, 105, 146; rap and, 149, 186n12; ritual in, 68, 78–79, 87; scholarship on, 69–70, 167n7; teaching career, 72, 75–76, 149; Teer and, 26, 36, 67, 78–79
PLAYS: *The Bronx Is Next*, 14, 68, 74, 77, 81, 82–88, 91, 178n59; *Dirty Hearts*, 14, 68, 93–96; *I'm Black When I'm Singing, I'm Blue When I Ain't*, 149; *Malcolm/Man Don't Live Here No Mo'*, 14, 68, 76, 96–99; *Sister Son/ji*, 14, 68, 72, 77–78, 79, 81, 88–93; *2 X 2*, 149; *Uh, Uh; But How Do It Free Us?*, 9, 14, 68, 76, 77–78, 99–106
POEMS AND ESSAYS: "blk/rhetoric," xi–xii; *Does Your House Have Lions?*, 150; *Homecoming*, 81; "Ruminations/Reflections," 68; "Solution to Sonia Sanchez," 76; "we a baddDDD people," 96
Sell, Mike, 43, 69, 88, 167n13
sexism, 13, 36, 55, 76, 80, 102, 117; in academia, 6, 52, 107; in black communities, 7, 13, 46, 69, 75; Sanchez's critique of, 69, 75, 76, 80, 81, 85
Shabazz, Betty, 97
Shange, Ntozake, 6, 9, 80, 146
Sharon Waite Community Center, 115
Shine, Ted, 56
Shogola Oloba (dance troupe), 39, 172n6
Simone, Nina, 49, 50, 98, 137
16th Street Baptist Church bombing, 50
slavery, 10, 21, 59, 95, 102; Evans-Charles and, 38, 46, 47, 49, 51–53, 58, 60; Franklin and, 124, 138
Smethurst, James, 6–7, 12–13, 18
Smith, Helene C., 149
Springer, Kimberly, 7
Staples, Robert, 84
Student Nonviolent Coordinating Committee (SNCC), 26, 50, 124–25
Stubbs, Louise, 134
superwoman mythology, 142–43
Supremes, the, 120
Sweatt, Heman Marion, 129

Taumann, Beatrix, 39, 111
Teer, Barbara Ann, 3–15, 17–36, 67, 114, 118, 152; awards, 25, 150–51; backlash against, 23, 24; Broadway career of, 19, 21, 35; "decrudin" process of, 25, 34; on feminist movement, 5, 36; "Five Cycles of Evolution" theory of, 25–26; later career of, 150–51; photographs of, 20, 31, 35; ritualistic revivals concept, 13–14, 17–18, 20–21, 26–34, 78–79, 150; scholarship on, 18–19. *See also* National Black Theatre
ESSAYS: "The Black Woman: She Does Exist," 21–22; "The Great White Way Is Not Our Way—Not Yet," 22; "Needed: A New Image," 22; "Ritual and the National Black Theatre," 30; "We Can Be What We Were Born to Be," 22
PLAYS: *The Legacy*, 150; *A Revival: Change! Love Together! Organize!*, 13, 18, 30–33; *A Ritual to Regain Our Strength and Reclaim Our Power* (and *The Ritual* film), 13, 18, 28, 29; *Softly Comes a Whirlwind, Whispering in Your Ear*, 150; *Soljourney into Truth: A Ritualistic Revival*, 13, 18, 28–29, 33–36; *Soul Fusion*, 150
Theatre DeLys, 118, 143
Third World Theatre, 58
Thomas, Lundeana, 18–19, 21, 150
Thompson, Howard, 61
Toussaint Louverture, 31
trickster folklore, 56–57

University of the Streets, 88
US Organization, 75

Vierow, Wendy, 150

Walker, Alice, 3, 5, 19, 49, 67, 98, 176n1
Wallace, Michele, 12, 142
Wallace-Sanders, Kimberly, 59
Ward, Douglas Turner, 134
warrior mother persona, 12–13; Evans-Charles and, 49, 50, 66; Franklin and, 132–33; Sanchez and, 68, 91, 93; Teer and, 21, 23–24, 33

Wasgindt, Isabel, 39, 40
Washington, Booker T., 81, 125
Wells, Ida B., 134
Wesley, Richard, 39, 42
West, Mae, 138
white hegemony, 5, 26, 48–49, 102–3,
   113, 126–27
Williams, Delores, 70
Williams, Mance, 25
Williams, Sherley Anne, 49
Wilson, August, 148

Wilson, Ted, 25
Woll, Allen, 63
womanism, 5, 176n1; Franklin and,
   114; Sanchez and, 67, 70–71, 76,
   79–80, 82, 106
Wood, Jacqueline, 69–70, 88, 94, 149
Woodard, Komozi, 6
Wright, Richard, 130

Yoruba religion, 12; in Teer, 14, 20–21,
   32–34